Complex Interpersonal Conflict Behaviour: Theoretical Frontiers

Evert Van de Vliert

*Department of Social and Organisational Psychology,
University of Groningen, The Netherlands*

Psychology Press
a member of the Taylor & Francis group

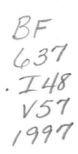

BF
637
.I48
V57
1997

Psychology Press Ltd, Publishers
27 Church Road
Hove
East Sussex, BN3 2FA
UK

British Library Cataloguing in Publication Data

A catalogue record for this book is availiable from the British Library

   ISBN 0-86377-716-3 (Hbk)
   (Essays in Social Psychology: ISSN 1367-5826)

Typeset by Lucy Morton, London SE12
Printed and bound in the United Kingdom by TJ International Ltd, Padstow, Cornwall

COMPLEX INTERPERSONAL
CONFLICT BEHAVIOUR

Contents

Foreword

Advice about how to behave in social conflict probably reaches back to the origins of man, but systematic theory and research on this topic are virtual newcomers. This book shows that a coherent scientific discipline of conflict studies has arisen and that this discipline is capable of explaining an ever-increasing range of phenomena. The author makes order out of the past and charts a challenge for the future.

The book is unusual in its emphasis on intellectual history. It shows how the field started with a five-part taxonomy of strategies for conflict: avoiding, accommodating, compromising, problem solving, and fighting. Scholars then developed a dimensional scheme (the "X-cross" model) for efficiently describing these strategies, and they finally constructed a theory (the "L-angle" theory) that has been quite successful at explaining and predicting their occurrence.

There is, however, a distinct limitation to what has been done so far: scholars have been dealing with only one strategy at a time, while actual conflict behaviour is usually much more complex. To correct this deficiency, the author proposes the development of a theory of "conglomerated" patterns—combinations of the basic strategies—such as "firm-flexibility" (holding firm on basic interests while seeking a formula that will satisfy the other party) and "thromises" (the union of threats and promises). He provides a fascinating initial statement of such a theory.

There are theoretical insights throughout the book: for example, the observation that changes in concern for the other party's goals determine *whether* cooperation or escalation will occur, whereas changes in concern for one's own goals influence the *form* that these processes will take. Research findings are described in every chapter, and several original data sets are presented. Some of the author's findings dramatise the importance of studying conglomerated patterns. For example, a combination of problem solving and fighting was found to be more effective at resolving conflict than either of these strategies alone.

The book ends with a challenge to students of social conflict, to develop a fuller understanding of the nature and sources of conglomerated patterns—how strategies blend and the turning points at which one strategy is replaced by another. The field of conflict studies will move much more rapidly once this challenge is met.

Dean G. Pruitt
26 February 1996

Acknowledgements

More than a decade of theoretical and empirical research work has gone into the preparation of this monograph on conflict behaviour. I am grateful to the Dutch National Science Foundation and to the Royal Netherlands Academy of Sciences for a series of grants that have made the research in this field at the University of Groningen possible. And I am very much indebted to all those who have been members of our great team, and particularly to Carsten de Dreu, Martin Euwema, Onne Janssen, and Aukje Nauta. They have participated in the research that is reported in this text. They have also read successive drafts and have detailed valuable comments, criticisms, and suggestions. Among the friends and colleagues who have reviewed the manuscript, or portions of it, I want especially to thank Bram Buunk, Peter Carnevale, Boris Kabanoff, Dean Pruitt, Shalom Schwartz, and Dean Tjosvold.

Stanley Frankel, Boris Kabanoff, Kamil Kozan, Linda Putnam, Afzal Rahim, Robert Sternberg, Deborah Weider-Hatfield, and Deanna Womack were kind enough to provide me with data sets that I needed for secondary analysis. To Fop Coolsma go sincere thanks for supplying the artwork. During the final phase of the project, Gün Semin helped me find a publisher, Miles Hewstone kept a careful watch on the editorial process, and Tanya Sagoo and Paul Dukes skilfully saw the book through production. Finally, the publishers and I would like to acknowledge that Figure 4.2 on page 81 was reprinted by permission of Sage Publications, Inc., from C.G.

McClintock, Social motivations in settings of outcome interdependence, in D. Druckman (Ed.), *Negotiations*, 49–77, 1976.

Evert Van de Vliert
Groningen, 11 August 1996

PART ONE

Introduction

CHAPTER ONE

Preview

Social conflicts abound. Conflict-free families, organisations, or nations do not exist. We detect conflict in people's frustrations and actions. Conflict becomes perceptible when individuals are annoyed by the actions of another person or a group. This is a phenomenon so omnipresent in social life that we too easily take it for granted. People react by choosing from well-trodden paths: they avoid a reproach, they accommodate a poor plan, they negotiate on a price or a problem, and sometimes they fight an opponent on principle. Social scientists first describe such conflict behaviour, then try to explain it. They picture behavioural outcomes and then recommend or prescribe effective methods of conflict management.

This book, written primarily for social and organisational psychologists and advanced psychology students, covers the domain of interpersonal conflict behaviour. Its six chapters challenge common typologies and models, which implicitly assume that a conflicting individual uses only one distinct mode of behaviour. Building on a decade of research, a new perspective is suggested. I assume that nearly every individual reaction to a conflict issue is complex. It consists of multiple components of behaviour rather than a single and pure mode of behaviour. That is, mixtures of avoiding, accommodating, compromising, problem solving, and fighting are the rule rather than the exception (cf. Blake & Mouton, 1964, 1970; Falbe & Yukl, 1992; Knapp, Putnam, & Davis, 1988; Rubin, Pruitt, & Kim, 1994; Van de Vliert & Euwema, 1996; Van de Vliert, Euwema, & Huismans, 1995; Williams, 1983, 1993; Yukl, Falbe, & Young Youn, 1993). For example,

3

"tacit coordination" is a merger of reactions in which one sticks to one's guns and withholds relevant information while revealing obligingness and real interests through nonverbal cues (e.g. Borisoff & Victor, 1989; Pruitt, 1981; Putnam, 1990). Such intertwinements of several reactions are the subject matter of the current monograph.

The introductory chapter presents my own definitions of conflict, conflict issue, conflict behaviour, and conflict outcome. The conflict definitions are followed by a brief discussion of two-, three-, four-, and five-part taxonomies of conflict handling. These taxonomies are then contrasted with the novel paradigm of complex conflict behaviour, which asks for the description and explanation of multiple behaviours rather than pure types of conflict handling. It will be argued that one particular theory, Blake and Mouton's (1964, 1970) "conflict management grid," presents the most promising descriptive and explanatory framework for future work in the area of complex conflict behaviour. As will be discussed in detail, the visual representation of the conflict management grid allows four figure–ground articulations, or faces. These differ in degree of theoretical value; that is, the extent to which they represent useful rules of correspondence between manifestations of behaviour, as well as between these behavioural manifestations and their antecedents and consequences. These grid faces serve as the basis for the design of the book in such a way that each chapter aims to add theoretical value to the preceding chapters.

CONFLICT DEFINITIONS

Conflict refers to a person's experience of discord due to a socially induced subject matter. It elicits complex, goal-directed reactions and produces benefits or costs for all people involved. This fairly extensive definition is not public property. For most people, "conflict" is just another word for fighting in the sense of attacking and defending actions. They are right, of course, in that any conflict with other people involves social behaviour. They are wrong, however, in that they conflate the issue and the reaction of fighting. Scientists working in the field of social conflict have made a sharp distinction between conflict issue and conflict behaviour. This distinction broadens one's perspective on conflict management from attacking and defending to alternative modes of conflict handling such as nonconfrontation and negotiation (Bartunek, Kolb, & Lewicki, 1992; Lax & Sebenius, 1986; Lewicki & Litterer, 1985; Rubin, Pruitt, & Kim, 1994; Wall, 1985). Here I shall use the following more specific concepts of conflict, conflict issue, conflict behaviour, and conflict outcome.

Conflict. Individuals are in conflict when they are obstructed or irritated by another individual or a group and inevitably react to it in a beneficial or costly way. If a husband is annoyed because he has wishes different from those of his wife about the desirable number of children, if a manager accuses a subordinate of laziness, or if ministers of two countries are seeking hegemony over the same piece of land with military aid, the parties have a conflict. Obviously, this concept is much too broad to be scientifically useful. It thus needs specification. Nevertheless, we can derive some preliminary insights from it. Important aspects and implications of this general definition of conflict include:

- a conflict is social because another individual or a group is involved;
- a conflict can be one-sided, when only one party experiences discord but avoids any communication about the problem;
- the existence of one-sided conflicts asks for a conceptualisation of conflict handling in terms of one-sided rather than two-sided response.

Conflict issue. A conflict issue is an experience of a subject matter of discord due to obstruction or irritation by one or more other people. In the above illustrations, the desired number of children, the laziness of the subordinate, and the ownership of the piece of land are the issues. One is taking them personally if one feels threatened, anxious, damaged, devalued, or insulted (Dallinger & Hample, 1995). Important aspects and implications of this specific definition of conflict issue include:

- a conflict issue is a subjective experience and does not necessarily have a real objective basis;
- the nature of a conflict issue may be cognitive or affective, or both (perception of blocked goals and disagreement, or feelings of repulsion, hostility, fear);
- the magnitude or intensity of a conflict issue may vary: a conflict de-escalates when the discord decreases, but it escalates when the discord increases;
- a conflict issue is not necessarily coupled with particular conflict behaviour toward the other party.

Important types of conflict issues are: incompatible beliefs about reality, disagreement about goals or actions, competition for scarce resources, and discontent bringing a person's identity into play (similar and other typologies may be found in Coombs, 1987; Deutsch, 1973; Fink, 1968; Glasl, 1980; Rahim, 1992; Walton, 1987). Deutsch (1973) called such issues veridical conflicts when they exist objectively and are perceived accurately. Additionally, he distinguished them from illusory conflicts based on misperception, misunderstanding, or displacement of the discord.

Conflict behaviour.   Conflict behaviour is defined as an individual's intended or displayed outward reaction to the conflict issue experienced. As a rule, people intend or display several reactions in varying degrees, which they aggregate into a unique manifestation of components of conflict behaviour, henceforth referred to as *conglomerated conflict behaviour*. For example, a seller who sees a stalemate coming will often threaten a potential buyer with the existence of alternative buyers, which represents an interesting mixture of seeking a settlement, attacking the opponent, and possible withdrawal. Similarly, when a manager accuses a subordinate of laziness, this predominant reaction of fighting will almost always be bound up with smaller or larger, verbal or nonverbal, components of compromising or problem solving, or even accommodating.

Each component of such conglomerated conflict behaviour may be either goal-directed or an expression of one's feelings. The current text deals exclusively with goal-directed behaviour. This is not to say that all components of conflict behaviour are driven by a conscious plan to achieve certain outcomes. Reactions may be strategic or spontaneous; that is, deliberately or *not* deliberately directed at the realisation of certain outcomes. The terms conflict behaviour, conflict handling, and conflict management are used interchangeably for both strategically and spontaneously goal-directed reactions aggregated into conglomerated conflict behaviour. Moreover, unless otherwise stated, these terms will refer to both covert behavioural intentions and overt actions.

Experienced conflict issues and enacted conflict behaviour are unique ingredients of tense human interaction. The *issue* represents a predominantly intrapersonal experience, whereas the *behaviour* is interpersonal in the first place. Also, predominantly, the *issue* is seen as "received" from the other party, and one's own *behaviour* as "sent" back to the other party. Most importantly, different *issues* may be reacted to in roughly the same way. Conversely, the same issue may elicit quite different *behaviours* from different people or from the same person at different times. In other words, conflict issues and conflict behaviours are basically independent phenomena. When authors discern only compounds of issue-plus-behaviour (e.g. anger-plus-fighting), connections such as anger–avoiding and anger–compromising, or disappointment–fighting and distrust–fighting are excluded. As a case in point, Burton (1990) couples issue and behaviour by contrasting negotiable "dispute issues" and intractable "conflict issues" deeply rooted in human behaviour (e.g. role negotiation versus ethnic discrimination).

Conflict outcome.   Outcomes as a consequence of both parties' behaviour are end states of benefits or costs for both oneself and one's opponent. For example, the husband and wife who disagree about the desirable number of children might end up with no offspring at all and a mutual relationship that has taken a turn for the worse. Similarly, the manager and the "lazy" subordinate might end up with a settlement about the appropriate level of work effort, and the disputed piece of land might be occupied by one country's army. Taken together, the total chain of causation consists of issue-based desired outcomes, conglomerated conflict behaviour, and ultimately resulting benefits or costs. It implies that complex conflict handling is viewed as capable of fulfilling one's own desires and/or the desires of the other party.

My definitions of issue, behaviour, and outcome relate to conflict in terms of an individual rather than a collective level of analysis. They reflect my viewpoint that *a group cannot experience discord and cannot display conflict behaviour*. Only the individual members of a family, organisation, or nation can experience conflict and can produce interactions and outcomes. Consequently, intergroup conflicts are conflicts only because they are carried by individuals who manifest conglomerated conflict behaviour vis-à-vis other individuals. Of course, this viewpoint does not ignore the fact that individual group members often act on behalf of the welfare of their group or on the basis of decisions made in their group (cf. Carnevale and Probst, 1997; Fisher, 1990, 1994; Putnam, 1997; Tajfel & Turner, 1979; Van de Vliert, 1996).

TAXONOMIES OF CONFLICT BEHAVIOUR

Conflict scholars have classified the multitude of possible reactions to conflict issues into distinct categories. There are dichotomies, trichotomies, four- and five-part typologies, and so on. The most well-known taxonomies are examined here, and are then criticised because they all undervalue behavioural complexity.

Dichotomy.   Like animals, human beings as "social animals" can exhibit a "fight-or-flight" response that prepares the organism to attack or flee (Baxter, 1982; Cannon, 1929). The fight–flight bifurcation ignores behavioural alternatives such as the ones used in bargaining. A more comprehensive dichotomy sets cooperation against competition. For instance, experimental gaming studies have used cooperation and competition as mutually exclusive reactions to social conflict (e.g. Axelrod, 1984; Deutsch, 1949, 1973; Pruitt & Kimmel, 1977; Tjosvold, 1988). Cooperation is typically seen as an agreeable and constructive process that tempers the discord, while competition is usually viewed as a disagreeable and destructive process that fuels the discord. Note that several scholars have rejected the fight–flight and cooperation–competition dichotomies by demonstrating that a single dimension is insufficient to reflect the abundance of behaviours used in handling interpersonal or small-group conflicts (e.g. Daves & Holland, 1989; Ruble & Thomas, 1976; Sternberg & Dobson, 1987; Van de Vliert & Prein, 1989).

Trichotomy. Horney (1945) initiated the taxonomy of "moving away" from people, "moving toward" people, and "moving against" people. In factor analyses of questionnaire data from employees in nonuniversity settings and students, Putnam and Wilson (1982) found essentially the same three forms of handling conflict, designating them as nonconfrontation (moving away), solution orientation (moving toward), and control (moving against). Very similar results of factor analyses have been reported by others (Bell & Blakeney, 1977; Fitzpatrick, 1988; Lawrence & Lorsch, 1967; Ross & DeWine, 1988; Schaap, Buunk, & Kerkstra, 1988; Weider-Hatfield, 1988; Wilson & Waltman, 1988).

Four-part typology. According to Rubin, Pruitt, and Kim (1994; see also Cahn, 1994), conflicting parties typically choose among four fundamentally different sorts of strategies. They can be inactive, withdrawing from the controversy either temporarily or permanently. They can yield to their opponent. They can take a problem-solving approach and try to locate a mutually acceptable or even completely satisfactory agreement. Or, finally, they can take a contentious approach, trying to impose their preferred outcomes on the adversary. However, there is no empirical evidence for this four-part classification of conflict behaviours.

Five-part typology. A still less parsimonious taxonomy is embedded in the so-called conflict management grid (Blake & Mouton, 1964, 1970; Rahim, 1992; Thomas, 1976, 1992b). As an extension of the four-part typology, this framework proposes five main ways or styles of managing conflict, which can be summarised by means of the following designations: (a) neutrality, withdrawal; (b) smooth over, peaceful coexistence; (c) compromise, bargaining; (d) problem solving, working through; and (e) suppress, win–lose power struggle (Blake & Mouton, 1970). Hall (1969) and Filley (1975) defined the above five types of conflict management as lose–leave, yield–lose, compromise, synergistic, and win–lose styles. Elsewhere, different terminological versions of essentially the same taxonomy have been proposed by Thomas (1976, 1988, 1992b), Rahim (1983b, 1992), and others.

The confusing mixture of labels of the five types of conflict management begs for an explicit nomenclature. In this book the catchwords for the five components of conflict handling mentioned above are *avoiding* (moving away from the conflict issue), *accommodating* (giving in to the opponent), *compromising* (settling through mutual concessions), *problem solving* (reconciling the parties' basic interests), and *fighting* (contending the adversary in a direct or indirect way). Although many authors, notably Blake and Mouton (1964, 1970), have referred to the five types as "styles," I prefer the term "mode," to avoid the impression of presupposed regularities in an individual's conflict behaviour.

A major problem.   These and similar taxonomies of conflict behaviour have proved to be invaluable for mapping and developing the scientific field of social conflict. They provided valid insight into the nature of various reactions to conflict issues, they stimulated the construction of measuring instruments (for an overview, see Chapter 3), and they made possible the development of elegant theories about the antecedents and consequences of particular types of conflict behaviour (notably Bacharach & Lawler, 1981; Blake & Mouton, 1964, 1970; Deutsch, 1973; Johnson & Johnson, 1989; Lax & Sebenius, 1986; Leary, 1957; Neale & Bazerman, 1991; Pruitt, 1981; Rubin, Pruitt, & Kim, 1994; Tjosvold, 1991; Wall, 1985; Walton & McKersie, 1965). However, we might soon reach the point where the reliance upon taxonomies of conflict behaviour is going to decelerate rather than accelerate theoretical progress. All of the above taxonomies undervalue both the frequency of occurrence and the scientific relevance of behavioural complexity. Indeed, "it may be commonplace for disputants to express preferences for several strategies simultaneously, or at least sequentially" (Knapp, Putnam, & Davis, 1988, p. 421; see also Putnam, 1990).

If the further use of taxonomies of conflict behaviour does follow the law of diminishing returns, we have a period of crisis ahead of us, in the sense proposed by Kuhn (1970) for natural science. Kuhn has argued that when the normal problem-solving activities in a discipline have for the time being failed, the odds are that major scientific advances emerge. A crisis often leads to a paradigm shift. I have gradually become convinced that continued investments in the manifestations, determinants, and outcomes of pure types of behaviour will deadlock the field of social conflict. If I am right, this field may be in need of a paradigm shift that replaces taxonomies of conflict behaviour by another shared way of looking at and investigating conflict behaviour. The perspective of conglomerated conflict behaviour outlined in this book could probably become the novel paradigm that guides research and intervention.

As will now be elaborated, Blake and Mouton's (1964, 1970) classic "conflict management grid" offers not only a five-part typology but also an appropriate foundation to support the building of viewpoints and propositions on conglomerated conflict management.

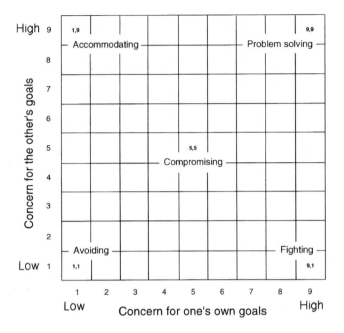

FIG. 1.1   Conflict management grid (after Blake & Mouton, 1970).

CONFLICT MANAGEMENT GRID

Blake and Mouton (1964, 1970) proposed two factors to describe and explain the aforementioned five basic ways of handling conflict: concern for production of results, and concern for people. To allow unequivocal operationalisation I label these two behavioural determinants *Concern for one's own goals* and *Concern for the other's goals*, respectively (cf. Rahim, 1983b, 1992; Rubin, Pruitt, & Kim, 1994; Thomas, 1992b). When the two-dimensional grid appeared, in 1964, Blake and Mouton restricted it to managerial behaviour, including managerial conflict behaviour. In 1970, when they focused on conflict management, they claimed that the concerns and the resulting modes of conflict handling also apply to actors other than managers and to conflicts other than managerial conflicts. This part of my introductory chapter presents the conflict management grid, using the terminology of avoiding, accommodating, compromising, problem solving, and fighting. It discusses the two concerns as independent variables, the five behaviours as dependent variables, the strengths and a weakness of the grid theory, and four grid manifestations.

Concerns as independent variables.   Blake and Mouton (1964, 1970) diagrammatically depicted concern for one's own goals and concern for the other's goals at an angle of 90 degrees (see Fig. 1.1). They thus implicitly saw these dimensions as mutually independent. Each concern was conceptualised as a nine-point scale at an interval rather than ordinal level of measurement (1 = minimum concern; 9 = maximum concern). It is the amount and kind of emphasis one places on the two dimensions that determines which mode of conflict management one uses. Put under the microscope, the two nine-point dimensions of concern produce $9 \times 9 = 81$ locations of conflict behaviour. Each combination of dual concern results in a unique behavioural compound, in which the two concerns lose their identities like hydrogen and oxygen turning from gas into liquid form (Blake & Mouton, 1981).

Dominant behaviours as dependent variables.   Blake and Mouton (1964, 1970) focused on developing their theory with regard to the following five locations of conflict behaviour: 1,1; 1,9; 5,5; 9,9; 9,1. These behavioural locations result from low (1), intermediate (5), and high (9) levels of concern for one's own goals and concern for the other's goals. In the 1,1 corner of very low concern for the goals of both self and opponent, the actor stays out of a situation that provokes controversy, turns away from an issue that promotes disagreement, or remains neutral (*avoiding*). The one-sided concern for the other's goals in the upper left corner (1,9) determines actions to maintain harmony. The actor smoothes over the conflict by cajolery, appeals to reason, or appeases the quarrel (*accommodating*). People with intermediate concerns, who apply the 5,5 theory in the centre, settle the conflict through bargaining a middle-of-the-road compromise (*compromising*). Under high concern for everyone's goals (9,9) creative problem solving results in complete satisfaction of all parties involved (*problem solving*). Lastly, an individual in the bottom right corner having a one-sided concern for his or her own goals (9,1) believes that the conflict can be controlled by overpowering it and suppressing the adversary. Winning for one's own position predominates over seeking an escape route, a way back, or a way out (*fighting*).

Because Blake and Mouton (1964) distinguished only five pure conflict behaviours (1,1; 1,9; 5,5; 9,9; 9,1), the overwhelming majority of the other 76 behavioural locations in the grid were viewed as mixtures of the five pure behaviours. Hence, by implication, the behavioural locations were seen as resulting from mixtures of low, intermediate, and high concern for one's own goals and for the other's goals, respectively (e.g. $3 = 1 + 5$; $7 = 5 + 9$). I conceptualise these behavioural mixtures as conglomerated conflict behaviours, which are the rule rather than the exception.

Additionally, Blake and Mouton (1964) devoted two chapters to a variety of what they called complex or mixed grid theories, in which two or more of the five pure modes of conflict behaviour are either simultaneously or successively used in conjunction with one another. A good example is paternalism, involving tight control in work matters, flowing from high concern for one's own goals (9,1), coupled with being generous and kind in a personal way, flowing from high concern for the other's goals (1,9). A related illustration is the "two-hat approach," in which high one-sided concern for one's own goals determines 9,1 behaviour, followed by high one-sided concern for the other's goals and 1,9 behaviour. Whereas under paternalism aspects of fighting and accommodating operate in juxtaposition, under the two-hat approach either one or the other is operating, never both together. Clearly, paternalism and the two-hat approach are examples of simultaneously and sequentially conglomerated conflict behaviour, respectively.

Strengths and a Weakness

Given my conflict definitions, and given the above taxonomies of conflict behaviour, the conflict management grid theory has several strengths. One strength is that its explanations of conflict handling are restricted to a single party's behaviour. This restriction allows the model to be applied to one-sided conflicts, in which only one party is aware of the discord. It also allows us to conceptualise two-sided conflicts in which the parties use different modes of conflict handling. Some authors claim that the grid framework is useful for conceptualising not only interpersonal conflict but also dyadic conflict between organisational groups or even nations (e.g. Fisher, 1990).

A second advantage is that the theory explains conflict behaviours rather than conflict outcomes. Behaviours are the means by which one tries to realise certain outcomes, but these attempts can and do sometimes fail. For example, problem solving can after all produce a winner and a loser, whereas fighting can result in a sudden solution.

As a third strong aspect, the theory applies to conflicts that involve all kinds of issues; that is, it does not couple a certain issue to a particular conflict behaviour toward the other party. Different issues such as a lie and a betrayal may thus lead to the same combination of concerns and associated behaviour. Conversely, the same issue may under different circumstances, such as trust or time pressure, lead to different combinations of concerns and different modes of conflict management.

The fourth strength of the theory is its recognition that disputants take the opponent's outcomes and reactions into account. The traditional model of thought that dominates behavioural research on conflict management, including negotiation, assumes only a concern for one's own outcomes. According to Pruitt and Carnevale (1993, p. 8), this "dominant paradigm is overly simplistic. It relies too much on the assumption that negotiators are always trying to maximize self-interest. It ignores the social context of negotiation, overlooking such important phenomena as social norms, relationships between negotiators, group decision processes, and the behaviour of third parties" (for a similar view, see Greenhalgh, 1995). These authors adopted the dual concerns framework with the explicit aim of correcting for the one-sidedness of prior theory.

As a fifth merit, the theory shows that either concern has a double-edged effect. Two examples should clarify this. A high concern for one's own goals leads to problem solving in conjunction with a high concern for the other's goals, but it leads to fighting in conjunction with a low concern for the other's goals. Likewise, a low concern for the other's goals leads to avoiding in conjunction with a low concern for one's own goals, but it leads to fighting in conjunction with a high concern for one's own goals. No doubt these and similar insights implied by the grid paradigm are remarkable for their clarity, testability, and practical applicability.

The sixth strength of the theory is that it can also explain why disputants change their behaviour, and predict the direction of that change. When at least one of an actor's two concerns changes, this actor will shift from a certain conflict reaction to another. Given a change in the dual concern, Fig. 1.1 specifies what behavioural shift will occur; that is, which of the five main reactions will replace the currently active mode of conflict management. The "conflict concerns theory" in Chapter 4 will elaborate on changing concerns as crucial factors in the explanation of unfolding conglomerated conflict behaviour and (de-)escalative processes.

The virtue that stands out most in the present context is that Blake and Mouton (1964) explicitly addressed behavioural complexity. The above-mentioned examples of paternalism and the two-hat approach nicely illustrate the fact that some reactions to conflict issues cannot be explained by a single level of concern for one's own goals combined with a single level of concern for the other's goals. Neither can these reactions be placed in a single location of conflict behaviour within the grid space of 81 behavioural locations. This important feature of the theory has not been noticed by the many researchers who have based their work on the conflict management grid over the last 30 years. In an attempt to correct that neglect of behavioural complexity, this book asserts that most conflict behaviour cannot be placed in one of the five pure grid locations of avoiding, accommodating, compromising, problem solving, and fighting. Conglomerated conflict management is the rule rather than the exception.

The conflict management grid also has a weakness. It was visually represented in an ambiguous way. Fig. 1.1 gives rise to a multitude of perceptual organisations. Mathematically and logically, an abscissa and an ordinate representing two determinants of five behaviours form a quite simple and comprehensible model. As a perceived object, however, Fig. 1.1 constitutes a rather complicated visual field of catchwords at the corners and midpoint (originally brief circumscriptions), number combinations at the corners and midpoint, concern captions indicating horizontal and vertical axes, and squares all over the diagram. We can focus on each of these parts of the differentiated visual field. However, inevitably, there is always one part that stands out in a distinctive way. Gestalt psychologists call the part that stands out the Gestalt (the German word for "form") or *figure*, and all other parts the background or just *ground*. The grid's main figure–ground manifestations deserve further exploration because, in my view, they provide different theoretical contributions. More than that, this book makes an attempt to transform the weakness of the grid's ambiguity into a strength by connecting distinct grid pictures and levels of theoretical value.

Grid Manifestations

In Fig. 1.1 the same parts of the visual field—words, numbers, and lines—may appear either as figure or as ground. Thus, on closer examination, Blake and Mouton's (1964, 1970) grid diagram is a classic example of an ambiguous visual field. It lends itself to four forms of figure–ground manifestation, to wit: the five *catchwords* at the corners and midpoint of Fig. 1.1, the symmetric (1,1; 5,5; 9,9) and asymmetric (1,9; 9,1) *pairs of numbers*, the *horizontal and vertical axes*, and the 81 *squares*. These four grid manifestations are elaborated in the remainder of this introductory chapter.

Catchwords.   If one focuses on the five catchwords, the following resemblances and differences come to the fore. To the left are two variants of nonconfrontation: avoiding and accommodating. In the middle and upper right are two variants of negotiation: striving for a mutually acceptable compromise, or a totally satisfactory solution to the problem. At the bottom right is the mode of fighting. Viewed like this, Fig. 1.1 manifests itself as a classification of conflict behaviours. Standing out is a simple verbal framework for the definition and operationalisation of five qualitatively different modes of conflict handling, henceforth called the "five-part typology."

Pairs of numbers.   If the number combinations hold a prominent place in the field of vision, there are three symmetric (1,1; 5,5; 9,9) and two asymmetric (1,9; 9,1) pairs of two digits. The first number denotes the actor's level of own outcomes, while the second number denotes the actor's estimation of the counterpart's level of outcomes. The pairs of behavioural outcomes describe variable sums on the 1,1–5,5–9,9 dimension, but constant sums on the 1,9–5,5–9,1 dimension. In addition, the variable-sum dimension is at right angles to the constant-sum dimension, so that all paired numbers together form a cross. Indeed, it is easy to recognise orthogonal dimensions in the very elegant whole of an "X-cross model."

Horizontal and vertical axes.   The horizontally and vertically placed concern captions, with the segmented scales to which they refer, are yet another view of the grid. Both concern for one's own goals and concern for the other's goals range from one to nine. One's low (1), intermediate (3), or high (9) position on the two concern dimensions determines which conflict behaviour one uses. Captions, scales, and low–high indications all call up the salient and good form of the grid's right-angled sides. Henceforth the two explanatory dimensions are referred to as the "L-angle of concerns."

Squares.   The last manifestation of the ambiguous picture in Fig. 1.1 is based on the Gestalt of the checkerboard of squares. The nonoverlapping and mutually related squares, neatly arranged in nine columns and nine rows of concern, are from now on given the apt name of the "grate of concerns." Recall that each square indicates a unique combination of dual concern, which explains how a person operating under that dual concern is likely to handle conflict. Unlike the five-part typology and the X-cross model, the squares of the grate of concerns refer to the determinants of conflict behaviour instead of the conflict behaviour itself. Unlike the L-angle of concerns that can explain only one unsegmented conflict behaviour at a time, several "squared" concerns can explain several components of conglomerated conflict behaviour such as paternalism and the two-hat approach (for details and additional examples, see Chapter 5).

To recapitulate, the original conflict management grid can now be seen as a *five-part typology* (catchwords), then as an *X-cross model* (pairs of numbers), as an *L-angle of concerns* (horizontal and vertical axes), or as a *grate of concerns* (nonoverlapping, interrelated squares). Each of these four grid faces is represented in Fig. 1.2.

THE SUBJECTIVE GRID

The visual field is organised in such a way that one sees what one is predisposed to see at the moment of perception. Momentary predispositions may be based on past experience, wishful thinking, or current goals. As an example of the latter, interventionists and researchers will approach the

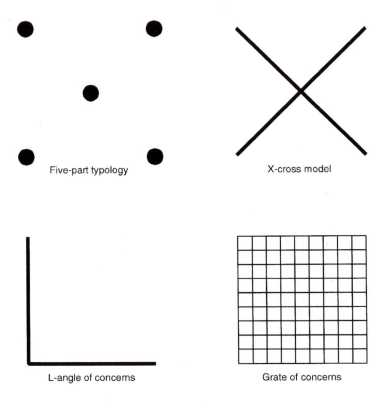

FIG. 1.2   Four faces of the conflict management grid.

conflict management grid with their own lens and filters. The intervention-ist wanting to change conflict behaviour will probably see the five-part typology or the X-cross model, whereas the researcher wanting to predict conflict behaviour might concentrate on the L-angle of concerns or the grate of concerns.

The following examples from the literature highlight the rather subjec-tive use of the five-part typology, the X-cross model, the L-angle of con-cerns, and the grate of concerns. They illustrate my view of the grid as an ambiguous stimulus that is perceived by social scientists to fit their mo-mentary predispositions.

Five-Part Typology

Thomas has written more on the conflict management grid than anyone else (Kilmann & Thomas, 1977; Ruble & Thomas, 1976; Thomas, 1976, 1979, 1988, 1992a, 1992b; Thomas & Pondy, 1977). He saw the grid as a five-part typology and then as an X-cross model, or as an L-angle of concerns. However, in more recent work he defined his ultimate position as being in favour of the five-part typology: "The model ... is purely a taxonomy ... It attempts to describe what the conflict modes *are*" (Thomas, 1988, pp. 432–433); "I now emphasize that the ... model is purely a classification scheme or *taxonomy* of five conflict-handling intentions" (Thomas, 1992a, p. 269). He also noted that other frameworks seek to explain the conflict modes as a function of the two concern dimensions. However, Thomas now rejects this approach because it reduces the complex causes of conflict behaviour to only two factors. His current preference is to use the descriptive five-part typology and then to construct more complex theories of the causes of these modes of conflict handling.

X-Cross Model

Several questionnaires have been created for the self-assessment of the five modes of conflict handling (see Chapter 3). In this line of research, Prein (1976) developed his own instrument and applied factor analysis to uncover the simple structure underlying the items. Unlike others, Prein (1976) predicted that factor analysis would result in the simple structure of the diagonals rather than the horizontal and vertical dimensions. That is, he recognised that the largest distances exist between avoiding and problem solving on the one hand, and between accommodating and fighting on the other. A rotation of these relatively long diagonals is necessary to find the relatively short horizontal axis (avoiding–fighting; accommodating–problem solving) and the equally short vertical axis (avoiding–accommodating; problem solving–fighting). This is a relevant insight because larger distances have more descriptive power; they discriminate better between distinct modes of conflict behaviour.

In successfully showing that his factor analyses reflected the diagonals and not the sides of the conflict management grid, Prein became one of the very first authors to recognise the real nature of the grid as a descriptive device. The grid's descriptive dimensions form an X-cross model of a variable-sum and a constant-sum dimension of potential outcomes rather than an L-angle of two concerns. Moreover, Prein was well aware of the fact that the results of his analyses did not explain the behaviours. He used the factor solution only to describe the content of each mode of conflict management in terms of the general behavioural factors of the X-cross model.

L-Angle of Concerns

Rubin, Pruitt, and Kim (1994) were interested in the determinants of choice among the basic strategies used by parties experiencing conflict. They saw the grid as an L-angle theory with concern for one's own outcomes and concern for the other's outcomes as intermediating between many sources of each of these concerns and strategic choice. Concern was defined as the importance placed on one's own and/or the other's interests. The theory contains four predictions. A preference for withdrawal or inaction results from a low concern about both parties' outcomes. Accommodating or yielding is encouraged mainly by a high concern for the other party's outcomes. When one's concern about both parties' outcomes is high, one will prefer problem solving. Finally, contentious fighting follows mainly from a high concern for one's own outcomes.

In the original L-angle of concerns theory, compromising is conceptualised as an additional 5,5 mode amidst all other modes. Rubin, Pruitt, and Kim (1994), however, limited themselves to a two-dimensional model with four strategies of preferred conflict handling, feeling no need to postulate a fifth strategy of compromising, resulting from intermediate levels of concern for one's own and other's outcomes. Interestingly, Pruitt and Rubin (1986) saw splitting the difference or steering a middle course as arising from one of two sources—either lazy problem solving or simple yielding by both people or groups.

Grate of Concerns

Earlier sections made it clear that Blake and Mouton (1964) addressed behavioural complexity in the form of, for instance, paternalism and the two-hat approach. Under paternalism, fighting and accommodating operate in a simultaneous aggregation, whereas under the two-hat approach they operate in a sequential aggregation. In both cases the aspects of fighting result from high concern for one's own goals and low concern for the other's goals, while the aspects of accommodating result from low concern for one's own goals and high concern for the other's goals. So, both paternalism and the two-hat approach result from a low as well as a high level of each of the two concerns. In fact, in both cases the grate of concerns is applied twice to predict both fighting and accommodating as aggregated locations of conflict management.

Blake and Mouton (1964, e.g. pp. 212, 221–222) explicitly stated that one can also be influenced by more than two combinations of the two concerns; sometimes a manager even "operates all over the grid." Apparently, any main cell of low, intermediate, or high concern in the grate of concerns (1,1; 1,9; 5,5; 9,9; 9,1) can occur together with one or more of the other four main cells, as the 76 mixed cells indicate already. Upon closer consideration, Blake and Mouton introduced the metatheory that their L-angle of concerns theory sometimes has to be applied repeatedly to predict a number of entwined locations of conflict behaviour—that is, components of conglomerated conflict behaviour.

Clearly, in their metatheory, Blake and Mouton (1964, 1970) went beyond the views of five-part typology, X-cross model, and L-angle of concerns, which share the assumption that any conflict behaviour occupies only a single position in the behavioural space. The five-part typology and the X-cross model cannot describe, neither can the L-angle of concerns explain, conglomerated conflict behaviour reflecting several positions in the behavioural space. Henceforth explanations of conglomerated conflict behaviour based on the grate of concerns are called "complexity explanations."

Levels of Theoretical Value

The grid's figure–ground manifestations portrayed in Fig. 1.2 differ in the emphasis that is placed on the description, the two-dimensional structure, and the explanation of conflict management, respectively. As will be discussed now, the underlying factors of description, dimensions, and explanation further clarify what each subjective grid manifestation represents. They also allow a particular theoretical rank order of the four grid faces.

Description.   Both five-part typology and X-cross model stress the descriptive rather than the explanatory nature of the grid. Of course, the five-part typology of conflict behaviours can be related to antecedents and consequences in a theoretical way, which has been done with great success (for recent overviews, see Rahim, 1992; Rubin, Pruitt, & Kim 1994; Thomas, 1992b; Van de Vliert, in press). But the five-part typology in and of itself does not contain any explanatory relationship that goes beyond simple description. Also, the X-cross model of a variable-sum and a constant-sum dimension has been used as a predictor of both conflict behaviour (e.g. Deutsch, 1949, 1973; Schelling, 1960) and conflict outcomes (e.g. Lax & Sebenius, 1986; Walton & McKersie, 1965). But the X-cross model is not an unequivocal predictor because, as will be elaborated from Chapter 4 onward, both the variable-sum and the constant-sum dimension mix up the potential outcomes of self and opponent. Consequently, one never knows whether a resulting conflict behaviour or outcome results from the potential outcomes for oneself, from the potential outcomes for one's opponent, or both. Rather than as a predictor, the X-cross model qualifies as a descriptor that specifies whether a particular behaviour treats oneself and the opponent equally or differentially (for details, see Chapter 3).

Although both five-part typology and X-cross model describe the differences among avoiding, accommodating, compromising, problem solving and fighting, they do so at a different theoretical level. The five-part typology specifies the behavioural content only at a nominal level of description, whereas the X-cross model reaches at least an ordinal level of description (e.g. compromising is higher on the variable-sum dimension than avoiding, but lower than problem solving). This book is therefore based on the viewpoint that nominal behavioural descriptions such as the five-part typology have less theoretical quality than dimensional behavioural descriptions such as the X-cross model.

Dimensions.   Both the X-cross model of the grid's diagonals and the L-angle of concerns of the grid's sides put forward two-dimensional frameworks. Whereas the X-cross model provides dimensional descriptors, the L-angle of concerns provides dimensional predictors. Granted, the L-angle of concerns is often used as a pair of descriptive rather than explanatory dimensions. However, because the concerns are intrapersonal and cannot be observed well by others, they are not unequivocal features of intended or displayed conflict behaviour. Moreover, predictors such as the L-angle of concerns are rarely good descriptors (Nicotera, 1993). The pair of concerns only indicates the preferred strategy of conflict behaviour. "But for a strategy actually to be adopted, it must also be seen as minimally feasible. If not, another strategy will be chosen, even if it is less consistent with the current combination of concerns" (Rubin, Pruitt, & Kim, 1994, p. 37). Overall, the common practice of using the L-angle of concerns as a pair of descriptive instead of explanatory dimensions is not to be recommended.

This book is also based on the viewpoint that descriptions in terms of the X-cross model have less theoretical quality than explanations in terms of the L-angle of concerns. The L-angle rather than the X-cross may serve as a backbone of conflict behaviour theory because explanations account for what has been described first. Chomsky (1965) told us much the same thing in his dictum that observational and descriptive adequacies are prerequisites for viable explanatory efforts.

Explanation.   Both the L-angle of concerns and grate of concerns constitute determinants of conflict behaviour. As outlined already, the L-angle theory and the grate metatheory of concerns predict singular and complex modes of conflict handling, respectively. The novel paradigm of behavioural complexity to be unfolded in this book reflects my presupposition that explanations of singular conflict behaviour have less theoretical quality than explanations of conglomerated conflict behaviour. Indeed, explanations that can account for complex conglomerations of conflict behaviour, such as trench warfare in which the parties may avoid and fight each other at the same time, have the highest level of theoretical quality.

Typology, model, theory, metatheory. The above viewpoints imply that the theoretical value increases if the grid manifestations are placed in the following order: typology, model, theory, and metatheory. The five-part *typology* is a classification or taxonomy based on the nominal character-istics and particulars of distinct conflict behaviours. The X-cross *model* is a set of leading ideas about the nature of conflict handling and the dimen-sional differences among distinct conflict behaviours. The L-angle of con-cerns *theory* is a set of rules of correspondence between distinct conflict behaviours and their determinants and consequences. A *metatheory* is an overarching rule of correspondence, or a set of such overarching rules, regarding one or more distinct theories. Thus the grate of concerns, with its implicit rule that the L-angle of concerns theory has to be applied repeatedly to predict separate components of conglomerated conflict behaviour, constitutes a metatheory.

At the bottom level of theory building we find conflict definitions, including those that were given earlier in this chapter. The increases in scientific value from that point onward can be portrayed as a four-step theoretical ladder of conflict behaviour (see Fig. 1.3). Each step includes the preceding steps. Specifically, the five-part typology of avoiding, accom-modating, compromising, problem solving, and fighting provides good tools for defining and confining the distinct components of a behavioural aggregation. In addition, the more advanced X-cross model can be used to describe the interrelationships among the components in terms of a variable-sum and a constant-sum dimension of potential outcomes of the conflict. Next, each of these components separately can be explained by applying the L-angle theory of concern for one's own goals and concern for the opponent's goals. Finally, the metatheory, which explains complex conglomerations of conflict behaviour, includes the preceding steps of typology, model, and theory.

RECAPITULATION

In this book conflict refers to an individual's experience of discord due to at least one socially induced issue. It elicits complex goal-directed inter-action and subsequent outcomes for all parties involved. Previous authors have classified modes of conflict handling into dichotomies, trichotomies, and four- and five-part typologies. Although these taxonomies have en-riched and advanced the scientific field of social conflict, they might lead

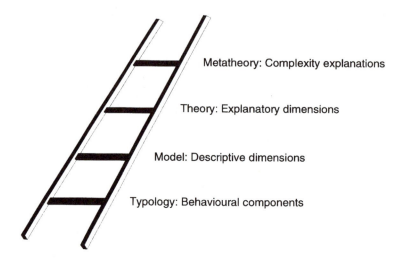

Metatheory: Complexity explanations

Theory: Explanatory dimensions

Model: Descriptive dimensions

Typology: Behavioural components

FIG. 1.3   The four-step theoretical ladder of conglomerated conflict behaviour.

to a paradigmatic crisis because they neglect behavioural complexity. Conglomerated conflict behaviours, defined as aggregations of intended or displayed reactions, could probably bring about a paradigm shift. Blake and Mouton's (1964, 1970) classic theory of the conflict management grid (see Fig. 1.1) offers some promising points of departure for further theory building about conglomerated conflict behaviour, including paternalism (simultaneous aggregation of fighting and accommodating) and the two-hat approach (sequential aggregation of fighting and accommodating).

The conflict management grid has four manifestations or faces, portrayed in Fig. 1.2, which may be used to describe and explain con-glomerated conflict behaviour. First, the components of conglomerated conflict behaviour can be described by applying the manifestation of the five-part typology of avoiding, accommodating, compromising, problem solving, and fighting. Second, a more advanced description of the compo-nents in terms of their variable-sum and constant-sum character results from the application of the manifestation of the X-cross model. Third, the manifestation of the L-angle of concerns for one's own and the opponent's goals can be employed to explain a single component of conglomerated conflict behaviour (see Fig. 1.1). The fourth grid manifestation, the grate of concerns for one's own and the opponent's goals, allows the explanation of all components of conglomerated conflict behaviour.

The manifestations of the conflict management grid may be represented as a ladder with stepwise increases in theoretical quality (see Fig. 1.3). The first step leads to the *five-part typology*, the description of five qualitatively different components of conglomerated conflict behaviour. The second step leads to the *X-cross model*, the description of a behavioural conglomeration in terms of a variable-sum and a constant-sum dimension of potential outcomes. The third step leads to the *L-angle of concerns*, the explanation of a single component of conglomerated conflict behaviour through the dimensions of concern for one's own and the other's goals. The fourth step leads to the *grate of concerns*, which can explain more than one component of a conglomeration of conflict management.

PLAN OF THE BOOK

Figures 1.2 and 1.3 are used as the cornerstones of the book. The sequence of chapters on the distinct manifestations of conglomerated conflict behaviour is designed in such a way that the theoretical value increases step by step.

As a first step, Chapter 2 gives an overview of the five-part typology for describing behavioural components and integrates it with the aforementioned two-, three- and four-part taxonomies of conflict handling. An observational experiment in Dutch police organisations is reported to test the validity of the proposed overarching typology. At the same time the study further typifies the five generic components of conglomerated conflict behaviour.

Chapter 3 takes the second step by illuminating the X-cross model for describing behavioural components with the help of the variable-sum dimension of integration and the constant-sum dimension of distribution. The two-dimensional model clarifies how one overcomes behavioural dilemmas between integration (equal treatment of self and opponent) and distribution (differential treatment of self and opponent). The last part of the chapter tests the generalisability of the dimensions of integration and distribution across assessment instruments and a variety of components of behavioural conglomerations.

The third step is from the description to the explanation of conglomerated conflict behaviour. Chapter 4 focuses on the L-angle of explanatory dimensions of concern for one's own goals and concern for the other's goals—that is, on the social motives of individualism and altruism. The validity of this dual concern theory is examined theoretically and empirically. In addition, an extended theory is suggested in which the concerns are conceptualised as mediating variables between a conflict issue and a single component of dominant conflict behaviour. The position is taken that concern for the other's goals rather than concern for one's own goals determines whether the conflict takes a de-escalative or escalative course.

The last step leads to the highest level of theoretical value, dealing with full-complexity explanations of conflict handling. At this level, Chapter 5 explores the metaphor of the grate of concerns producing simultaneous and sequential components of behaviour. The conflict concerns theory is extended into a theory of conglomerated conflict behaviour, a metatheory that explains more than one behavioural component at the same time. This more advanced theory describes and explains instances of conglomerated conflict behaviour such as walk-away negotiation, tacit coordination, firm flexibility, and the use of promises. The chapter ends with empirical demonstrations of simultaneous and sequential conglomerations of conflict behaviour as powerful predictors of the substantive and relational outcomes of interpersonal conflict.

An overview of the book from different perspectives is presented in Chapter 6. Handling conflict is pictured as processing issues, developing goal concerns, overcoming choices, and producing (de-)escalation. Special attention is paid to conglomerated conflict behaviours that tend to produce short-term de-escalation but long-term escalation, or short-term escalation but long-term de-escalation. The chapter closes with a concluding discussion and evaluation of the four-step theoretical ladder from Fig. 1.3.

Each chapter ends with five or six propositions. The function of these axioms, suppositions, and corollaries is to emphasise the most basic and most innovative contributions of the foregoing chapter. All scattered propositions are brought together in the Appendix "Thirty-Four Propositions" to sketch a bird's-eye view of the book.

PROPOSITIONS

1a.   Conflict refers to an individual's cognitive and/or affective discord due to a socially induced issue, which elicits goal-directed reactions and subsequent outcomes for all parties involved (pp. 4–7).

1b.   As a rule, a conflict issue elicits a complex aggregation of intended or displayed behavioural components, referred to as conglomerated conflict behaviour (pp. 3, 6).

1c.   Blake and Mouton's (1964, 1970) conflict management grid has four distinct manifestations or faces, which can be used to describe and explain conglomerated conflict behaviour (pp. 14–19).

1d.   The theoretical value of the four grid manifestations increases in the following order: descriptions of behavioural components, descriptive dimensions, explanatory dimensions, complexity explanations (pp. 19–22).

1e.   The dimensions of the grid's diagonals *describe* conglomerated conflict behaviour, whereas the goal concern dimensions of the grid's sides also *explain* it (pp. 20–22).

PART TWO

Description

CHAPTER TWO

First Step: Description of Behavioural Components

• •

•

• •

The very first result of studying the reactions of principal parties to their mutual conflict is, of course, a simple description of what each person is doing. The main behavioural components are identified, named, and their characteristics listed. People may typically react agreeably or disagreeably, passively or actively. For example, a psychologist who is at loggerheads with a social worker about the "conservative and formalistic" procedures in their mental-health-care institution can avoid the issue, accommodate the social worker's wishes, pursue a compromise, seek a resolution, and fight the social worker. These main components of conglomerated conflict behaviour are labelled the five-part typology. Their definition and confinement is a modest first move towards the development of knowledge about complex reactions to conflict issues.

Categorisations of behavioural components such as the five-part typology represent the lowest level of theory development. At this level the determinants and consequences of the reactions have a rather superficial descriptive function at most. This chapter deals with such classifications of components of conflict handling. First, the five generic behavioural components of avoiding, accommodating, compromising, problem solving, and fighting are discussed. Next, the two-, three-, four-, and five-part taxonomies of conflict behaviour, reviewed in Chapter 1, are mutually related. An attempt is made to integrate all types of conflict handling that are part of these taxonomies on the basis of two features: agreeableness and activeness. Closing the overview of descriptions of behavioural components is a global report of an observational study undertaken to test the validity of the leading idea in the integrated taxonomy.

FIVE-PART TYPOLOGY

As outlined in Chapter 1, all intended and displayed outward reactions to social discord come under the general heading of conflict behaviour. The behavioural modes at the corners and midpoint of the conflict management grid were labelled avoiding, accommodating, compromising, problem solving, and fighting. People can be asked to describe the occurrence of these components of conflict handling. One may have them indicate to what extent each component is used by themselves (for a brief review of five instruments, see the Box "Self-Assessments Based on the Five-Part Typology"). One may also have respondents indicate to what extent each component is used by their opponents, or by other persons. The resulting descriptions originate from biased actors, biased observers, or neutral observers, respectively.

Actors will have difficulty entangling their inner frustrations or attitudes and their outer conflict behaviours. They will tend to overplay the behavioural intentions they experience. For observers, on the other hand, it will not be easy to read other people's behavioural signs because the same conflict action must be interpreted differently depending on the purpose of that action. For example, if the protagonist is silent for a while, this may predominantly reflect a form of nonconfrontation, a form of negotiation, or even a tactic that is part of a fight. In other words, outsiders can categorise conflict behaviour more easily when the actor's behavioural intention is better known or attributable with more certainty. All this should be kept in mind whenever one encounters descriptions such as the ratings of others' conflict handling in Study 1 reported at the end of this chapter.

The five-part typology can be criticised for underrepresenting relatively aggressive components of conflict behaviour. Fighting is accompanied by the four much less contentious components of avoiding, accommodating, compromising, and problem solving. In an effort to correct this skewed distribution, one may distinguish between 2 x 2 components of fighting, namely indirect versus direct fighting, by fair versus unfair fighting (cf. Van de Vliert, 1990b). Indirect or cold fighting is characterised by covertness

Self-Assessments Based on the Five-Part Typology

Hall's (1969) *Conflict Management Survey* (CMS) measures an individual's use of the five modes across personal, interpersonal, small group, and intergroup contexts. It consists of 60 items (4 contexts x 3 statements x 5 modes). The items are rated on a 10-point scale ranging from "completely characteristic" to "completely uncharacteristic." For each mode of conflict management the sum of the 12 behaviour reports becomes the respondent's overall score for that mode. Shockley-Zalabak (1988) reviewed high item–test correlations, as well as moderate to low coefficients for the internal consistency and test–retest reliability of the mode subscales. Additionally, she reported relationships between the CMS and other instruments that provide some support for the concurrent validity of the CMS.

Thomas and Kilmann's (1974) *Management Of Differences Exercise* (MODE) is a forced-choice questionnaire consisting of 30 sets of paired items, with each item describing the likelihood of one of the five modes. A person's score on each mode is the number of times that person selects statements representing that behavioural intention over other mode statements. The mode subscale measures appear to have rather low levels of homogeneity and test–retest reliability (Womack, 1988). Support for the MODE's validity includes demonstrated correlations between measures of the five modes and scores on related instruments (Brown, Yelsma, & Keller, 1981; Kilmann & Thomas, 1977). However, Kabanoff (1987), who used peer ratings of conflict behaviours as criteria, failed to find evidence of predictive validity.

The *Organisational Communication Conflict Instrument* (OCCI; Putnam & Wilson, 1982) assesses communicative tactics that individuals use. On 30 seven-point scales it is indicated how frequently one engages in each of the five modes of conflict handling. Principal components analysis indicated that avoiding and accommodating both represent nonconfrontation (mean Cronbach's $\alpha = .88$), that compromising and problem solving may both be interpreted as solution orientation (mean $\alpha = .83$), and that fighting reflects control (mean $\alpha = .77$). Wilson and Waltman (1988) discussed validity, particularly that the OCCI converges at moderate levels with measures of similar instruments.

Rahim's Organisational Conflict Inventory (ROCI) is a series of 28 five-point Likert items ranging from "strongly agree" to "strongly disagree" with the use of a mode of conflict handling (Rahim, 1983a). It is available in three forms, which refer to conflict with a boss, peer, or subordinate, respectively. The parts of the questionnaire containing the five mode clusters are internally consistent (mean $\alpha = .74$) and stable (mean retest reliability $= .76$; Weider-Hatfield, 1988). Evidence for ROCI's validity has been provided by the invariance of its factor model across groups, its ability to discriminate between groups known to differ in their conflict behaviour, its meaningful relations with other conflict manifestations, and its associations with measures of organisational effectiveness and climate (Rahim, 1983a, 1983b, 1992; Rahim & Magner, 1995; Weider-Hatfield, 1988).

The *Dutch Test of Conflict Handling* (DUTCH; Janssen & Van de Vliert, 1996) was designed to remedy the poor ability of instruments to discriminate between avoiding and accommodating, and between compromising and problem solving. It consists of 20 seven-point items, assessing the five components of conflict behaviour on bipolar response scales from very likely to very unlikely. In police organisations and hospitals alpha coefficients of internal consistency ranged from .60 to .85 for conflicts with superiors (mean α = .74) and from .59 to .81 for conflicts with subordinates (mean α = .72). The validity of the DUTCH has been assessed by comparing the 10 correlations among the subscales of conflict handling with the 10 theoretical interrelationships predicted by the conflict management grid (for the details of this approach, see Van de Vliert & Kabanoff, 1990).

and reliance on procedures, whereas direct or hot fighting is an overt, almost explosive form of straightforward contentious behaviour (cf. Glasl, 1980; Sheppard, 1984; Volkema & Bergmann, 1989). Both fighting components are fair or unfair to the extent that the combatants do or do not follow mutually agreed-upon behavioural rules (cf. Bach & Wyden, 1969). These four subdivisions of fighting are elaborated below, after a more detailed discussion of the four noncompetitive components of conflict handling.

Avoiding

Avoidance is the prevention or termination of efforts to yield openly, to negotiate constructively, or to win completely. Prevention takes place, for example, if a person suppresses awareness of a minor controversy, or if one ignores a conflict issue by denying that it is present or by not paying any attention to it. Likewise, showing seemingly issue-independent behaviour is a very popular way of avoiding other components of conflict handling. Such "avoiding by implication" may surface as a premature topic shift or as the "fact" that more important matters are pressing. It includes coping behaviours to alleviate the discomfort created by a stressful conflict—for example, engaging in physical exercise to take one's mind off the issue, having a drink, or seeking emotional support from friends.

Deliberate prevention or termination of more active reactions may represent a kind of nonoption, a choice not to choose. For instance, a lottery approach as a device for settlement represents a conscious decision not to take responsibility for any other component of conflict management. Some other illustrations of how people may deliberately demonstrate avoidance are: speaking about an issue in abstruse terms, making distracting or procedural remarks, and asking unfocused and conflict-irrelevant questions. Borisoff and Victor (1989) discussed the following additional ways of not really dealing with the conflict issues: making excuses, underresponsiveness, trivialisation of the problem through joking or sarcasm, silencing, using generalisations and stereotypes, and definitional side-tracking.

An interesting form of making excuses is the use of social accounts to explain one's own actions that may upset others (Bies, 1989; Sitkin & Bies, 1993; Thomas & Pondy, 1977). A social account attempts to influence the other party's perception of the unfavourability of the incident or action, one's own responsibility for what happened, or one's own intention to obstruct or irritate the other. According to Bartunek, Kolb, and Lewicki (1992), in organisational settings these and other forms of avoidance are the most commonly described type of dealing with conflict.

As a component of negotiation, avoiding often takes the shape of adopting a walk-away alternative, notably by turning to another buyer or seller. This no-agreement component is also known as the Best Alternative To a Negotiated Agreement, or BATNA (Fisher & Ury, 1981). It occurs when a bargainer's prospective outcomes do not equal or exceed this party's comparison level of alternatives (Wall, 1985). The possibility of a getaway via one's BATNA helps a negotiator "determine whether to negotiate at all, whether to continue the process, whether to accept a proposal, and whether an agreement, once reached, will be secure." (Lax & Sebenius, 1986, p. 47).

As a concept, avoiding is difficult to grasp and, for that reason, has given occasion for plenty of misconceptions. The following three considerations may further clarify the phenomenon of avoidance. First of all, the absence of a verbal reaction is a deed of avoidance only if this component is coupled with the absence of other components including nonverbal concessions, signals of a need for agreement, and expressions of aggressiveness. Second, active flight can be seen as a passive form of avoidance because there is no disagreeable interaction whatsoever with the counterpart. Similarly, an open declaration of withdrawal or neutrality is still a hardly agreeable form of nonconfrontation, because the actor is dealing with the issues and interests one-sidedly without giving in. Third, a distinction between short-term and longer-term avoidance provides additional insight. Rubin, Pruitt, and Kim (1994) defined inaction as a temporary move of doing nothing that leaves open the possibility of resuming efforts to deal with the controversy, whereas withdrawing was seen as a permanent move of leaving the conflict by terminating efforts to yield, to negotiate, or to fight.

Accommodating

Accommodation occurs when one gives in to the opponent's point of view or demand. It can be described best as open cooperation by nonconfrontation. Social psychologists concur that this type of behaviour derives its significance from different sources, including altruism, normative beliefs, the obtainment of benefits, and the prevention of costs. Some annotations may help frame these types of accommodating components more precisely.

A relevant observation is that many definitions of accommodation contain elements of self-sacrifice, thus ignoring one's own pay-offs of nonconfrontation through yielding. However, people also accommodate when that is fair, when they are wrong, and when they feel obliged to do so. Similarly, it is anything but self-sacrificing if accommodation forms a means to a further end that is more important than the immediate conflict issue. Sometimes giving in means building social credits for later interactions with the adversary or outsiders. In such cases, accommodating is setting a sprat to catch a mackerel. Sometimes acceptance of the opponent's position reflects minimising loss when one is outmatched and losing. Notice, however, that accommodation is bound up with components of negotiation if one seeks to guarantee restricted loss. Any proposal to surrender on certain conditions is a complicated attempt to safeguard certain interests in return for giving up the less important interests involved in losing the conflict. If the loser negotiates very skilfully, what seems to be accommodation at first sight may even turn into a Pyrrhic victory for the opponent in the end.

A clever complex strategy of accommodating is the involvement of a third party that paves the road for giving in without losing face. A skilful intermediary can be used to maintain one's own personal dignity and reputation. For example, a principal party may have a third party suggest proposals that help avoid the appearance of defeat on an issue, or help handle problems with a constituent. The outside helper may even be enlisted to take responsibility for particular concessions.

Compromising

Components of compromising refer to the pursuance of a mutually acceptable settlement in which each of the conflicting parties makes some concession. They cover tactics of temporary avoidance, accommodation, or contention, which are embedded in an intention to negotiate a settlement. Compromising is a ubiquitous phenomenon, occurring in all social relationships and governing much social behaviour. A typical compromise stands part way between the parties' preferred positions about each other's outcomes. Two classes of compromises, resulting from two components of negotiation—claiming versus trading—are discussed. Claim-negotiating is primarily making decisions, whereas trade-negotiating is primarily making exchanges. One may also change the game by converting a claim-negotiation into a trade-negotiation, or vice versa.

Claim-negotiation.   In the case of claiming outcomes, the intended compromise applies to an allocation of benefits or costs that nobody "owns" at present (e.g. manganese nodules at the seabed, a collective debt, a new position, part of the housekeeping money). Almost by definition compromising about incompatible claims is negotiating about the criterion or criteria on the basis of which the outcomes must be allocated. Important principles of allocative justice are those of equity, equality, and need (Deutsch, 1985; Pruitt, 1981; Folger, Sheppard, & Buttram, 1995; Zartman & Berman, 1982). A hypothesis exists "that the tendency for economically oriented groups will be to use the principle of equity, for solidarity-oriented groups to use the principle of equality, and for caring-oriented groups to use the principle of need as the basic value underlying the system of distributive justice" (Deutsch, 1985, p. 44).

Trade-negotiation.   In the case of trading outcomes, the intended compromise is an exchange of benefits or costs that one party "owns" for benefits or costs that the other party "owns" (e.g. remission of debts for promises of political support, hostages for unopposed withdrawal of hijackers, money for goods). This type of settlement includes compensation, whereby a conceding conflict party is repaid in some unrelated coin. Subject to several benefits or costs being under consideration, each party may get that outcome that it deems most important. This integrative trading of concessions on each party's high-priority issues in multi-attribute negotiations, called logrolling, can also be posited as a contingent splitting of differences (Greenhalgh, 1987). In my own terminology, logrolling can be conceptualised as either a simultaneous or a sequential conglomeration of the behavioural components of accommodating and fighting.

On closer examination, trade-negotiators often attempt to agree upon a package of four issues. They negotiate about the kind of outcome that they themselves will obtain, the kind of outcome that the other party will obtain in return, the relative weight of the two sorts of outcome, and the magnitude of the transfer of material or immaterial property. In essence it is a matter of conglomerated conflict behaviour directed at three part-settlements dealing with the means, the rate, and the magnitude of exchange.

Changing the game of compromising.   Because the distinction between claiming and trading is not well established in the bargaining literature, we hardly know anything about the tactics of defining the situation as a claim- or trade-negotiation. A new line of research might concentrate on conglomerated conflict behaviour meant to convert claim-compromising into trade-compromising, or vice versa. Illustrative are actions such as denying the ownership of costs (a poor plan, a tough job, being a long way behind), appropriating benefits (a promising idea, a pleasant chore, a lead), contesting that the opponent is the owner of benefits, and labelling the opponent as the owner of costs. A particularly fruitful area for theory development might be the situation in which one party sees no owners and therefore wants to pursue a claim-negotiation by reason of justice arguments, whereas the other party does see owners and therefore wants to pursue a trade-negotiation on the basis of things to be done in return.

It is worthwhile noting also that the literature predominantly, albeit implicitly, associates claim- and trade-negotiations with compromising about profits. Insufficient light has been shed on bargaining about costs. Most authors do not satisfactorily discuss such allocation rules as the cause-of-damage principle and the ability-to-pay principle. The topic of claiming or trading protection for costs clearly warrants further consideration, however, because negotiators react differently to gains and losses. In general, potential benefits appear to tend toward compromising by making concessions, whereas potential costs encourage inflexibility (Bazerman, Magliozzi, & Neale, 1985; De Dreu, Carnevale, Emans, & Van de Vliert, 1994, 1995; De Dreu, Emans, & Van de Vliert, 1992a, 1992b; Neale & Bazerman, 1985, 1991). Therefore, other things being equal and compared with compromising about benefits, compromising about costs elicits a tougher negotiation process and is attended with a greater risk of stalemate.

A relatively complex and indirect way of compromising is enlisting the services of a third party to facilitate the attainment of a settlement. More so than the conflicting individuals or groups themselves, the intermediary will be in a position to stress public interests and the importance of an agreement, to turn a claim-negotiation into a trade-negotiation, or to reframe gains as losses or losses as gains.

Problem Solving

Resolving the conflict is a sequential conglomeration of active and creative components of conflict behaviour. It is a process of open negotiation to reconcile completely the counterparts' basic interests in the end. Claim- and trade-negotiations may both lead to resolutions. Unlike compromising, problem solving is a win/win strategy aimed at optimising rather than at satisficing for the parties. If, for instance, two managers are competing for personnel, their problem ends in a compromise if both have to share one extra member of staff half-time during summer and winter. It is solved if they discover that one party only needs an extra member of staff during the summer whereas the other only needs one during the winter.

Usually problem solving is a more ambiguous activity than compromising. With compromising the goal is clear (a distribution or an exchange) and so is the road that leads to it (splitting the difference). With problem solving, on the other hand, both the goal and the means to achieve it are less obvious. Often both parties' seemingly incompatible goals must be redefined to reach a mutually satisfactory win/win agreement (Burton, 1990; Filley, 1975; Lax & Sebenius, 1986), sometimes termed "synergic" (e.g. Craig & Craig, 1974), or "Pareto optimal" (e.g. Luce & Raiffa, 1957). Problem solving "involves invention, and the clever thing is to recognize this, and not to let one's thinking stay within the boundaries of two alternatives which are mutually exclusive." (Follett, 1940, p. 33).

A somewhat different conceptualisation of conflict resolution has been worked out by Satir (1972). She envisioned three essential ingredients of social conflict: the issue, the self, and the other. Denying wipes out the issue, whereas placating wipes out the self (cf. accommodating); blaming wipes out the other (cf. fighting); and avoiding wipes out the issue and the other. Superrationalising wipes out all ingredients: the issue, the self, and the other. Only if one rejects wiping out any ingredient does one utilise conflict creatively by affirming the issue, the self, and the other (cf. problem solving). It may be noted in passing that Satir (1972), like Pruitt and Rubin (1986), feels no need to postulate an additional mode of compromising or splitting the difference, in which the issue, the self, and the other are all wiped out in part.

Problem-solving components are tentative and exploratory, seeking to expand rather than to control alternative courses of action. They communicate questions rather than statements. As Fisher and Ury (1981) have noted, questions generate answers, whereas statements generate resistance. Unlike statements, questions allow the other side to get standpoints and basic interests across. Consistent with this point of view, Tutzauer and Roloff (1988) demonstrated that seeking information, rather than giving information, led to insight into the opponent's priorities, which in turn resulted in integrative outcomes and subsequent satisfaction with how the conflict was handled. Furthermore, fully integrative outcomes appear to be linked to frequency of initiations, procedural suggestions, explorations, proposals, and other-supporting as well as positive affect statements (Putnam & Wilson, 1989).

Rubin, Pruitt, and Kim (1994) have identified and elaborated the following three routes for moving from opposing demands to a real solution of the conflict: *expanding the pie* by increasing the available resources such as money, time, and power, in cases where the discord hinges on a resource shortage; *cost cutting* by eliminating the disadvantages or trouble of an agreement for the parties involved; and *bridging* by devising a new option that does not satisfy the parties' initial demands, but that does satisfy the interests underlying the parties' opposing positions. Trade-negotiating, including logrolling, may shift from compromising into problem solving by expanding the pie, cost cutting, or bridging.

To create resolutions the disputants must reach beyond themselves. They have to bring in an extra piece of information, a new relation between old pieces of information, or a novel frame. In this vein Väyrynen (1991) discussed issue transformation, rule transformation, actor transformation, and structural transformation. The principal parties can also bring in a mediating third party, who can take over that almost impossible task of excelling oneself. A mediator can successfully emphasise a superordinate goal that might otherwise become caught up in the conflict if it was initiated by one of the principal parties (Johnson & Lewicki, 1969). Or a mediator can be used to discourage the opponent's avoidance or aggression so as to bring about a more constructive level of tension, which enhances the chances of solving the conflict (Van de Vliert, 1985, 1997; Walton, 1987).

Inherent in the effective solving of small or common problems is a sequential conglomeration of conflict intensification and reconciliation. The phase of integration produces better results when preceded by a phase of detailed confrontation during which the conflict issues are defined and analysed (Fisher, 1997; Johnson, Johnson, & Smith, 1989; Turner & Pratkanis, 1997; Walton, 1987). Conflict stimulation generally enhances joint outcomes when the tension level is low rather than high, when conflict focuses on task issues rather than identity issues, and when disputants' goals are positively rather than negatively interdependent (Amason & Schweiger, 1997; Jehn, 1997; Putnam, 1997; Van de Vliert, 1997). In such cases, limited escalation facilitates differentiation, stimulates the search for new means and goals, and prevents rash pseudosolutions. Self-evidently, controlled escalation as part of a process of creating high joint benefit must not be mistaken for a win–lose battle.

Fighting

One who seeks to prevail at the expense of the adversary engages in conglomerated fighting behaviour, which has also been called a win–lose power struggle. Indeed, in order to defeat a protagonist who offers resistance one must overpower such an "enemy." Since there are many forms of power, many corresponding components of fighting exist. One may notably use positive or negative sanctions, legitimate claims, and convincing information. Above fighting has been subdivided into indirect and direct fighting on the one hand, and fair and unfair fighting on the other. Indirect, direct, and fair fights will now be considered subsequently.

Indirect fight.   People at war relatively often prefer to deal with one another as little as possible while attempting to beat the adversary with the help of procedures. The resulting covert, cold fights are an intriguing conglomeration of avoidance and enforcement by manipulating the agenda and the rules of the game to one's own advantage. An example is the statement "Let's take turns to explain why each of us thinks to have done the right thing." If at all possible, face-to-face contacts are avoided while one obstructs the other's plans, talks behind the other's back, or forms hidden alliances with third parties. Bisno (1988) clustered the following three types of indirect fighting under the heading of passive resistance or concealment: *negativism*—when persons, by body language or terse verbalisation, manifest disagreement or hurt, without overtly engaging in hostility; *noncompliance*—running the gamut from simple noncooperation to the covert sabotage of policies by inadequate implementation; and *stonewalling*— adamantly refusing to comment on something or to admit to an action or statement. Why and when people prefer such "hidden" aggressive strategies to straightforward fights are still largely unanswered questions.

Direct fight.   Volkema and Bergmann (1989) investigated concrete interactions that occur during overt and hot fights between individuals at work, including: shouting at the person; trying to get even; pushing, striking, or punching the person; throwing things; and sabotaging the person's work. No less familiar are laughing at the adversary, making presumptive remarks, belittling, accusing, and using abusive language. On empirical grounds set forth by Straus (1979), all such hot fighting could be subdivided into verbal aggression, physical force, and the potentially lethal use of a knife or a gun.

On a more general level of analysis direct, contentious tactics are an assortment of odd bedfellows ranging from ingratiation, feather ruffling, and persuasive argumentation, to promises, threats, and irrevocable commitments (Rubin, Pruitt, & Kim, 1994). Yet another interesting means of expression is whistle-blowing, in which an insider chooses to take frustrations to outside authorities or to the press. One form is filing a charge, a suit, or a petition in court. According to Glasl (1980), in strongly escalating conflicts the combatants start to make each other lose face, then use all-pervasive and determined threats, and ultimately deny the other's human value, thus clearing the way for manipulation, retaliation, and elimination of the enemy. All such sequential conglomerations of reactions indicate hot fighting if they are supposedly instrumental to beating the adversary. Yet if such behaviours are used to pursue an agreement, they indicate an escalatory component in a complex process of negotiation.

Fair fight. Though indirect and direct fights are not the pursuing of agreement between the conflicting parties, they may still be based on such an agreement. Fights are fair to the extent that the combatants follow agreed-upon rules of right and wrong behaviour to defeat each other. A sports competition, for example, is intended to be a fair fight. The family therapists Bach and Wyden (1969) were the first to teach people the conglomerated conflict behaviour of how to fight fairly (see also Brown, 1983; Deutsch 1973; Robbins, 1974; Van de Vliert, 1985). Although they did not make clear what they meant by a "fair fight," their descriptions indicated that they considered openness, honesty, equality, and reciprocity relevant criteria. The goal should be to pursue better mutual relationships through struggling instead of knockouts. The parties must learn not only to communicate better with one another but also to acquire skills in communicating about the rules laid down for fair conflict management. Rules could be: not leaving during a fight; no bluffing, generalisations, or ultimatums; no underhandedness; no aiming for the opponent's Achilles heel; no deliberate actions in the presence or the absence of certain third parties; or no physical violence. To fight fairly implies that one must learn not only to inflict fair blows but also to receive and absorb blows in a fair manner (Van de Vliert, 1985, 1990b). With regard to violent communications and treatments, Bies and Moag (1986) also identified various principles of fairness, including the propriety of questions, justification for decisions, and truthfulness (candidness and no deception).

The refined distinctions between indirect, direct, and fair fighting have not been introduced into the instruments designed to assess the use of modes of conflict behaviour. Neither are they part of taxonomies of conflict handling other than those operationalised in measuring instruments. In Chapter 5 of this book, however, indirect and direct fighting are further conceptualised and explained as components of conglomerated conflict management.

INTERRELATING FOUR TAXONOMIES

The five-part typology does not hold the monopoly on classifications of components of conglomerated conflict behaviour, as is apparent from the review of taxonomies in Chapter 1. A more parsimonious or less parsimonious categorisation of conflict management may be preferred with regard to the purposes of a research or intervention project. There simply is no "right" number of behavioural components. By clarifying commonalities and differences, this section attempts to facilitate justified choices between the most well-known two-, three-, four-, and five-part taxonomies (Blake & Mouton, 1964, 1970; Deutsch, 1949, 1973; Horney, 1945; Rubin, Pruitt, & Kim, 1994; Putnam & Wilson, 1982; Rahim, 1983b, 1992; Thomas, 1976, 1992b; Walton, Cutcher-Gershenfeld, & McKersie, 1994). A perusal of these taxonomies and empirical research (Bales, 1950; Sternberg & Dobson, 1987) suggests that the behavioural components can be very well discriminated on the basis of their degrees of agreeableness and activeness.

Agreeableness is the extent to which a component of conglomerated conflict behaviour has pleasant and relaxed, rather than stressful, qualities. Agreeable reactions reflect agreement, tension release, and solidarity (Bales, 1950). *Activeness* is the extent to which the conflict behaviour has responsive and direct rather than inert qualities (cf. Lazarus & Launier, 1978). Active reactions provide or solicit suggestions, opinions, and orientations (Bales, 1950). Agreeableness and activeness are real, relevant, and readable features of a party's reactions, which make them suitable indeed for distinguishing among the following conflict behaviour taxonomies.

Cooperation–competition.   Often conflict handling is analysed as a simple dichotomy in which cooperation and competition are seen as mutually exclusive reactions to social conflict (see Chapter 1). Some scholars view cooperation and competition as social value orientations to maximise joint outcomes or relative advantage in favour of self (e.g. Liebrand, Wilke, Vogel, & Walters, 1986; MacCrimmon & Messick, 1976; McClintock, 1972; McClintock & Liebrand, 1988). For others, who are more strongly influenced by Deutsch (1949, 1973), cooperation typically represents an agreeable activity, whereas competition constitutes a disagreeable activity.

The cooperation–competition bifurcation is a relatively undifferentiated division in which cooperation varies from hardly agreeable and hardly active noncompetition to pre-eminently agreeable and active resolution of the conflict issue. In fact, the dichotomy conceptualises cooperation as a residual category of noncompetition ranging from passive to active cooperation (Ruble & Thomas, 1976).

Nonconfrontation, negotiation, competition.   Horney (1945) introduced the conceptual scheme of passively moving away or withdrawing from confrontation, actively moving towards people and towards a negotiated agreement, and moving against people through aggressive competition. Her taxonomy can be seen as a result of refining the concepts of noncompetition–competition along the lines of passive and active noncompetition or cooperation. And the same holds for Putnam and Wilson's (1982) equivalent scheme of nonconfrontation, solution orientation, and control. Much empirical evidence supports this trichotomy (e.g. Fitz-patrick, 1988; Lawrence & Lorsch, 1967; Walton, Cutcher-Gershenfeld, & McKersie, 1994; Weider-Hatfield, 1988; Wilson & Waltman, 1988).

Four-part taxonomy.   Rubin, Pruitt, and Kim's (1994) taxonomy of four available strategies—inaction, yielding, problem solving, and contending—can be understood in the light of the following conceptual refinement of the above trichotomy. It makes sense to assume that inaction and yielding are different categories by which one can move away and refrain from a proactive stance. Nonconfrontation will tend to take the form of no sig-nals of agreement or disagreement whatsoever during avoidance, but of signals of agreement if one accommodates. In about the same vein Ruble and Thomas (1976) and Cosier and Ruble (1981; see also Ruble & Cosier, 1982) showed that an avoiding opponent is perceived as less friendly, soft, and fair, as well as more greedy and stubborn than an accommodating opponent. So, less agreeable avoidance and more agreeable accommodation can well be subsumed under passive nonconfrontation.

It is interesting to note that essentially the same breakdown of conflict management has been used for the description and prediction of mediator behaviours. The strategic choice model of mediation in particular (Carnevale, 1986, 1992; Van de Vliert, 1992) distinguishes between four fundamental third-party strategies designed to produce agreement between conflicting parties: inaction, compensation, integration, and pressing.

Five-part taxonomy.   The taxonomy of avoiding, accommodating, com-promising, problem solving, and fighting can be understood as a further conceptual refinement of the above trichotomy as follows. Active co-operation by negotiation can be broken down into settling for a compro-mise through a less agreeable process of give and take, and solving the problem through a more agreeable process of satisfying all parties' wishes completely (cf. Putnam & Wilson, 1989; Van de Vliert & Hordijk, 1989; Walton & McKersie, 1965). This further subdivision indeed results in the five-part typology, which has repeatedly been supported empirically (e.g. Janssen, 1994; Janssen, Euwema, & Van de Vliert, 1994; Kilmann & Thomas, 1977; Prein, 1976; Rahim, 1983b; Rahim & Magner, 1995; Van de Vliert & Prein, 1989).

Again, essentially the same breakdown of conflict handling has been used for the description and prediction of third-party behaviours. More specifically, the theory on siding in a conflict (Laskewitz, Van de Vliert, & De Dreu, 1994; Van de Vliert, 1981) proposes that outsiders pressured to show their colours choose one of the following behaviour alternatives: avoidance, compromise, conflict resolution, and taking sides by accom-modating one party's wishes and fighting the other party's wishes.

Of course, five is an arbitrary rather than the "right" number of behavioural components. Notably, fighting also varies in activeness. Though fighting is never as passive as nonconfrontation through avoiding or accommodating, indirect fighting certainly is the most moderately active variant of contentious activity that contrasts with highly active moves of direct fighting.

In sum, classifications of components of conglomerated conflict behaviour can be integrated into a metataxonomy on the basis of agreeableness and activeness as linking concepts. Fig. 2.1 shows the main lines of thought. Agreeable cooperation can be first broken down into passively moving away by nonconfrontation, and actively moving toward by negotiating an agreement. These, in turn, have more specific conflict management components subsumed under them. Less agreeable avoiding and more agreeable accommodating are both subsumed under nonconfrontation. Similarly, compromising and problem solving represent subdivisions of negotiation. Disagreeable competition, equally called moving against, contending or fighting, can be broken down into moderately active indirect fighting and active direct fighting. The postulated degrees of agreeableness and activeness of the six components of conflict handling were tested in the following field experiment.

STUDY 1: OBSERVATIONAL SPECIFICATIONS

The integrated taxonomy of behavioural components in Fig. 2.1 can be translated into a considerable number of testable hypotheses. The first and most critical question, however, is whether agreeableness and activeness can indeed be used to discriminate between main components of conglomerated conflict behaviour. Hence the following hypotheses on the basis of the similarities and differences discussed above and represented in Fig. 2.1.

The main components of conglomerated conflict behaviour are less positively or more negatively related to agreeableness in the following order: (a) accommodating and problem solving; (b) avoiding and compromising; and (c) indirect and direct fighting (*Hypothesis 1*). At the same time the main components of conglomerated conflict behaviour are more positively or less negatively related to activeness in the following order: (a) avoiding and accommodating; (b) indirect fighting; and (c) compromising, problem solving, and direct fighting (*Hypothesis 2*).

The two hypotheses were put to the test by Martin Euwema and myself (Euwema, 1992; Van de Vliert & Euwema, 1994). We had neutral observers rate how police officers handled a standardised conflict with a subordinate or a superior.

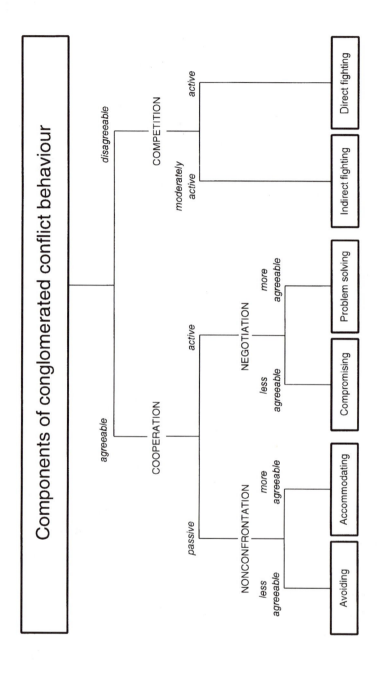

FIG. 2.1   A characterisation of components of conglomerated conflict behaviour in terms of agreeableness and activeness.

44

Method

Subjects. Eighty-two first-line supervisors in Dutch police organisations (hereinafter: police sergeants) were chosen as subjects because they occupy a conflict-prone position in their organisation (Kahn et al., 1964; Ritzer, 1972). The subjects were male, their age ranged from 28 to 51 (Mdn = 38 years), and their experience in the present position as supervisor ranged from less than 1 year to 10 years (Mdn = 3 years). The supervisors were randomly assigned to the condition of superior (N = 40) or subordinate (N = 42).

Conflict simulation. The police sergeants volunteered to participate in the simulation as the first part of a four-day course in conflict management. The incendiary issue was that the other person took away and used a reserved car for more than an hour without reporting this to the station sergeant responsible for all cars. Taking a car without permission was seen as a highly realistic and serious violation of the rules. All sergeants in both conditions said that they would confront the offending party (police constable or warrant officer).

Four male professional actors had been trained to start with trivialisation of the incident, to continue with discord about the underlying policy, and to end with a personal attack on the behaviour of the sergeant in this matter. Each played the role of police constable (superior condition) or warrant officer (subordinate condition) for about 15 minutes on average.

Scoring conflict behaviour. To begin with, each videotaped conflict simulation was rated twice to assess the units of analysis and the components of the sergeant's conglomerated conflict behaviour, respectively.

The subsequent stages of trivialisation, underlying policy, and personal attack were chosen as the psychologically meaningful units during which the behavioural components were described. Two women and two men independently assessed and then reached consensus about when the professional actor shifted from the first to the second and from the second to the third stage of conflict simulation.

Next, after being trained for two days, the same observers rated the use of the behavioural components mentioned in Fig. 2.1, to wit: avoiding, accommodating, compromising, problem solving, indirect fighting, and direct fighting. For each of these six components of conglomerated conflict behaviour separately, each observer independently completed a single five-point rating scale anchored by *not at all* (1) and *to a great extent* (5). This rating procedure was repeated for each of the three stages of escalation separately, after which a sergeant's average use of each of the six components of conglomerated conflict behaviour was calculated (for interobserver reliabilities and other details, see Van de Vliert & Euwema, 1994).

Scoring agreeableness and activeness.   A completely independent group of two women and three men rated the videotapes once again. These judges had to apply Bales's (1950) interaction process analysis. In this observation device, six behavioural features refer to social-emotional expressions that are agreeable (show agreement, tension release, and solidarity) or disagreeable (show disagreement, tension, and antagonism). Six other features refer to the task-oriented activeness of giving information (give suggestion, opinion, and orientation) or asking for it (ask for suggestion, opinion, and orientation).

The observers independently counted the number of times the sergeant used specific actions or statements reflecting each of the 12 behavioural features. After these codings were done for each of the three stages of escalation separately, a sergeant's average scores for agreeableness, disagreeableness, activeness, and passiveness were calculated (details about the construction of these scores as well as their reliability levels can be found in Van de Vliert & Euwema, 1994).

Data analysis.   In line with Fig. 2.1, the two hypotheses predict the extent to which the main components of conglomerated conflict behaviour are characterised by the features of agreeableness and activeness. The hypotheses were therefore tested by calculating (a) Pearson correlations between each of the six behavioural components and each of the four operationalisations of agreeableness and activeness, and (b) Spearman correlations between the hypothesised and the observed rank order of associations between the six behavioural components and the respective features of agreeableness, disagreeableness, passiveness, and activeness. These tests were repeated for each of the subsequent conflict stages of trivialisation, underlying policy, and personal attack, as well as for the hierarchical conditions of superior and subordinate.

Results and Discussion

Whereas Hypothesis 1 was not supported for differences in agreeableness, it could be accepted for differences in disagreeableness, regardless of the conflict stage and the relative hierarchical position. Not surprisingly, accommodating qualified as the least and direct fighting as the most disagreeable behavioural component. The complete rank order of the behavioural components in terms of their disagreeableness is as follows: accommodating, problem solving, indirect fighting, avoiding, compromising, and direct fighting. The only deviation from the picture in Fig. 2.1 lies in the position of indirect fighting as less rather than more disagreeable than avoiding and compromising. An obvious explanation for this last finding is that indirect fighting was operationalised as controlling the process rather than undermining the opponent (cf. Euwema, 1992; Sheppard, 1984).

Likewise, whereas Hypothesis 2 was not supported for differences in passiveness, it could be accepted for differences in activeness, regardless of the conflict stage and the relative hierarchical position. Quite clearly, on a dimension of increasing activeness the behavioural components have to be ordered as follows: avoiding, accommodating, indirect fighting, direct fighting, compromising, and problem solving. It is especially interesting to note that compromising and problem solving emerge as even more active ways of responding to conflict than direct fighting.

Together, the findings imply qualified support for the integrated taxonomy in Fig. 2.1. That overarching typology is corroborated if one operationalises agreeableness in terms of unpleasantness and stressfulness, and activeness in terms of responsiveness and directness. Thus, disagreeableness and activeness may well pave the way for the integration of now-separated taxonomies of reactions to social conflicts.

The conclusion that disagreeableness discriminates between components of conflict behaviour better than agreeableness is an intriguing one. It might simply be a consequence of the fact that disagreeableness appeared to overlap activeness. More disagreeable actions might be more salient and distinctive because they are also more active actions. An alternative or supplementary explanation of the descriptive power of disagreeableness might lie in the escalating nature of the conflict. It is conceivable that agreeableness is a better descriptor in de-escalatory conflicts, whereas disagreeableness is a better descriptor in escalatory conflicts. Another reason why the extent of disagreeableness tells us so much about distinct behavioural components might be the presence of a negativity effect (e.g. Fiske, 1980; Martijn, Spears, Van der Pligt, & Jakobs, 1992; Skowronski & Carlston, 1987). In comparison with agreeableness, our judges may have overemphasised disagreeableness because it contains negative information about the police sergeant's conflict handling.

As for the limitations, our study used an all-male sample, and it was restricted to a particular simulation of a conflict in a formal organisational setting: a police sergeant having a fight with his subordinate or superior about the latter's deviant role behaviour. Disagreeable or active behaviour that might be common between men may be exceptional between man and woman or between women. Similarly, behaviour that might occur frequently between police officers within a naturally confrontational profession may be a rarity between members of other groups. Also, behaviour that might be seen as only mildly disagreeable or moderately active between equals may be seen as very disagreeable or active when displayed by a lower-status person to a higher-status person, or vice versa. Lastly, the conflict interaction was a videotaped simulation rather than a naturally occurring event. So, all in all, replications of the study would be most welcome.

Conclusion.   The behavioural components of avoiding, accommodating, compromising, problem solving, indirect fighting, and direct fighting differ from each other in terms of disagreeableness and activeness. Systematic observations of videotaped simulations by male police sergeants handling a standardised hierarchical conflict showed that the differences are in line with the integration of several taxonomies in Fig. 2.1.

PROPOSITIONS

2a.   Components of conglomerated conflict behaviour can be categorised more easily as avoiding, accommodating, compromising, problem solving, and indirect or direct fighting if the actor's behavioural intention is known better (p. 30).

2b.   Two kinds of compromising components exist: claim-negotiating resulting in an allocation of something nobody owns, and trade-negotiating resulting in an exchange of belongings (pp. 35–36).

2c.   A component of fighting is direct to the extent that it is overt and straightforward, and fair to the extent that it follows mutually agreed-upon behavioural rules to defeat the other party (pp. 30, 32, 39–40).

2d.   A fair-fighting component is different from a negotiating component in that it is based on an agreement about right and wrong behaviour, but is not directed at a further agreement in the form of a compromise or a resolution (pp. 34–35, 40).

2e.   The dichotomy of cooperative and competitive components, the trichotomy of moving away–toward–against, and the typology of avoiding, accommodating, compromising, problem solving, and indirect or direct fighting, are interrelated in terms of the agreeableness and activeness of the postulated components (pp. 41–48).

CHAPTER THREE

Second Step:
Descriptive Dimensions

A shop assistant who catches a small child in the act of stealing typically mixes integrative and distributive moves to handle that conflict. Predominantly integrative components of a person's salient reaction to a conflict issue are avoiding, compromising and problem solving. Predominantly distributive behavioural components are accommodating and fighting. In Chapter 2 it has been shown that these behavioural components can also be characterised in terms of agreeableness and activeness. However, agreeableness and activeness were introduced especially to integrate two-, three-, four-, and five-part taxonomies of conflict management. Other features may constitute equally or more relevant characteristics for description.

The question of which factors discriminate best between components of conflict behaviour goes beyond simple classification. To ask this question is to move from the lowest to the next level of theoretical quality, from typology to model. Whereas a typology provides us with nominally distinct behavioural descriptions, a model provides us with behavioural descriptions that are mutually related in terms of inlaying dimensions. As will be elucidated, the grid's X-cross of diagonal dimensions discriminates best between components of conflict management.

This chapter first addresses the two generic X-cross dimensions in depth. They are viewed as very different, independent factors dealing with integrative and distributive outcome allocations. Behavioural dilemmas are also discussed. Two reports of empirical investigations to further test and advance the model follow on from there (numbered Studies 2 and 3, subsequent to Study 1 in Chapter 2). Study 2 tested whether the model is the backbone of measuring instruments because their measurements reflect the interrelations among the conflict management components as predicted by the X-cross. Study 3 was concerned with the generalisability of these descriptive dimensions of integration and distribution across a variety of behavioural components.

X-CROSS MODEL

Given a two-dimensional space of components of conflict behaviour such as the one represented in the grid in Fig. 1.1, what dimensions best describe the salient behavioural locations in this space? Theories and methods of factor analysis and multidimensional scaling suggest two criteria. First, the two dimensions should especially capture the smallest and largest distances between the behavioural components to be described. Second, the two dimensions should capture totally different subsets of the smallest and largest distances between the behavioural components to be described. That is, the two dimensions should be independent, or at least as close to orthogonality as possible.

The conflict management grid was designed as a two-dimensional space in the form of a square with a centre. The smallest distances are between the middle point and the four corners. The largest distances are between the two pairs of opposite corners. Hence the requisite of smallest and largest distances points to the diagonals as the most appropriate descriptors of behavioural locations in the grid. The diagonals, forming an X-cross, also meet the criterion of independence. So, the grid's diagonal dimensions rather than the dimensions of the grid's sides describe the components of conflict behaviour best (cf. proposition 1.e).

In Figs 1.1 and 1.2 the X-cross dimensions run from avoiding at the bottom left hand to problem solving at the top right hand, and from accommodating at the top left hand to fighting at the bottom right hand. According to Thomas (1976, 1992b), this X-cross indicates that an integrative and a distributive way of allocating benefits and costs to the parties can be taken. His point of view is discussed further to see what conflict management is all about. The integrative and distributive dimensions are portrayed as basic features of any component of conflict handling, which are unequal and mutually independent.

Integrative and Distributive Dimension

Irrespective of what others expect to achieve, each conflicting individual can anticipate positive or negative outcomes for him- or herself on the one hand, and positive or negative outcomes for the opponent on the other. By implication, one can treat oneself and the other party equally or differentially. Again relying on the conflict management grid in Fig. 1.1, equal treatment or integration, and differential treatment or distribution will now be set alongside each other.

Integrative dimension.   The 1,1–2,2–3,3–4,4–5,5–6,6–7,7–8,8–9,9 or integrative dimension represents the extent to which a conflicting party minimises or maximises outcomes for the conflicting parties together. In other words, the size of a joint pie is at stake. The variable sum of the pie ranges from sum 2 to 18. In this range the total absence of integrative activity (0,0) is omitted because it can only occur when there is no conflict at all. The anticipated result is a less or more satisfying agreement in which both parties are treated equally. This 1,1–9,9 scale has been labelled variously as cooperation (Deutsch, 1949, 1973), integrative dimension (Thomas, 1976, 1992b), relationship dimension (Hocker & Wilmot, 1985), and the principle of creating value for all (Lax & Sebenius, 1986). The adjective "integrative" is used here as it is a widely accepted term.

Distributive dimension.   The 1,9–2,8–3,7–4,6–5,5–6,4–7,3–8,2–9,1 or distributive dimension (Thomas, 1976, 1992b) represents the extent to which the conflicting party minimises or maximises its relative gain or loss of outcomes vis-à-vis the other party. The size of each party's proportion of a fixed pie is at stake. That is, wholly or partly, the prospective end state is one of a loser and a winner, or of an equal split. Note that the constant sum is 10, and that the 100% winner versus 100% loser divisions are omitted because total defeat and total victory are inconceivable. This second diagonal of the conflict management grid is also known as competition (Deutsch, 1949, 1973), zero-sum dimension (Bacharach & Lawler, 1981; Zartman, 1976), and the principle of claiming value for each (Lax & Sebenius, 1986).

Unequal Diagonals

A more systematic exploration of the nature of integrative and distributive components reveals several differences. Integrative behaviour refers to a unipolar dimension of anticipated variable-sum outcomes that portrays compromising as suboptimal for the conflicting parties. In contrast, distributive behaviour refers to a bipolar dimension of anticipated constant-sum outcomes that portrays compromising as optimal for both parties together. Those differences between the arms of the X-cross will now be elaborated to build a common platform between the hitherto divergent literature on general conflict management and negotiation. The 5,5 component of compromising gets special attention because the differences between the two dimensions are most clearly expressed at their 5,5 intersection.

Unipolar versus bipolar dimensions.   First of all, the integrative dimension is a unipolar scale ranging in only one direction, from 1,1 to 9,9. As a consequence, avoiding must be associated with the absence rather than with the opposite of problem solving; it is not the active sabotage of problem solving. The distributive dimension, on the other hand, is a bipolar scale ranging in two directions, from 5,5 to 1,9 and from 5,5 to 9,1. Therefore accommodating must be associated with the presence of anti-fighting rather than with the absence of fighting, and vice versa.

Variable-sum versus constant-sum dimensions.   As for the anticipated benefits and costs, the integrative 1,1 $\rightarrow$ 9,9 dimension refers to variable-sum outcomes for the two conflicting parties, hypothetically ranging from 2 to 18. The distributive 1,9 $\longleftrightarrow$ 9,1 dimension, on the other hand, refers to anticipated constant-sum outcomes for the parties involved, hypothetically set at 10. Since some conflict issues are bound up with variable-sum outcomes, whereas other issues are confined to constant-sum outcomes, the suitability of each descriptive dimension also depends on the subject matter of the discord.

The chameleonic identity of compromising.   The above differences are most salient at the 5,5 intersection of the two dimensions. Take, for example, two politicians who use the 5,5 option of compromising in addition to other reactions to a policy matter. The unipolar integrative dimension frames that component of compromising as a mixture of avoiding and problem solving. The bipolar distributive dimension, on the other hand, frames precisely the same behaviour of compromising as a point of balance between accommodating and fighting. The position of 5,5 between avoiding (1,1) and problem solving (9,9) is clear, but the distributive framework of 5,5 is indistinct. The midpoint between 1,9 and 9,1 could stand for neither accommodating nor fighting, a mixture of both accommodating and fighting (simultaneous conglomeration), or an alternation of accommodating and fighting (sequential conglomeration).

Compromising might even represent an overall conglomeration of avoiding, accommodating, compromising, problem solving, and fighting. Blake and Mouton (1964, pp. 221–222) described this mammoth conglomeration as a "mixed grid theory": "The 'statistical' 5,5 manager employs all five styles in his daily supervision.... In other words, the 'statistical' 5,5 manager operates all over the grid. His managerial styles average out to 5,5." Such an alternative interpretation of compromising does justice to the fact that compromising exhibits a mutable character and fits wonderfully well into both more integrative and more distributive environments. Compromising has a chameleonic identity. The same ultimate compromise may result from quite different behavioural configurations. Some scholars, probably misled by this variety of appearances, see no need to postulate a mode of compromising. Others thinly portray compromising as satisficing; still others colourfully paint it as optimising.

Suboptimal versus optimal compromising.   Compromising is viewed as the realisation of a halfway resolution of conflict about a variable-sum issue if one wants an agreement and focuses on the integrative dimension (e.g. Pruitt, 1983). Seen like this, the opponents are settling on a satisfactory alternative that meets or exceeds their ultimate fall-back positions rather than an alternative that they prefer to all other agreements. To paraphrase March and Simon (1958, p. 141), compromising is like searching a haystack to find a needle sharp enough to sew with, rather than searching the haystack to find the sharpest needle in it.

In contrast, compromising is viewed as the realisation of an attractive equilibrium between winning and losing a conflict about a constant-sum issue if one wants an agreement and focuses on the distributive dimension (e.g. Lewicki & Litterer, 1985). In negotiations about really scarce means such as money or manpower, compromising can achieve such a positive identity between the more negative anchor points of stalemate and surrender. The same holds true when people, due to a so-called fixed pie bias, erroneously expect the counterpart's interests to be opposed to their own (Bazerman & Neale, 1983; Neale & Bazerman, 1991; Thompson & Hastie, 1990).

It is no coincidence, of course, that the intersection of compromising provides most information about the main directions of conflict handling. On the same route from 1,1 via 5,5 to 9,9 the intersection will be perceived as a point on the road rather than the destination: compromising will be seen as suboptimal. However, on the different routes from 1,9 to 5,5 and from 5,5 to 9,1 the crossing of 5,5 will mark an end and a new beginning at the same time. Within the latter, distributive framework, the fifty–fifty split may be adopted more easily as the destination rather than just a point along the road, thus experiencing compromising as optimal. As a case in point, Loewenstein, Thompson, and Bazerman (1989) showed that in a dispute context most disputants prefer equal pay-offs to either advantageous or disadvantageous inequality (see also De Dreu, Emans, & Van de Vliert, 1991; Messick & Sentis, 1985).

Ample evidence exists that scientists conceptualise compromising on different dimensions of the X-cross. The fact that some authors view compromising as less socially desirable than problem solving attests to the use of the integrative 1,1–5,5–9,9 frame (e.g. Kilmann & Thomas, 1977; Prein, 1976; Rahim, 1983b). On the other hand, the 1,9–5,5–9,1 dimensional view is adopted by scholars who consider the fifty–fifty settlement fairer than less equal distributions of outcomes or concessions (Deutsch, 1985; Pruitt, 1981). Against this background, the different manifestations and effects of the above conglomerations of compromising could become a rich research topic in itself.

Mutually Independent Diagonals

The grid conceptualises the integrative and distributive dimensions as principal axes with an orthogonal interrelationship. That is, manifestations of integration and distribution are seen as two independent factors. Consequently, various degrees of integrative treatment and various degrees of distributive treatment may or may not occur simultaneously (cf. Bartos, 1995; Donohue & Roberto, 1996; Lewicki, Weiss, & Lewin, 1992; Putnam, 1990; Raiffa, 1982; Thomas, 1992b). However, some scholars, in some of their papers, tend to view integrative and distributive conflict behaviour as the two poles of one and the same dimension rather than two separate dimensions. I am not thinking of Deutsch (1949, 1973) and Schelling (1960), who conceptualise integration and distribution as antecedents rather than manifestations of conflict behaviour. Instead, as will now be discussed, I am primarily thinking of Walton and McKersie (1965), Pruitt (1981), and Lax and Sebenius (1986), who tend to conceptualise integration and distribution as opposite poles of a behavioural dimension.

Hints in the direction of uni-dimensionality. Walton and McKersie (1965), who did not relate their concepts of integration and distribution to the grid, were the very first to disseminate implicit suggestions of bipolarity. They described *integrative bargaining* as a system of activities directed at problem solving, and *distributive bargaining* as a system of activities primarily concerned with one's own gains and losses as a function of the adversary's gains and losses. The implementing techniques for these classes of conflict behaviours were supposed to stand in an antithetical relationship: "While the integrative and distributive processes are related and are sometimes difficult to separate ... the techniques for fostering the integrative process are generally the reverse of the techniques for implementing the distributive process" (Walton & McKersie, 1965, p. 144).

They later discussed mixed integrative and distributive bargaining as a choice between mutually exclusive allocative behaviours: "the alternate strategies ... are an integrative, increasing-sum strategy (I) and a distributive strategy (D), which treats the situation as a fixed-sum issue." (Walton & McKersie, 1965, p. 163). "Parties engage in mixed bargaining in order to achieve the most from each of the two processes. Generally speaking, the tactics appropriate for pure distributive bargaining conflict with those appropriate for pure integrative bargaining." (Walton & McKersie, 1965, p. 182). Apparently, these authors tended to assume a negative interrelationship rather than a relationship of coexistence of integrative and distributive conflict handling at one point in time (cf. Bartos, 1995; Donohue & Roberto, 1996; Putnam, 1990; Tracy & Peterson, 1986).

Pruitt (1981, p. 15) followed Walton and McKersie. He used the terms coordinative and competitive strategies to refer to integrative and distributive behaviour, respectively, and stated that they "can be combined, but [that] this does not ordinarily happen because of various psychological and practical contradictions among the strategies." As a consequence, Pruitt employed the following two principles throughout his monograph: (a) the choice of integrative behaviour makes the choice of distributive behaviour less likely, and vice versa, and (b) conditions that enhance/diminish the probability of adopting integrative behaviour diminish/enhance the probability of adopting distributive behaviour, and vice versa. Apparently, Pruitt also tended to assume a negative rather than a neutral relationship between integrative and distributive conflict management.

Similarly, throughout their book on negotiation, Lax and Sebenius (1986) set creating value against claiming value. Integratively *creating value* was described as: being open; sharing information about preferences and beliefs; and being honest about minimum requirements. The opposite, distributively *claiming value*, was described as: being cagey and misleading about preferences, beliefs, and minimum requirements; making commitments; and using threats. In addition, the stand was taken that value creating and value claiming are not independent reactions: "In tactical choices, each negotiator thus has reasons not to be open and cooperative. Each also has apparent incentives to try to claim value. Moves to claim value thus tend to drive out moves to create it." (Lax & Sebenius, 1986, p. 35).

Implicit assumptions of bipolarity are embedded in the fabric of Western scientific thinking (Bobko, 1985). It is either flight or fight, either cooperate or compete, either 1,9 or 9,1 distributive behaviour. And if the authors in the last paragraphs are right, handling conflict is choosing either integrative or distributive enactments. The transformation of such assumptions of bipolarity into a two-dimensional perspective can enhance both the quality of behavioural descriptions and the progress of theory construction. Seen like this, the X-cross has to be preferred to a simpler image of opposition between integrative and distributive components of conflict management.

Two-dimensionality. If the diagonals do indeed represent independent higher-order constructs, these concepts can be used well to describe acts of conflict management. That is, each component of conflict handling is identifiable by means of its degrees of integration and distribution. Consider the examples in the X-cross space of components of conflict behaviour in Fig. 3.1. Nonconfrontation (1,4) and hard consolidation (4,1) are hardly integrative, whereas soft negotiation (6,9) and hard negotiation (9,6) are predominantly integrative. At the same time, nonconfrontation and soft negotiation are distributive in favour of the other party, whereas hard consolidation and hard negotiation are distributive in favour of oneself.

Though a behavioural component's degrees of integration and distribution are distinguishable, they are not separable. A component of handling conflict is a unique and unsplittable phenomenon. To put it metaphorically once more, if the X-cross does reflect reality, any component of conflict behaviour can be thought of as having an integrative and a distributive arm. Even extreme forms of accommodating (1,9) and fighting (9,1) have a very small amount of integrative content indicated as "1." Even extreme forms of avoiding (1,1) and problem solving (9,9) reflect distribution in the form of an equal split.

As a consequence, each component of conflict behaviour is conceptually related to each other component of conflict behaviour in terms of the common factors of integration and distribution. The X-cross is thus a model not only for describing but also for interrelating components of conflict handling. The inlaying integrative and distributive dimensions structure the abundance of acts into a system of interrelated, though distinct, behavioural components. Two components of conflict behaviour are conceptually distant if they have a contradictory integrative and distributive content (e.g. problem solving and direct fighting). Conversely, two components of conflict behaviour are conceptually close if they have a compatible integrative and distributive content (e.g. compromising and problem solving)

Behavioural Dilemmas

The integrative and distributive dimensions make very relevant contributions to the field of complex social behaviour. Not only do they represent statements full of insight on components of conflict handling as being directed at the minimisation or maximisation of outcomes for oneself and for one or more others. They also highlight the fact that a conflicting party faces an approach-avoidance choice between integrative and distributive

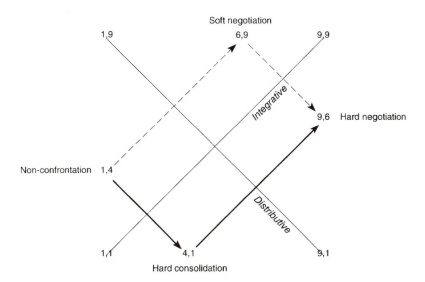

FIG. 3.1 Locations of non-confrontation, soft negotiation, hard consolidation, and hard negotiation in the X-cross space of components of conglomerated conflict behaviour, and two routes from 1,4 non-confrontation to 9,6 hard negotiation.

behavioural alternatives. This dilemma presents itself in two shapes: regardless of and with regard to the subsequent reaction of the opponent. These two manifestations of essentially the same dubiety are discussed here as the intrapersonal and the interpersonal behavioural dilemma.

Intrapersonal behavioural dilemma.   By its very nature, managing social conflict is the facing of choices between either joint pie or fixed pie definitions of the situation, and between either equal or differential treatment of oneself and the opponent. Each option is attractive for some reasons and unattractive for others. For example, integrating may produce a better relationship but worse commodity outcomes than fighting. In Lax and Sebenius's (1986, p. 30) words: "There is a central, inescapable tension between cooperative moves to create value jointly and competitive moves to gain individual advantage. This tension affects virtually all tactical and strategic choice ... Neither denial nor discomfort will make it disappear."

So, in the terminology of the current chapter, there is an inescapable dilemma between the integrative and the distributive content of conflict behaviour. Taking integrative action may build mutual trust but runs the risk of undermining one's position and competitive advantage. Or, as Pruitt (1981, p. 92) would put it: integrative moves are risky because they entail the possibility of four kinds of loss—image loss, position loss, information loss, and loss of opportunity for distributive behaviour. Taking distributive action, on the other hand, may result in competitive advantage but runs the risk of undermining potential agreements and a good mutual relationship in the future.

An inescapable behavioural dilemma is not necessarily an insoluble dilemma. The two horns of equal versus differential treatment of oneself and the other may exhibit an apparently contradictory nature. Indeed, if integrative and distributive reactions are mutually independent dimensions, as stated above, the intrapersonal dilemma constitutes a paradox. The contradiction evaporates like snow in summer as soon as a party adopts a perspective wherein low–low and high–high combinations of integration and distribution are possible. Putnam (1990) reviewed that perspective as "the interdependence model of integrative and distributive bargaining." Quite correctly, I think, she concluded that negotiating tactics represent a unique paradoxical role by contributing to both integrative and distributive functions simultaneously. In my own words: the intrapersonal behavioural dilemma is overcome by the simultaneous conglomeration of more and less integrative and distributive components of conflict behaviour. The grid's X-cross represents that paradoxical role of negotiations in an elegant way. The X-cross model even implies that Putnam's conclusion is not restricted to negotiations. All conflict behaviours serve integrative as well as distributive functions.

Interpersonal behavioural dilemma.   Self-evidently, the opponent has an important part to play in the process of shaping a party's reactions to the conflict. Usually the opponent's past actions and future reactions both have an impact on a person's present integrative and distributive initiatives. However, the experience of the dilemma is especially elicited by uncertainty about the opponent's future reactions. The following considerations and illustration may clarify this.

Whereas moving in the direction of an anticipated outcome allocation is solely in the hands of each individual actor, actually realising that outcome allocation needs an appropriate response from the opponent. Specifically, one cannot successfully avoid, compromise, or solve the problem if the other party does not avoid, compromise, or solve the problem as well. In other words, realisation of *variable-sum outcomes* on the integrative dimension needs *behavioural symmetry* on the part of the opponent. Similarly, one cannot successfully accommodate if the other party does not want to win, and one cannot successfully fight either if the other party does not want to lose (unless the opponent is eliminated once and for all).

So, realisation of *constant-sum outcomes* on the distributive dimension needs *behavioural complementarity* on the part of the opponent.

There is much empirical support for those behavioural regularities. For example, Weingart et al. (1990) showed that highly efficient dyads differed from less efficient dyads in their reciprocation of integrative behaviours and complementarity of distributive behaviours (see also Kabanoff & Van de Vliert, 1993; Nauta, 1996; Putnam & Jones, 1982). Likewise, Leng (1993) convincingly demonstrated that national leaders who effectively managed a militarised interstate crisis realised better joint outcomes by acting symmetrically on the integrative dimension. In contrast, when the parties' interests and military capabilities were skewed, the crisis managers tended to act complementarily on the distributive dimension by creating a winner and a loser.

These different forms of behavioural interdependency make it important to note next that the opponent's reaction is never completely beyond doubt. There are always possibilities that the other party does not react symmetrically on the integrative dimension and complementarily on the distributive dimension. As a consequence one can be, and often is, in two minds about the opponent's response to one's own integrative and distributive actions. This uncertainty about the occurrence of the adversary's necessary reaction lies at the root of the interpersonal behavioural dilemma (for an analogous dubiety, see the Box "The Prisoner's Dilemma in the Grid").

The dilemma can be illustrated by reproducing the possible thoughts of someone who is facing a choice between maximum integration to everybody's advantage and maximum distribution to one's own advantage: "If I share information and help create a solution, and he does the same, I shall be better off than if I fight him until I win. In particular, we will get along better after reaching a satisfactory agreement than after my victory. However, if I open up and try to resolve our problem, whereas he appears to fight to the finish, I will be worse off than if I fight back. He will most probably take undue advantage of my confessions, concessions, and constructive proposals." This difficult choice between integrative and distributive moves is overcome, as indicated above, by blending more and less integrative and distributive moves into a conglomeration of components of conflict management. One may use more integrative and more distributive components at the same time (simultaneous aggregation) or in succession (sequential conglomeration).

Alternation as a way out. One may adopt an integrative stance without permanently giving up a distributive stance, or the other way round. This change from a predominantly integrative to a predominantly distributive phase, or vice versa, is worked out in stage models of spontaneous escalation (e.g. Folger & Poole, 1984; Glasl, 1980) and strategic negotiation

The Prisoner's Dilemma in the Grid

The conflict management grid's spatial structure of allocating benefits and costs is basically the same as that of the typical 2 x 2 outcome matrix used in the well-known prisoner's dilemma game (e.g. Axelrod, 1984; Deutsch, 1973; Kelley & Thibaut, 1978; Pruitt & Kimmel, 1977). In this game each player can make either a competitive choice with a relatively low or high pay-off, or a cooperative choice with a relatively low or high pay-off, whereby the pay-off always depends on the opponent's competitive or co-operative choice. If both players choose to compete, both will lose (e.g. both get only 1), but if both players make a cooperative choice, both will win (e.g. both get 9). This first pair of opposite cells in the outcome matrix closely corresponds to the integrative grid corners of avoiding (1,1) and problem solving (9,9). If the players of the prisoner's dilemma game make different behavioural choices, the competitor will win while the coopera-tor will lose (e.g. they get 9 versus 1). This second pair of opposite cells in the outcome matrix closely corresponds to the distributive grid corners of accommodating (1,9) and fighting (9,1).

(e.g. Donohue & Roberto, 1996; Douglas, 1962; Gulliver, 1979; Morley & Stephenson, 1977; Putnam, 1990). Escalative processes typically proceed down the integrative dimension, from 9,9 problem solving towards 1,1 avoiding, and/or across the distributive dimension, from 1,9 accommodat-ing towards 9,1 fighting. In contrast, processes of de-escalative negotiation typically progress up the integrative dimension and/or towards the middle of the distributive dimension.

All such alterations of conflict management are transitions from one location to another in the two-dimensional X-cross space of conflict be-haviours. A salient route is to change the magnitude of the integrative content first, followed by changing the magnitude of the distributive content (e.g. from 1,4 nonconfrontation via 6,9 soft negotiation to 9,6 hard negotiation; see Fig. 3.1). A salient alternative route is to change the magnitude of the distributive content first, followed by changing the magni-tude of the integrative content (e.g. from 1,4 nonconfrontation via 4,1 hard consolidation to 9,6 hard negotiation; see Fig. 3.1). Many other routes are possible, not only from 1,4 to 9,6, but from any location in the behav-ioural space to any other. Indeed, the principle of equifinality applies, as one can attain the same location proceeding from initially different locations, passing a variety of still other locations. There are always various behavioural sequences that can overcome the dilemma between integrative and distributive reactions.

Overall recapitulation. The X-cross of the diagonals of the conflict management grid can be conceptualised as consisting of an integrative and a distributive dimension. The unipolar integrative dimension represents variations in anticipated variable-sum outcomes and portrays compromising as suboptimal for the conflicting parties. Effectuation of integration requires behavioural symmetry on the part of the opponent with both parties avoiding or negotiating. In contrast, the bipolar distributive dimension represents variations in anticipated constant-sum outcomes and portrays compromising as optimal for the conflicting parties together. Effectuation of distribution requires behavioural complementarity on the part of the opponent with one party accommodating and the other party fighting.

Though the X-cross dimensions are mutually independent, they elicit intra- and interpersonal dilemmas between either equal or differential treatment of oneself and the opponent. The behavioural dilemmas are handled by adopting conglomerated conflict behaviour; that is, by blending, and sometimes also alternating, behavioural components consisting of predominantly integrative and distributive moves. Therefore the X-cross makes an elegant model for describing and interrelating components of conflict behaviour in terms of the magnitude of their integrative and distributive content.

STUDY 2: DIMENSIONS INLAYING MEASURES

If components of conflict behaviour are indeed pre-eminently interrelated in terms of an integrative and a distributive dimension, measures of conflict behaviours should contain this information. Specifically, any questionnaire instrument designed to assess avoiding, accommodating, compromising, problem solving, and fighting should be characterised by inlaying factors of integration and distribution. Moreover, across instruments, different sets of 10 empirical correlations among the five subscales of conflict management should have much in common because they share the same higher-order constructs of integration and distribution. In operational terms, all instruments' sets of 10 correlations among the five subscales of conflict handling should reflect the modes' conceptual distances specified by the two independent factors.

Larger conceptual distances between components of conflict behaviour in the two-dimensional space should produce lower positive (or higher negative) values of correlations. Thus, the X-cross model can be broken down into three main hypotheses. *Hypothesis 1* primarily refers to the integrative dimension: avoiding is less positively related to problem solving than both avoiding and problem solving are related to accommodating and fighting. *Hypothesis 2* primarily refers to the distributive dimension: accommodating is less positively related to fighting than both accommodating and fighting are related to avoiding and problem solving. The next, twofold, hypothesis refers primarily to the intersection of compromising. *Hypothesis 3a*: avoiding is less positively related to problem solving than both avoiding and problem solving are related to compromising. *Hypothesis 3b*: accommodating is less positively related to fighting than both accommodating and fighting are related to compromising.

Method

Measures.   Self-report sets of the 10 correlations among the five subscales of avoiding, accommodating, compromising, problem solving, and fighting have been used to test the above hypotheses. Single-item assessments of the five modes of conflict handling (Baron, 1984, 1989; Blake & Mouton, 1964; Renwick, 1975a, 1975b, 1977; Van de Vliert & Hordijk, 1989) were left aside because there is insufficient guarantee that they can be considered adequate. Also excluded were instruments that do not provide separate scores for avoiding and accommodating, or for compromising and problem solving (Lawrence & Lorsch, 1967; Ross & DeWine, 1988). These restrictions left the following questionnaire measures for further consideration: Conflict Management Survey (CMS), Management Of Differences Exercise (MODE), Organisational Communication Conflict Instrument (OCCI), Rahim's Organisational Conflict Inventory (ROCI), and Dutch Test of Conflict Handling (DUTCH). These instruments were briefly reviewed in the Box "Self-Assessments Based on the Five-Part Typology" in Chapter 2.

Re-analysis.   A secondary analysis of the sets of correlations was carried out. It involved four steps. The first was the selection of 12 studies that gathered data through CMS, MODE, OCCI, ROCI, or DUTCH. Second, sets of the 10 correlations among the five types of conflict behaviour were formed for each instrument. Third, the hypotheses were tested through systematic comparisons of correlation coefficients. Though the tests were done for the 12 studies together, special attention was paid to differences between the five measuring instruments.

By way of illustration, and to explore the mutual independence of the integrative and distributive dimension, some research results were visually represented in a fourth and final step. Using the nonmetric distance-scaling programme MINISSA designed by Lingoes and Roskam (1973), a set of 10 correlations was reproduced spatially by portraying each mode's subscale of conflict handling as a point in a plane. The purpose of the MINISSA procedure is to find a configuration of points whose Euclidian output distances reflect the rank order of the input dissimilarities as closely as possible. A stress index ranging between 0 (perfect fit) and 1 (no fit) indicates how well a one-dimensional, a two-dimensional, or a multidimensional picture represents the configuration of associations within the data.

Results and Discussion

How the first operations were effected is accounted for in the Box "Data on Five Instruments." It concerned the selection of empirical data and the reduction into one set of 10 intercorrelations for each of the instruments.

Tests of hypotheses.   In point of fact, Hypothesis 1 predicted that the correlation coefficients between avoiding and problem solving (third column in the Box "Data on Five Instruments") have a less positive or more negative value than the correlation coefficients between avoiding and accommodating (first column), avoiding and fighting (fourth column), accommodating and problem solving (sixth column), and problem solving and fighting (last column). Indeed, 43 of those 48 paired comparisons were in the predicted direction ($z = 5.34$, $p \leq .001$); Hypothesis 1 held for CMS, ROCI, and DUTCH, in particular. Similarly, in support of Hypothesis 2, accommodating and fighting were less positively or more negatively related to each other than each of them was related to avoiding and problem solving (first, fourth, sixth, seventh, and last column). Forty-two of the 48 paired comparisons were in the predicted direction ($z = 5.05$, $p \leq .001$), notably due to CMS, MODE, and OCCI.

The third hypothesis sets column 3 alongside columns 2 and 8 (Hypothesis 3a) and column 7 alongside columns 5 and 9 (Hypothesis 3b). Again, both parts of the hypothesis were supported. Avoiding and problem solving did have less in common than each of them had in common with compromising (24 paired comparisons, 22 correct predictions; $z = 3.88$, $p \leq .001$), and accommodating and fighting did have less in common than each of them had in common with compromising (24 paired comparisons, 21 correct predictions; $z = 3.47$, $p \leq .001$). Clearly, compromising had a position between avoiding and problem solving and between accommodating and fighting, most perfectly in CMS and DUTCH. Compromising is a mixed behavioural component indeed, which can be conceptualised as integrative, distributive, or both.

The fact that all hypotheses could be accepted is rather convincing evidence for the soundness of the descriptive X-cross model. Apparently, very different data sets on conflict behaviour are characterised by an integrative dimension ranging from avoiding to problem solving, a distributive dimension ranging from accommodating to fighting, and a location of compromising between the poles of both dimensions.

Data on Five Instruments

Data were gathered regarding each of the instruments reviewed in the Box "Self-Assessments Based on the Five-Part Typology" in Chapter 2 (CMS, MODE, OCCI, ROCI, DUTCH). The data consisted of correlations between the five modes of conflict behaviour. Eleven sets of correlations, which were published or placed at my disposal, satisfied two requirements for inclusion in a secondary analysis.

The 11 sets of correlations used different samples of respondents; that is, parallel studies and retest studies were discarded. Furthermore, to guarantee comparability of the results for different instruments, they assessed how managers or other organisation members handle conflict at work. A 12th study, using only students as respondents, was included to add a second set of CMS correlations for reasons of reliability. The nature and sources of the sets of correlations between conflict behaviours will now be listed in the order in which the measuring instruments are mentioned above:

1. *CMS*:   59 board of education members (Nichols, 1984).
2. *CMS*:   86 graduate students (Kilmann & Thomas, 1977).
3. *MODE*:   96 managers from a law enforcement agency (Kravitz, 1987).
4. *MODE*:   158 deans of baccalaureate programmes in nursing (Woodtli, 1982).
5. *MODE*:   140 first-line supervisors in a large retail store chain (O'Reilly & Weitz, 1980).
6. *MODE*:   199 project managers working in a matrix organisation or two-boss system (Mills, Robey, & Smith, 1985).
7. *OCCI*:   217 members from a newspaper company, an insurance firm, and a metropolitan bank, as well as 143 students (Putnam & Wilson, 1982).
8. *ROCI*:   1219 managers from a national random sample (Rahim, 1983a).
9. *DUTCH*:   128 police-sergeants in the role of subordinate (Euwema & Van de Vliert, 1990).
10. *DUTCH*:   135 police-sergeants in the role of superior (Euwema & Van de Vliert, 1990).
11. *DUTCH*:   239 head-nurses in the role of subordinate (Euwema & Van de Vliert, 1994b).
12. *DUTCH*:   215 head-nurses in the role of superior (Euwema & Van de Vliert, 1994a).

The details of the 12 sets of 10 correlations between avoiding (*1,1*), accommodating (*1,9*), compromising (*5,5*), problem solving (*9,9*), and fighting (*9,1*) are as follows:

Pair of modes	1,1 1,9	1,1 5,5	1,1 9,9	1,1 9,1	1.9 5,5	1,9 9,9	1,9 9,1	5,5 9,9	5,5 9,1	9,9 9,1
1. CMS	.52	−.03	−.73	−.54	.38	−.47	−.79	.03	−.61	.31
2. CMS	.32	.05	−.17	−.01	.22	.03	−.26	.33	.12	−.07
Mean	**.43**	**.01**	**−.50**	**−.30**	**.30**	**−.24**	**−.58**	**.18**	**−.29**	**.12**
3. MODE	.11	−.13	−.35	−.48	−.17	−.28	−.34	−.31	−.41	−.06
4. MODE	.19	−.21	−.09	−.22	−.12	−.11	−.29	−.09	−.14	−.02
5. MODE	.17	−.20	−.36	−.47	−.15	−.25	−.53	−.34	−.27	.00
6. MODE	.05	−.35	−.41	−.24	−.09	−.38	−.53	−.03	−.28	−.12
Mean	**.13**	**−.22**	**−.31**	**−.36**	**−.13**	**−.26**	**−.43**	**−.20**	**−.28**	**−.05**
7. OCCI	.26	.18	.12	−.11	.43	.36	−.27	.53	−.28	−.22
8. ROCI	.33	.16	−.08	.01	.26	.14	.11	.23	.07	−.04
9. DUTCH	.56	−.05	−.58	−.38	.15	−.22	−.30	.42	.02	.16
10. DUTCH	.60	−.39	−.78	−.41	−.16	−.49	−.48	.57	.27	.37
11. DUTCH	.64	−.01	−.45	−.16	.10	−.24	−.19	.25	.03	.00
12. DUTCH	.61	.05	−.25	−.05	.20	−.16	−.24	.35	−.20	.10
Mean	**.60**	**−.11**	**−.55**	**−.26**	**.07**	**−.28**	**−.31**	**.40**	**.03**	**.16**

The CMS sets 1 and 2 correlate .68 ($p \leq .02$), which justifies their combination into a mean set. Therefore, using Fisher's r to Z transformation, a mean CMS measure was computed and reproduced in bold type. The same procedure was followed for the four MODE measures with mutual correlations ranging from .56 to .91 ($M = .75$, $p \leq .01$), and for the four DUTCH measures with mutual correlations ranging from .74 to .94 ($M = .88$, $p \leq .01$). This results in one set of 10 correlations for each of the five instruments.

Explorations. The only questionnaire that supported all three hypotheses was CMS. To gain a better insight into this "ideal" instrument, it was visually reproduced through the multidimensional scaling technique MINISSA. The one-dimensional representation of the CMS set of 10 conflict behaviour correlations did not fit the data satisfactorily (stress .10, n.s.). However, a two-dimensional representation of the interrelations between avoiding, accommodating, compromising, problem solving, and fighting had a perfect fit because all variance could be predicted (stress $\leq$ .001, $p \leq .001$; for acceptability of MINISSA solutions, see Wagenaar & Padmos, 1971). To facilitate comparison of this two-dimensional CMS configuration to the X-cross model, the two largest distances in Fig. 3.2

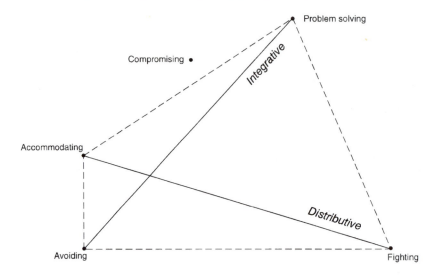

FIG. 3.2   The X-cross space of an integrative and a distributive dimension in Hall's
Conflict Management Survey.

were accentuated by drawing them as the diagonals of a quadrangle. The
quadrangle was then rotated until the axis of "avoiding–fighting" was in a
horizontal position at the bottom of Fig. 3.2. Finally, the diagonals were
labelled *integrative* and *distributive*.

Although the empirical data of the CMS appeared to produce an X-
cross, compromising did not figure as the midpoint of conflict behaviours,
located at the intersection of the integrative and distributive dimension.
Relying on Fig. 3.2, compromising is both a strongly integrative and a
strongly accommodation-directed distributive component of conflict behaviour. Other researchers have also reported that compromising refers to the
realisation of mutual agreement rather than to less cooperative and less
constructive reactions such as withdrawal and aggressive competition
(Cosier & Ruble, 1981; Kabanoff, 1987; Ruble & Thomas, 1976; Van de
Vliert & Hordijk, 1989). Consequently, despite the above acceptance of
Hypothesis 3, a slight revision of the X-cross model seems in order, removing compromising from the centre and placing this mode in between
accommodating and problem solving.

Interestingly, the arms of the X-cross in Fig. 3.2 are not mutually independent dimensions that are at right angles to one another. An unexpected
positive relationship exists between the integrative dimension and the
distributive dimension, reflected in supplementary angles of 67 and 113
degrees ($r = \cos 67° = .39$, $N = 145$, $p \le .001$). A similar secondary analysis

of Van de Vliert and Kabanoff's (1990) visual representations of the measures of MODE and ROCI underscored the fact that a significant positive correlation between the integrative and the distributive dimension exists. All this contradicts the model's assumption of orthogonality, let alone that there would be a negative relationship between integrative and distributive reactions to conflict issues.

Interpreting the acute angle between the arms of the X-cross as a positive conceptual association between the two descriptive dimensions is not the only possible explanation. The most superficial reason for the positive relationship between integration and distribution in Fig. 3.2 is the significant overlap between the subscales of avoiding and accommodating ($r = .43, p \leq .01$). That overlap in its turn might indicate the CMS instrument's failure to discriminate sufficiently between avoiding and accommodating (for a further interpretation of the findings in terms of measurement, see the Box "Measurement Validity"). Or it might reflect the respondents' tendency to frame avoiding and accommodating as corresponding variants of nonconfrontation (cf. Fig. 2.1).

Finally, it is worthwhile to signal that the above behavioural structure of obliquely crossed integrative and distributive dimensions was remarkably stable over different conditions. The high correlations between the MODE data sets in the Box "Data on Five Instruments" imply that the X-cross model is generalisable over completely different organisational contexts (cf. Mintzberg, 1979). At the one extreme, the data dealt with Kravitz's (1987) law enforcement agency, which is characterised by environmental stability, much formalisation, little decentralisation, and standardisation of work processes as coordinating mechanism. At the other extreme, there were data from Mills, Robey, and Smith's (1985) project-management personnel working in "adhocracies" characterised by environmental complexity, little formalisation, much decentralisation, and mutual adjustment as coordinating mechanism. The high correlations between the DUTCH data sets imply furthermore that the inlaying behavioural structure is also generalisable over the different roles of superior and subordinate.

STUDY 3: GENERALISABILITY ACROSS BEHAVIOURAL COMPONENTS

The central idea in the X-cross model is that all components of conflict handling are interrelated in terms of the magnitude of their integrative and distributive behavioural content. Because this postulate applies to the universe of behavioural components, a remaining question is whether avoiding, accommodating, compromising, problem solving and fighting constitute a representative sample of all possible methods of conflict handling. Does

Measurement Validity

Researchers who have to determine the value of an instrument for tapping the five modes of conflict handling usually assume that the five subscales can and must be validated separately. This is also reflected in the fact that the calculated relationship between a subscale and a validation criterion is never controlled for the relationships between that subscale and the other subscales. Such validation procedures are at odds with the perspective of conglomerated conflict behaviour, which sees the modes as co-occurring and covarying components of conflict behaviour.

The following alternative procedure of validation is based on the perspective of conglomerations of behavioural components. It compares an instrument's configuration of interrelations between subscales with the corresponding configuration of interrelations produced by (a) other methods of data gathering, or (b) the theoretical closeness of the components of conflict behaviour in the conflict management grid (Van de Vliert, Euwema, & Huismans, 1995; Van de Vliert & Kabanoff, 1990; Kabanoff & Van de Vliert, 1993). This approach leads to an evaluative judgement about the entire measuring instrument rather than about isolated subscales of conflict management. It differs from earlier validation studies in the following ways. First, it assumes that an instrument's subscales overlap. Second, it also assumes that the similarities and differences between the subscales constitute an appropriate validation criterion. Third, the criterion is complex, composed of as many subcriteria as there are pairs of distinct subscales. Fourth, each part of the criterion refers to the relationship between two subscales rather than to relative values on two subscales: one examines correlations instead of means.

Application of this novel validation criterion to the data in the Box "Data on Five Instruments" produces the following correlations between (a) the five sets of 10 correlations, and (b) each set of 10 correlations and the corresponding set of 10 criteria of closeness in the conflict management grid in Fig. 1.1.

	MODE	OCCI	ROCI	DUTCH	GRID
CMS	.88***	.56*	.68*	.87***	.63*
MODE		.36	.51	.81**	.34
OCCI			.63*	.32	.38
ROCI				.68*	.48
DUTCH					.56*

Notes: N = 10 interrelations among five subscales of conflict management.
* $p < .05$. ** $p < .01$. *** $p < .001$.
Abbreviations: CMS = Conflict Management Survey; MODE = Management Of Differences Exercise; OCCI = Organisational Communication Conflict Instrument; ROCI = Rahim's Organisational Conflict Inventory; DUTCH = Dutch Test of Conflict Handling.

As can be seen, CMS provides the only data set that significantly overlaps all the others (mean $r = .75$, $p < .01$). Since each correlation between two instruments can be considered an indication of their degree of concurrent validity, the results indicate that Hall's (1969) CMS has the highest degree of overall validity. In addition, CMS has the highest degree of overall construct validity because it resembles the interrelations in the conflict management grid best (see last column). These are remarkable conclusions. CMS, first published in 1969 and revised in 1973 and 1986, is the oldest questionnaire, which has been replaced by other instruments because of its disappointing psychometric qualities (e.g. Landy, 1978; Thomas & Kilmann, 1978). In a relatively recent review and critique of the CMS, Shockley-Zalabak (1988) cautioned researchers for social desirability bias and insufficient validity. The results reported in Study 2 and in this Box do not support those objections. On the contrary, together Fig. 3.2 and the above correlation matrix strongly suggest that the CMS validly measures the five-part typology, which can be described best with an integrative and a distributive dimension.

the X-cross inlay not only measures of the particular behavioural collection of the five-part typology, but measures of all other kinds of reactions to social conflicts as well (cf. Nicotera, 1993)? If so, the best description of all components of reactions to conflict uses integrative and distributive intentions, because these dimensions span the largest conceptual distances between widely divergent conflict behaviours by connecting the most opposite reactions (*Hypothesis 4*, replacing the more specific Hypotheses 1 to 3 from Study 2).

Method

Sternberg and his co-authors (Sternberg & Dobson, 1987; Sternberg & Soriano, 1984) investigated a sample of conflict behaviours, apparently unaware of the earlier work based upon the five-part typology. Initially they introduced the following reactions: physical action, economic action, wait and see, accept the situation, step down, third party, and undermine esteem. Later, after studying real-life conflicts, they expanded the list of behavioural alternatives to include withholding, bargain/compromise, avoidance, give in, manipulate, verbal force, prior history, confrontational discussion, mutual discussion, and separation. Data from an experiment using this enlarged set of conflict-handling methods (Sternberg & Dobson, 1987) were re-analysed to test Hypothesis 4 (for details, see Van de Vliert, 1990a).

Sternberg and Dobson (1987) had 40 Yale students—equally divided between men and women—describe four significant conflicts and the methods that they had applied to handle these conflicts with a parent, a teacher, a roommate, and a romantic partner, respectively. After subjects had completed these descriptions, they were asked to provide nine-point ratings regarding the extent to which each of 16 ways of dealing with conflict characterised these real and recent conflict interactions. So, viewed from the perspective of conglomerated conflict behaviour, Sternberg and Dobson (1987) included 16 behavioural components in their experiment. A matrix resulted of 120 correlations among each person's mean occurrence of each of the 16 components of conflict handling.

Once more using the multidimensional scaling programme MINISSA described above, the correlations were represented spatially in such a way that the distances between the methods of conflict handling reproduced the numerical value of the correlation coefficients. Repeated application of MINISSA to the set of 120 correlations resulted in one- and two-dimensional representations of the 120 conceptual distances between the 16 components of conflict behaviour (stress .38 and .16, respectively). The two-dimensional solution was certainly acceptable, since 84% of the variance could be predicted ($p \leq .05$, again relying on significance levels developed by Wagenaar & Padmos, 1971).

Results and Discussion

The statistical acceptability of the picture shown in Fig. 3.3 implied that it was not necessary to introduce more than two dimensions to describe conflict behaviour satisfactorily. Apparently, adhering to a two-dimensional structure for our research and intervention is not as "myopic and reductionistic" as Nicotera (1993, p. 286) believed.

Furthermore, the empirical configuration of components of conflict behaviour appeared to reflect the conflict management grid. To facilitate interpretation of the results, the two largest conceptual distances, drawn as solid lines, were rotated until they figured as the diagonals of an imaginary quadrangle extending from avoidance in the lower left corner (see quadrangle of broken lines in Fig. 3.3). As can be ascertained at a single glance the two descriptive dimensions, like the grid diagonals, were equally large. Clearly, the diagonal that connected avoidance and mutual discussion reflects an integrative dimension. Just as clearly, the other diagonal that ran from accept to physical force reflects a distributive dimension. The two dimensions, intersecting at supplementary angles of 71 and 109 rather than 90 degrees, support the X-cross model underlying Hypothesis 4 ($r = \cos 71° = .33$, $N = 40$, $p \leq .05$). Again, the integrative and the distributive behavioural content correlated significantly positive because of the overlap

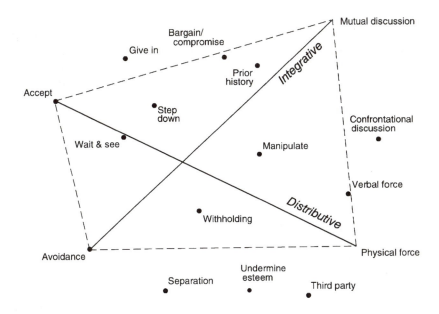

FIG. 3.3   The X-cross of an integrative and a distributive dimension in Sternberg's
components of conglomerated conflict behaviour.

between the nonconfronting components of conflict behaviour (see discussion of Study 2).

If acceptance is replaced by accommodation, mutual discussion by problem solving, and physical force by fighting, Fig. 3.3 appears to have much in common with Fig. 3.2. Sternberg's data reflect the same basic structure as the data gathered through established questionnaires. Here, too, the re-analysed interrelations among distinct components of conflict management are supportive of Hypotheses 1 through 3. Again, compromising did not represent the intersection of the integrative and distributive dimensions as the original X-cross model stipulates. Once again, compromising may support another feature of the conflict management grid. Bargain/compromise had a relatively high projection on the integrative dimension, in addition to a projection on the accommodating part of the distributive dimension. The findings seem to support the corollary that, for both parties together, compromising tends to be suboptimal in relation to fully integrative conflict resolution, whereas it tends to be optimal in relation to fully distributive victory and defeat.

Summary and conclusion.   Although Study 2 and Study 3 investigated different conflict reactions using different research methodologies, the results were quite consistent. Taken together, the findings strongly suggest that the X-cross of an integrative and a distributive dimension is a sound descriptive model that holds true for widely divergent components of conflict behaviour. However, the two dimensions are positively rather than negatively related, and compromising is a predominantly integrative and accommodation-directed component of conflict management.

PROPOSITIONS

3a.   The integrative dimension ranging from the component of avoiding to the component of problem solving, and the distributive dimension ranging from the component of accommodating to the component of fighting, have a positive or neutral rather than a negative relationship of co-occurrence (pp. 54–56, 66–67, 70).

3b.   The integrative dimension represents variations in anticipated variable-sum outcomes, whereas the distributive dimension represents variations in anticipated constant-sum outcomes for the conflicting parties (pp. 51–53).

3c.   Effectuation of variable-sum outcomes on the integrative dimension requires behavioural symmetry on the part of the opponent with both parties avoiding or negotiating, whereas effectuation of constant-sum outcomes on the distributive dimension requires behavioural complementarity on the part of the opponent with one party accommodating and the other party fighting (pp. 58–59, 61).

3d.   Conflicting parties handle behavioural dilemmas between equal and differential treatment of oneself and the opponent by conglomerating more and less integrative and distributive components of conflict behaviour (pp. 56–61).

3e.   Distinct components of conflict handling are interrelated in terms of the magnitude of their integrative and distributive behavioural content (pp. 56, 61, 69–70).

3f.   For the conflicting parties together, on the integrative dimension compromising is suboptimal in relation to conflict resolution, but on the distributive dimension compromising is optimal in relation to victory and defeat (pp. 52–54, 63, 71).

PART THREE

Explanation

CHAPTER FOUR

Third Step: Explanatory Dimensions

Descriptions and explanations go hand in glove; it does not make sense to give reasons for conflict behaviour that is not yet depicted in words. Paving the way for this chapter, Part II has therefore described five main components of conglomerated conflict behaviour and the elements of integration and distribution that they have in common. The next layer of theory building asks that old, short and pressing question: why? What determines how conflicting parties manage their inescapable behavioural dilemmas between integration and distribution? Guided by this question, attention now shifts from the characteristics to the antecedents of the principal party's complex reactions.

To begin with, the L-angle theory of concerns for one's own and the other's goals is reviewed by comparing it to the arms of the X-cross as predictors, and to a twin theory, the theory of social motives. Subsequent sections then develop an issue-based concerns theory. In this framework the conflict issue figures as the origin of the goals and the goal concern dimensions. The mutually independent goal concerns in their turn co-determine the dominant behavioural component and its (de-)escalative consequences. That is, the mutually independent concerns are mutually dependent in their consequences. Living apart together, as it were, the concerns have at least five offspring—avoiding, accommodating, compromising, problem solving, and fighting. A brief report of a questionnaire study that successfully tested some central assumptions from the conflict concerns theory closes this chapter.

L-ANGLE OF CONCERNS

Concerns for One's Own and the Other's Goals

Concerns as predictors. As set forth in Chapter 1, any actor in a context of social conflict is concerned about the achievement of goals. This concern has two directions: attaining one's own goals and attaining the other's goals. Both concerns arise from inside oneself and from the environment, and are "systems of pressures acting on an individual to manage [the conflict] in a certain fashion" (Blake & Mouton, 1964, p. 12). As behavioural predictors, the concerns go beyond pure description of how the conflict is handled. To be sure, the concerns have often been used to describe what the conflict management modes are (e.g. Cosier & Ruble, 1981; Folger & Poole, 1984; Hocker & Wilmot, 1985; Lewicki, Weiss, & Lewin, 1992; Ruble & Cosier, 1982; Ruble & Thomas, 1976; Thomas, 1988, 1992a). However, that either strips them of their causal core or it introduces the unjustified assumption that the concerns and the conflict behaviours are perfectly correlated.

Recall that too much research, especially in the field of bargaining, makes the impact of self-interest on conflict behaviour absolute, thus neglecting possible empathy with the other party. Therefore the addition of the second predictor, dealing with concern for the counterpart's welfare, is a great improvement on prior conceptual frameworks. Each of the two predictors ranges from 1 (low) to 9 (high), irrespective of the second amount of goal concern. Note that neither concern has a true zero point as its origin. The absence of a reference point of no concern may seem trivial, but it is not. It indicates that any conflict situation always elicits at least a very low amount of each of the two concerns. Consequently, a party's conflict behaviour vis-à-vis a particular adversary is always determined by both concerns (cf. Blake & Mouton, 1964, p. 9; 1970, p. 418; 1981). In other words, the basis of blending the two concerns into dominant conflict behaviour is co-determination. The resulting component of behaviour is unitary, holistic, and has a oneness in character. It is neither splittable into its integrative and distributive content nor into its two determinants of goal concern.

X-cross arms as predictors?   Sometimes the X-cross from Chapter 3 instead of the L-angle is viewed as the basic pair of motivational dimensions. For example, Schelling (1960) coined the term "mixed-motive" to refer to an X-cross mixture of preferences for integrative and distributive outcomes. In my view, the L-angle of concerns is a better predictor and explanator than the X-cross of integration and distribution in several regards. First, unlike integration and distribution, the concerns do not reflect the intended or displayed conflict behaviour that has to be explained. That is, L-angle-based predictions are less obvious and trivial than X-cross-based predictions. Second, unlike integration and distribution, the concerns are not closely associated with particular behaviour-based outcome allocations. Third, the concerns are elemental variables containing only information about either oneself or the opponent, whereas integrative and distributive aspirations are complex variables containing information about both oneself and the opponent. In other words, the integrative variable-sum dimension, as well as the distributive constant-sum dimension, confounds the potential outcomes for each of the principal parties. As a consequence, successfully predicted conflict behaviour and subsequent benefits or costs cannot be accounted for unequivocally by the potential outcomes for oneself, the potential outcomes for one's opponent, or both.

Behavioural predictions.   As outlined in Fig. 4.1, having hardly any concern for any party's goals leads to avoiding integrative and distributive interaction (1,1). A weak concern for one's own present goals but a strong

FIG. 4.1   Components of conglomerated conflict behaviour as a function of the twofold concern for one's own and the other's goals.

concern for the opponent's goals produces accommodating (1,9). Moderate and strong concern for both parties' goals co-determine compromising (5,5) and problem solving (9,9), respectively. Lastly, fighting is predicted when a strong concern for one's own goals exists, but only a weak concern for the adversary's goals (9,1).

Empirical evidence.   Pruitt et al. (1983) and Ben-Yoav and Pruitt (1984a) designed two studies to assess the combined effect of negotiator concerns about personal benefit and about the other party's benefit. Buyer–seller dyads had to simulate a trade negotiation to reach agreement on the price of three appliances. Each negotiator received a schedule showing the profit that their own firm would make at each price level for each appliance. The benefit schedules were constructed so that the parties could freely move up and down the integrative and distributive dimensions of conflict handling. What might be seen as high versus low concern for their own goals was manipulated by telling or not telling both negotiators privately that their firms required them to achieve no less than a particular profit level (lower limit). Note that higher goals are equated with higher goal concerns, which need not necessarily be the case. What might be seen as high versus low concern for the other's goals was produced by either putting or not putting both negotiators in a good mood, or giving or not giving them an expectation of continued future cooperation. The resulting patterns of negotiation and subsequent outcomes were similar in both studies: low concern for one's own goals embedded in high concern for the other's goals resulted in particularly profound accommodating and relatively low outcomes. Furthermore, high concern for one's own goals led to much problem solving and especially high outcomes when concern for the other's goals was also high, but much fighting and significantly lower outcomes when concern for the other's goals was low.

Building upon these earlier findings, Ben-Yoav and Pruitt (1984b) conducted a third experiment using the same buyer–seller task. This time the negotiators were or were not told that they had to report to the constituents; the company owners were or were not told how well they had negotiated (high versus low concern for one's own goals). In addition, they were told that they would have to cooperate with the other negotiator on a task following the negotiation session (high versus low concern for the other's goals). As predicted by the L-angle of concerns, high concern for both one's own and the other's goals produced especially high outcomes, apparently because it fostered heavy joint problem solving. But the impact of high concern for one's own goals was completely reversed when there was low concern for the other's goals. That condition encouraged fighting behaviour and especially low outcomes. The authors concluded that high concern for one's own outcomes is a two-edged sword: in the presence of high concern about the counterpart's outcomes both parties "win," whereas in the absence of high concern about the opponent's outcomes both parties "lose" as a consequence of their contentious behaviour.

Recently, Butler (1994) investigated the effects of four main components of conglomerated conflict behaviour, and the effects of self- and other-interest, on the outcomes of a negotiation with fully integrative potential. Students enacted the role of avoiders, accommodators, problem solvers, or fighters. Midway the role-play was interrupted and the negotiators answered two sets of questions about the pursuit of self- and other-interest, respectively. The problem solvers were the most efficient in terms of minutes needed to discover the logrolling solution, as well as the most effective in terms of joint outcome. The pursuit of one's self-interest, the pursuit of other-interest, and their interaction all had significant effects on joint outcomes. This pattern of findings indicates the superiority of the component of problem solving for achieving negotiating effectiveness.

Butler's negotiating role-play strongly suggested that the two concern dimensions co-determine dominant conflict behaviour, and so did the earlier creative series of experiments. A minor objection against Pruitt et al.'s (1983; Ben-Yoav & Pruitt, 1984a, 1984b) studies might be that both members of the dyad always received the same combination of concerns, and that heterogeneous dyads might yield other results. If one does not want to niggle, however, sufficient evidence exists to back up Blake and Mouton's (1964, 1970, 1981) conviction that conflict management always stems from a mixture of concern for one's own goals and concern for the other's goals. Put otherwise, the two mutually independent goal concerns determine one's dominant conflict behaviour in close conjunction with each other rather than independently.

Social Motives: A Twin Theory

Circumplex of motives as a predictor. In a letter to Einstein, entitled "Why War?," Freud divulged that as early as the eighteenth century Georg Christoph Lichtenberg invented a "Compass-card of Motives." Lichtenberg wrote: "The efficient motives impelling man to act can be classified like the 32 winds, and described in the same manner" (Freud, 1933, p. 43). Much later, basically the same idea reappeared in the theory of social motives, which—like the conflict management grid—gives a great deal of prominence to the two concerns for one's own and the other's goals (McClintock, 1972, 1976; see also Deutsch, 1973; Griesinger & Livingston, 1973; MacCrimmon & Messick, 1976).

McClintock (1972, 1976) proposed a circular array of behavioural orientations that operationalises the complex domain of social motives. A social motive was assumed to be made up of a subjective utility component that reflects the "rewardableness" of a particular outcome, and a subjective probability component that reflects the actor's expectancy of obtaining that outcome. McClintock subsequently defined several motives or orientations toward one's own and other's outcomes when dealing with opponents. Each social motive was geometrically represented as a motivational vector of infinite length and extending from the origin of the two-dimensional space defined by one's own and the other's outcomes. In this visualised framework the magnitude or quality of one's own outcomes was measured on the horizontal axis, and those of the adversary on the vertical axis (see Fig. 4.2).

McClintock postulated that individuals have a dominant motivational vector. The weights assigned to one's own and the other's outcomes, respectively, reflect several personal preferences for outcome allocations. Altogether he distinguished: *individualism*, maximising one's own outcomes; *altruism*, maximising the other's outcomes; *cooperation*, maximising both one's own and the other's outcomes (cf. integrative dimension in Chapter 3); *competition*, maximising the relative advantage of one's own over the other's outcomes, or minimising the other's relative advantage (cf. distributive dimension in Chapter 3); and *aggression*, minimising the other's outcomes. In Fig. 4.2 the vectors to the left of altruism and aggression represent goals that imply preferences for outcomes negative to oneself. They were not labelled because, rather interestingly, there are no self-evident descriptive terms to attach to these social motives. According to McClintock, individualism, altruism, cooperation, competition, and aggression dominate human action.

Behavioural predictions.   Given two alternatives of self/other outcomes defined as points in the conflict parties' joint outcome space, the theory of social motives makes the following prediction. The actor will choose the behavioural outcome with the greatest projection on his or her dominant motivational vector. For example, as can be seen in Fig. 4.2, a conflict party confronted with a choice between the behavioural alternatives A (1,5) and B (3,2) will select B if it is individualistic in orientation, but A if it is altruistically motivated. Similarly, conflict behaviour A will be preferred to B in the case of a cooperative orientation, but B will be chosen instead of A in the case of a competitive orientation.

Research into the basis of the theory of social motives has typically used individualism, altruism, cooperation, competition, and aggression as a convenient taxonomy of qualitatively different personality orientations. Thus, it was shown that the nominally distinct social motives are predictive of a person's conflict behaviour (e.g. De Dreu & Van Lange, 1995; Kramer, McClintock, & Messick, 1986; Kuhlman & Marshello, 1975; Liebrand & Van Run, 1985; McClintock & Allison, 1989; McClintock & Liebrand, 1988; Van Lange, 1991, 1992).

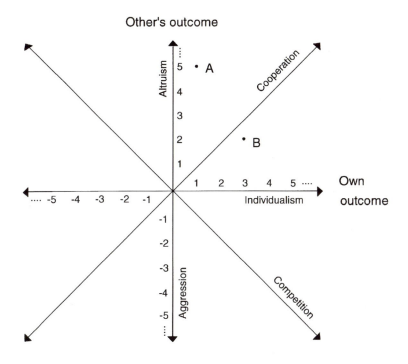

FIG. 4.2   Motivational vectors with two self–other outcome combinations
A (1,5) and B (3,2) (after McClintock, 1976).

Comparison of the Twins

The conflict management grid and the theory of social motives have a striking resemblance. Both frameworks present a coordinate system of concerns for one's own and the other's outcomes as conjunctive determinants of dominant conflict behaviour. They also present a second coordinate system of variable- and constant-sum outcomes. In the grid the variable- and constant-sum coordinates are represented by the X-cross of integration and distribution that was the subject of Chapter 3. In the theory of social motives basically the same coordinates are represented by the X-cross of the vectors of cooperation and competition in Fig. 4.2. Finally, the twins are reluctant to take negative concern about one's own outcomes seriously.

As for the differences, first of all, the social motives have a true zero point, whereas the concerns do not. Second, it is theoretically important that McClintock (1976) saw "goal concern" as a combination of outcome utility and outcome probability. The grid's L-angle, which defines "goal concern" in more global terms of emphasis and inner pressure, could benefit from McClintock's more specific operationalisation.

Third, it is immediately obvious that the theory of social motives includes negative concern about the opponent's outcomes, whereas the L-angle of concerns does not. Here, again, we are faced with the fact that the grid paradigm is weak on aggression. In Chapter 2 it was already noted that components of fighting are underrepresented in the grid's five-part taxonomy. For that reason more refined distinctions were introduced between indirect and direct fighting, and between fair and unfair fighting. But the bottom right quadrant of Fig. 4.1 offers room for further specification of fighting behaviours.

A fourth difference is that compromising is the pivot of the conflict management grid, whereas it is absent in the theory of social motives. As outlined in Chapter 3, the grid displays the hybrid character of compromising in a clear manner. For the parties together, the grid framework views compromising as suboptimal on the variable-sum dimension of integration, but as optimal on the constant-sum dimension of distribution. At the same time the grid conceptualises compromising as a mode with a moderately high projection on the basic orientations of looking after one's own and the other's conflict outcomes. In contrast, the theory of social motives lacks a vector of compromising. With reference to such behavioural heuristics as "one divides, the other chooses," "split it down the middle," and "take turns," McClintock (1976) observed that equality may also serve as a social motive, but that it cannot be defined by a single vector in the self/other outcome space.

Recapitulation.   Blake and Mouton's (1964, 1970) L-angle of concerns and McClintock's (1976) theory of social motives are twins. They both predict dominant conflict behaviour by means of the desired allocation of variable or constant outcomes to oneself and the opponent. Compared to the grid framework of dual goal concern, the theory of social motives gives a more specific operationalisation of the concept of concern in terms of outcome utility and outcome probability. It also pays more attention to fighting, but less attention to compromising.

CONFLICT CONCERNS THEORY

Does each of the concerns for one's own and the other's goals operate as an ultimate behavioural determinant or as an intermediator that transmits the influence from an originator to a conflict management mode? Blake and Mouton (1964) saw the concerns as pressures, in their turn arising from inside oneself, from the immediate external situation, or from characteristics of the social system (for analogous views, see Blalock, 1989; Giebels, De Dreu, & Van de Vliert, 1995; Griesinger & Livingston, 1973; Rubin, Pruitt, & Kim, 1994). Here, too, the concerns are conceptualised as intermediating variables, resulting from indirect behavioural determinants including the conflict issue. What follows is meant to develop an issue-based extension of the concerns framework, using linear mapping of the variables proposed to explain the handling of conflict. Note that this conflict concerns theory is not meant to explain how conflict comes about. On the contrary, the existence of a conflict issue is the starting point, the one and only stimulus that can activate the theory.

As depicted in Fig. 4.3, *concern for one's own goals* and *concern for the other's goals* are the central parts of the theory. They are inspired by *one's own and the other's goals*, of course. A *conflict issue* is a necessary but incomplete condition of an individual's goals and goal concerns. *Person* and *environment* are supposed to moderate its impact. To state the latter point differently, personal traits or states and contextual conditions can influence conflict behaviour only if an influential conflict issue exists in the first place.

Usually person and environment do indeed alter the relationship between the conflict issue on the one hand and the goals and goal concerns on the other. For instance, people differ in how sensitive they are to certain issues of norm violation. Likewise, different environments may potentiate and increase or buffer and reduce the seriousness of particular norm violations (De Ridder & Tripathi, 1992; Van de Vliert et al., 1996). Or, to give a specific example of issue–person–environment interaction: a minister may be especially sensitive to blasphemous cursing inside a church. The theory construes person and environment as having interactive rather than main effects to emphasise that each conflict goal and each goal concern is inevitably dependent on a conflict issue in every respect.

Subsequent to their formation, the two concerns have a joint effect on the selection of a dominant reaction to the conflict issue experienced. The *conflict behaviour*—avoiding, accommodating, compromising, problem solving, or fighting—is spontaneous inasmuch as it is not deliberately directed at the acquisition of benefits or the prevention of costs. It is strategic, however, inasmuch as the relationship between the concerns and the conflict behaviour is intermediated by a conscious plan to bring about certain outcomes for oneself and the opponent.

The feedback loops in Fig. 4.3 show that the actor's conflict behaviour has *de-escalative or escalative consequences*. As pointed out in a later section, de-escalative consequences temper the conflict issue or underpin the concern for the other's goals, whereas escalative consequences fuel the conflict issue or undermine the concern for the other's goals. Most consequences

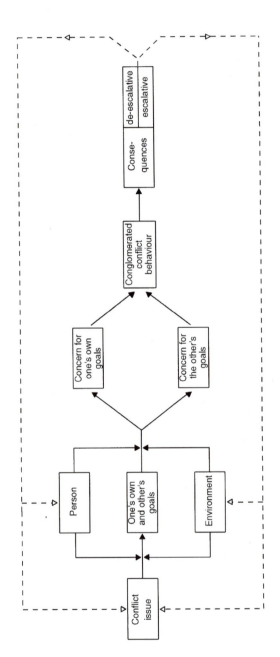

FIG. 4.3   A theory of goal concerns as intermediators between conflict issue and conglomerated conflict behaviour.

first influence the person or the environment, which then influences the goals and/or the goal concerns. Because the other individual or group is part of the actor's environment, a particularly relevant subset of consequences comes into being through the opponent's conflict behaviour.

The main parts of the above theory are the goal concerns as the intermediators, the conflict issue as the originator of the goals and goal concerns, and the (de-)escalative path as the ultimate consequent of the goal concerns. These three overlapping blocks of thought are further dealt with here in this order.

Concerns as Intermediators

Definitional specifications.   Concerns for goals are not goals or aspiration levels, as asserted by Thompson (1990; see also Rubin, Pruitt, & Kim, 1994, when summarising the studies of Ben-Yoav & Pruitt, 1984a, 1984b; Pruitt, et al., 1983). Whereas goals represent the outcomes capable of fulfilling desires, the goal concerns reflect desires. For example, in the case of a quarrel about an inheritance the perceived importance and feasibility of the respective claims may constitute the concerns for one's own and the other's goals, while the money, the real estate, and the movables may make up the parties' goals. Though the goal concerns are not the goals themselves, they imply that goals exist as they are directed at the realisation of these goals. Thus: no goals, no goal concerns.

In this book "concern" is understood to indicate the experienced amount of motivation to accomplish one's own goals and the other's goals. A motivation is not an emotion of discontent or a behavioural intention. Though a concern will usually be embedded in emotions, it is not considered an emotion as such. Similarly, though a concern may elicit one or more behavioural intentions, it is not considered an intention itself.

Motivational dilemma.   As the two goal concerns operate simultaneously, they create a motivational dilemma. While it is undesirable to give up one's own goals, it is also undesirable to obstruct or irritate the other party. This dilemma deserves some elaboration. My students often confuse the intra- and interpersonal behavioural dilemmas between integration and distribution discussed in Chapter 3 with the motivational dilemma between self-concern and other-concern broached here. The Chapter 3 dilemmas deal with a choice between *behavioural dimensions* containing *descriptive* information about the outcomes allocated to *both oneself and the opponent*. The current dilemma refers to a choice between *motivational dimensions* containing *explanatory* information about the outcomes desired by *either oneself or the opponent*.

The following is part of what I tell my students:

The two goal concerns do not co-determine a mixed-motive of integration or distribution, or both, which subsequently determines conflict management. Rather, the two goal concerns merge when they co-determine to what extent the conflict is handled integratively and distributively. Thus, the real mixed-motive nature of the conflict *is* the co-determination of conflict behaviour. Having said this, may I now demand your special attention to a most important implication. The co-determination of behaviour by the two concerns implies that, in fact, the choice between the two concerns constitutes a paradox. A 100% choice in favour of one concern is impossible. As conflicting parties, none of us can act upon one concern independently of and without reference to the other. We simply cannot escape from mixing these two motives.

Operationalisation.   Analogous to McClintock's (1976) definition of social motives, the actor's intermediating concerns are assumed to be made up of outcome utility and outcome probability. These motivational components are also known as the valence and the expectancy or feasibility of goal realisation (cf. Rubin, Pruitt, & Kim, 1994; Thomas, 1982; Vroom, 1964).

The outcome utility or *valence* of goal attainment reflects the reward-ableness or attractiveness of behavioural consequences, including costs which might result from the conflict management. The expectancy or *feasibility* of goal attainment reflects the likelihood of actually obtaining those desired consequences through particular conflict behaviour. Valence and feasibility can change, perhaps because of satiation or deprivation in the case of the valence, or the opponent's resources and reactions in the case of the feasibility (Blalock, 1989).

It might help future research if we expressed and operationalised each of the two intermediating concerns as a multiplicative function of outcome valence and outcome feasibility in the following way:

- concern for one's own goals $= f$ [valence × feasibility of attaining one's own objectives];
- concern for the other's goals $= f$ [valence × feasibility of attaining the other's objectives].

Keying this operationalisation to the concerns of the conflict management grid, one may have both valence and feasibility vary from 1 (small contribution to concern) to 3 (large contribution to concern). In consequence, the two final concern scores will range from 1 to 9.

A psychologically interesting fact is that concern for the other's goals is considered partially a function of the valence that the other's welfare has for oneself. The realisation of the counterpart's goals can have particular intrinsic valence for a conflict party holding altruistic norms or responsibility conceptions. Similarly, concessions can be a desirable means to a further end for oneself such as future repayment in some unrelated coin (cf. the section on accommodating in Chapter 2). For example, negotiators often have strong instrumental concerns for building interpersonal trust and confidence early in the process in order to facilitate jointly beneficial settlements (Lax & Sebenius, 1986). So, altruistic concern for the other's goals is often anything but self-sacrificing (cf. Cialdini et al., 1987).

Issue as Originator of Goals and Goal Concerns

This section starts with the viewpoint that the conflict issue is the birthplace of goals. It then proceeds to three types of goal interdependence evoked by conflict issues: positive interdependence, negative interdependence, and non-interdependence.

The birthplace of goals.   The main origin of the goals is not difficult to discover: with no conflict issue there are no goals and no goal-directed interaction. However obvious this point of departure may sound, it is at odds with the widely accepted assumption that conflict behaviour can be caused exclusively by either person or environment, or both (e.g. Filley, 1975; Folger & Poole, 1984; Greenhalgh, Neslin, & Gilkey, 1985; Hocker & Wilmot, 1985; Kelley & Stahelski, 1970; Rahim, 1992; Rubin & Brown, 1975; Terhune, 1970). Granted, the discord experienced will in its turn be influenced by both personal characteristics and surrounding milieu, including the antagonist. Moreover, as represented in Fig. 4.3, the conflict issue will often interact with person and environment to produce ultimately the conflict behaviour. However, neither of these impacts justifies person and environment, without regard to the conflict issue, being construed as the direct and sole origins of goal-directed conflict management (see, however, the Box "Concerns of Five Animals").

Conflict issue has been defined as the cognitive and/or affective experience of discord when at least one of the parties is being obstructed or irritated by the other. For example, marital conflict about the division of household labour is related to the wife's and not the husband's dissatisfaction with the status quo, whereas marital conflict about the division of paid work revolves around both spouses' dissatisfaction with the status quo (Kluwer, Heesink, & Van de Vliert, 1996). It is noteworthy that, almost by definition, dissatisfaction with the status quo evokes a need for attaining one or more objectives of change.

An axiom may now be deduced from the definition of conflict issue in Chapter 1. Discord acts to alert a conflict party to goals, particularly endangered own goals. Blocked objectives and negative emotions are alarm signals that divert people from pursuing the currently active goal hierarchy and goal sequence. Such signals of frustration point people toward

Concerns of Five Animals

Johnson and Johnson (1987; see also Filley, 1975) used the conflict management grid to identify five personality types: turtles, teddy bears, foxes, owls, and sharks. *Turtles* withdraw into their shells because they are hardly concerned about personal benefits and costs and good relationships with others. *Teddy bears* give up their own goals and try to smooth over the conflict out of fear of harming the other party. *Foxes*, having moderate concerns, seek compromises by giving up part of their goals and by persuading opponents to give up part of their goals as well. *Owls* value anybody's goals highly and, therefore, view conflict issues as problems to be solved fully. Lastly, egocentrically motivated *sharks* want to achieve their own goals at all costs by overpowering enemies. "These strategies are learned, usually in childhood, and they seem to function automatically." (Johnson & Johnson, 1987, p. 272).

Studies on the basis of the theory of social motives, discussed above, indicate that there is some truth in the existence of turtles, teddy bears, foxes, owls, and sharks. That is, experimentalists have consistently found that different individuals in a number of Western and Eastern countries systematically assign different weights to the realisation of their own and the other's goals (Kagan & Knight, 1981; Kelley & Thibaut, 1978; Kuhlman, Camac, & Cunha, 1986; Liebrand & Van Run, 1985; McClintock & Liebrand, 1988). People in individualistic cultures, including those of North America, Australia, and Great Britain, tend to value concern for their own goals over concern for the other's goals. In contrast, people in collectivistic cultures, including those of South America and Asia, tend to value concern for group goals over concern for personal goals (Hofstede, 1980; Ting-Toomey, 1988; Ting-Toomey et al., 1991; Triandis et al., 1988).

pursuing other goals that have meanwhile increased in importance (Simon, 1967; Fiske & Taylor, 1984). The axiom therefore postulates that a sensation of being obstructed or irritated makes goals salient.

All conflicts incorporate at least content and relationship goals (Fisher & Ury, 1981; Hocker & Wilmot, 1991), often supplemented by face-related identity goals (Fukushima & Ohbuchi, 1996; Roloff & Jordan, 1992; Wilson, 1992) and justice goals (Fukushima & Ohbuchi, 1996). From quite another perspective, negotiation researchers distinguish between (a) *limit level*—that is, the reservation value or resistance point to which one will eventually concede; (b) *aspiration level* or target point that one is trying to achieve; and (c) *demand level* of benefits claimed or costs disclaimed (Lax & Sebenius, 1986; Lewicki & Litterer, 1985; Pruitt, 1981; Walton & McKersie, 1965). The clarification or revision of those and still other goals refers to the assessment of future outcomes for both oneself and the opponent. One's own goals are set, and the other's goals are perceived or assumed, taking into account the particular conflict issue, personal traits or states, and contextual conditions (see Fig. 4.3).

Prominent determinants of the goals are the magnitude and intensity of the conflict issue at stake. Consider, for example, conflict involving a large amount of money, a precedent, a complicated topic, or a matter of principle. All such issues are likely to be associated with a high level of one's own goals and a low level of the other's goals (Brown, 1983; Deutsch, 1973; Euwema & Van de Vliert, 1994a; Fisher, 1964; Rubin & Brown, 1975). More relationally based issues also appear to trigger one-sided goals for oneself, thus locking the parties into an attack–defend state of mind (Donohue, 1991). The size, complexity, and relational base of a conflict increase if potential loss of face becomes a superimposed issue. A prospect of loss of face elicits superimposed goals and tends to heighten the concern about one's own rather than about the opponent's outcomes (cf. Brown, 1977; Folger & Poole, 1984; Pruitt, 1981; Tjosvold & Huston, 1978). However, one should keep in mind that person and environment moderate the relationship between goals and goal concerns. For example, concern may be low for an impracticably high goal, but one may be highly concerned about a reasonable and feasible target.

Goal assessment also includes the estimation of the possible covariation of one's own and other goals. In this connection Deutsch's (1949, 1973, 1985) theory of goal interdependence is most relevant. According to the goal interdependence theory, people pursue goals by the deployment of activities. A conflict exists whenever parties perceive that their activities are mutually incompatible. Whether this conflict will take a constructive or destructive course is determined by the relationship between the parties' respective goal attainments. Deutsch distinguished between positively interdependent, negatively interdependent, and noninterdependent goals. The three types of goal interdependence are discussed in some detail, because they shed novel light on the chain of antecedents of conflict behaviour.

Positive goal interdependence.   The term positive or promotive interdependence was used to characterise mutual exclusivity of activities in combination with a positive relation between the attainment of one's own and the other's goals. In other words, a combination exists of incompatible lower-order goals and compatible higher-order goals, to the ultimate effect that the conflicting parties stand or fall together. What is critical is whether this particular person in this particular conflict environment comes to *perceive* the ultimate goals as positively linked. Coombs and Avrunin (1988) viewed conflict in a context of positive goal interdependence as conflict that arises because the parties think they want different things and must settle for the same thing. Examples would be a conflict between husband

and wife about the number of children they wish to have, disagreement between manager and subordinates on a wage scale, and a fight between two statesmen on the location of their common national border. In all such cases, the goals are linked so that the conflicting parties have a shared responsibility and will "sink or swim" together.

The foxes and owls in the Box "Concerns of Five Animals" will tend to perceive positive goal interdependence, even when it does not exist. Others sometimes create such a situation of interdependency by establishing as a fact for themselves that, in spite of the conflict, the relationship with the opposite party is essentially one of unitedness and solidarity. Likewise, contextual conditions may promote perceptions of being thrown together. Just think of crises that can be solved only by mutual effort, ambiences of necessary teamwork as in a medical surgery team, and reward systems that remunerate the group as a whole.

Positive goal linkages refer back to and build on the integrative dimension of the X-cross in Chapter 3. Issues characterised by positive interdependence favour equal rather than differential treatment of oneself and the opponent. They foster integration, simply because self-interests require negotiation. In other words, such issues tend to equalise a conflict party's amount of concern for one's own goals and concern for the other's goals, because those goals have valence and feasibility of their realisation in common. Such issues create common ground, the perceived likelihood that mutually beneficial outcomes can be developed (Rubin, Pruitt, & Kim, 1994). Subsequently, people are bound to sink together on the grid location of 1,1 concern, but to swim together on the grid location of 9,9 concern.

In short, positive goal linkage tends to transform self-concern into joint-concern (Pruitt & Carnevale, 1993). In a questionnaire study and in a simulation experiment, Janssen (1994) recently showed that positive interdependence indeed equalises concern for one's own goals and concern for the other's goals ($r = .63/.67$, $p \leq .001$; valence .56/.22; feasibility .20/.74). Considerable research further supports the corollary that protagonists under circumstances of greater positive interdependence are more open-minded regarding the other party's arguments and desires, and more concerned about the opponent's outcomes (Deutsch, 1973; Johnson & Johnson, 1989; Johnson et al., 1981; Kramer, Pommerenke, & Newton, 1993; Tjosvold, 1989, 1990; Tjosvold & Deemer, 1980).

Negative goal interdependence. In Deutsch's theory, negative or contrient interdependence referred to the condition in which mutual exclusivity of activities is accompanied by a perceived negative relation between the attainment of one's own and the other's goals. Consequently, there is entrenched conflict as both lower- and higher-order goals are incompatible. Coombs and Avrunin (1988) viewed conflict in a context of negative goal interdependence as conflict that arises because the parties think they want the same thing and must settle for different things. Illustrations include two men courting the same woman, fights in competitive sports, and the ministers of two countries who are seeking hegemony over the same target. In such situations, if "one party swims, the other must sink."

Negative interdependence can be a realistic perception that one's gain is the other's loss, as when the environment is characterised by scarcity of certain disputed resources. Those scarce resources may be both material and social. In work organisations, for example, they regard not only money, facilities, materials, space, and manpower, but also information, attention, status, and social power as scarce resources. Under the influence of personal and contextual conditions, negative interdependence can also be an erroneous either–or conceptualisation of winning versus losing (cf. the teddy bears and sharks in the Box "Concerns of Five Animals"). Either–or conceptualisation may particularly result from a perceptual distortion, known as the *fixed pie error*: the parties expect the counterpart's interests to be opposed to their own (Bazerman & Neale, 1983; Neale & Bazerman, 1991; Thompson & Hastie, 1990). This cognitive bias is reinforced when the conflict intensifies (Rubin, Pruitt, & Kim, 1994).

The above illustrations and elucidations remind us of the distributive dimension of the X-cross in Chapter 3. Conflict issues characterised by negative interdependence favour differential rather than equal treatment of the opponent, because self-interests require a distributive win–lose attitude rather than a disposition to withdraw or to reconcile. Such issues tend to encourage asymmetrical—that is, opposite—quantities of concern about one's own and the other's goals, respectively; they destroy common ground. Put otherwise, a conflict party's valence and feasibility of obtaining desired outcomes tend to be high for the outcomes of oneself and low for the outcomes of the other (the reverse of low self-interest and high other-interest is a very rare case). Subsequently, the party's grid location near to 9,1 concern triggers swimming, which boils down to making the other party sink.

In short, negative goal linkage tends to transform self-concern into negative other-concern. In his above-mentioned studies, Janssen (1994) found that negative interdependence indeed produces much concern for one's own goals and little concern for the other's goals ($r = -.64/-.65$, $p \leq .001$; valence $-.60/-.64$; feasibility $-.84/-.80$). Considerable other empirical evidence also appears to support the relationship between negative interdependence and the vigorous pursuance of one's own interests (Deutsch, 1973; Johnson & Johnson, 1989; Johnson et al., 1981; Tjosvold, 1989, 1990; Tjosvold & Deemer, 1980).

Noninterdependence.   Still according to Deutsch (1949, 1973), both positive and negative goal interdependence can be absent despite the existence of incompatible activities. An extreme example is two strangers who are plunged into a row about who has to make space for the other, while accomplishing purely individualistic goals such as shopping and going to work. One can also think of sales representatives from different companies selling different products in different regions who have a conflict about the ethical permissibility of a selling tactic. As a result of this unrelatedness of the parties' respective goals, the conflict issue will tend to elicit neither equal nor opposite concern about outcomes for oneself and the other.

Relying on the L-angle of concerns, noninterdependence of goals, leading to mutually independent goal concerns, is the rule rather than the exception. However, conflict issues characterised by positive or negative goal interdependence, which tend to stimulate interrelated goal concerns, detract from the generalisability of the orthogonality of concern for one's own and the other's goals.

Conclusion.   A conflicting party's perception of the issue makes goals salient and triggers subsequent goal valuation and feasibility estimation. Notably, big issues, negative goal interdependence, and little perceived common ground tend to promote egocentric concern. Alternatively, small disagreements, positive goal interdependence, and much perceived common ground allow for altruistic concern. In interaction with characteristics of person and environment, therefore, the issue helps explain the degree to which conflict behaviour has de-escalative or escalative consequences.

The (De-)Escalative Path

De-escalation or mitigation and escalation or intensification of a conflict should not be confounded with the ultimate effectiveness of that conflict (for the effectiveness of conglomerated conflict behaviour, see Chapter 5). Instead, (de-)escalation is a process that relates to all the boxes in Fig. 4.3. The seriousness of the conflict issue, the level of and the concern for one's own and the other's goals, and the type of conflict behaviour and its consequences, in particular, all reflect and effect (de-)escalative change. Nevertheless, the cornerstones of the theory, the goal concerns, contribute to the explanation of (de-)escalation crucially. The three possibilities are, of course, change of concern for one's own goals, change of concern for the other's goals, and change of both.

Change of concern for one's own goals.   It can be concluded from Fig. 4.1 that a drastic change in concern for one's own goals produces a shift from avoiding to fighting or vice versa, or from accommodating to problem solving or vice versa. Avoiding and fighting are forms of nonagreeable noncooperation, whereas accommodating and problem solving are forms of agreeable cooperation (see Chapter 2). In the same vein, avoiding and fighting are found to bring about destructive consequences, whereas accommodating and problem solving produce more constructive outcomes (Burke, 1970; Euwema, 1992; Renwick, 1977; Tjosvold, 1991; Van de Vliert, Euwema, & Huismans, 1995). Clearly, then, a change in concern for one's own goals alters the form that noncooperation or cooperation takes, but it does not cause a U-turn from the track of de-escalation to the track of escalation, or vice versa.

Change of concern for the other's goals.   Figure 4.1 also indicates that a drastic change in concern for the other's goals produces a shift from avoiding to accommodating or vice versa, or from fighting to problem solving or vice versa. Avoiding is less agreeable and provides less beneficial and more costly substantive and relational outcomes than does accommodating (see Burke, 1970; Van de Vliert, Euwema, & Huismans, 1995). Similarly, fighting and problem solving are poles apart on the dimension of disagreeableness–agreeableness (see Chapter 2), and fighting provides fewer benefits and more costs than problem solving. So, the person who changes his or her concern for the opponent's goals swings in the opposite direction, either from the track of de-escalation to the track of escalation, or from the track of escalation to the track of de-escalation.

The how and why of (de-)escalation.   Taken together, the conflict concerns theory enunciates that concern for one's own goals determines *how* the conflict either de-escalates or escalates, whereas concern for the other's goals determines whether and explains *why* the conflict de-escalates or escalates. This corollary about the how and why of (de-)escalation underscores the one-sidedness of previous theory building that restricted itself to the impact of concern for one's own goals.

To illustrate the "how and why" rule, consider a highly educated employee with little experience who comes up against a lowly educated employee with much experience. In this case *de-escalation* flows from appreciating and making use of the other's experience and expertise by conceding or creating solutions. A reduction in the importance and likelihood of applying "book knowledge" might lead to accommodating or it might go off the rails of de-escalation via avoiding. *Escalation* flows from under-appreciating and bypassing the opponent's practical know-how and skills by withdrawing from or enforcing a course of action. An enlargement of the importance and likelihood of applying "book knowledge" might lead to fighting or it might go off the rails of escalation via problem solving. Consequently, conflicting parties wanting to de-escalate their discord should switch over to promoting each other's interests more, instead of promoting their own interests less. Conversely, when escalation is needed they are advised to switch over to promoting each other's interests less, instead of promoting their own interests more.

There is abundant support for the main thesis that de-escalation and escalation result from high and low concern for the opponent's goals, respectively. This support is implied in hundreds of studies on goal interdependence. Both positive and negative interdependence elicit high concern for one's own goals. The only factor that varies is the concern for the other's goals, being high in the case of positive interdependence but low in the case of negative interdependence. Viewed like this, conflicting parties with high rather than low concern for the other's goals accept the opposing party more readily and react to that party in a more cooperative and de-escalative way (Butler, 1995; Deutsch, 1973; Johnson & Johnson, 1989; Sherif, 1966; Tjosvold, 1989, 1990).

The "how and why" rule of (de-)escalation may also shed a different light on entrapment as an explanation for intensifying conflict. An entrapped party, it is proclaimed, escalates his or her commitment to a detrimental course of action to justify prior investments in the conflict (Bazerman, 1983; Brockner & Rubin, 1985; Teger, 1980). This gradual increase in the valence of one's own objectives is especially likely to occur when one's conflict behaviour is highly salient (e.g. high in publicity), when it elicits irrevocable consequences, and when one feels personally responsible for taking that action. Rather than an increasing dedication to one's own interests, the actual cause of entrapment might well be a decreasing dedication to the other party's interests. If so, a fighter is entrapped not so much in an overcommitment to his or her own goals as in an undercommitment to the adversary's goals. Only further research can pass judgement on these intriguing alternative explanations of conflict escalation.

Summary. The conflict concerns theory holds that the conflict issue, the person, and the environment have interactive effects on the parties' goals and concerns for one's own and the other's goals. The dual goal concern, in its turn, especially concern for the other's goals, has a pivotal function in the further process of handling and (de-)escalating the conflict.

STUDY 4: IMPACT OF THE CONCERNS

The crucial postulate of the conflict concerns theory states that concern for the attainment of one's own goals and concern for the attainment of the other's goals co-determine the dominant conflict behaviour. This general postulate can be broken down into more specific hypotheses. *Hypothesis 1*: higher concern for one's own and for the other's goals results in less avoiding, more compromising, and much more problem solving. This hypothesis deals with the integrative dimension of conflict behaviour. *Hypothesis 2*: higher concern for one's own goals and lower concern for the other's goals results in less accommodating and more fighting. This hypothesis deals with the distributive dimension of conflict behaviour.

One of the theory's supplementary postulates addresses the impact of the concerns on the (de-)escalative consequences. Concern for the other's goals, rather than concern for one's own goals, is supposed to de-escalate or escalate the conflict. The theory also states that the behaviour intermediates between the dual goal concern and the further (de-)escalative course of the conflict process. Taken together, concern for the other's goals, rather than concern for one's own goals, produces conflict behaviour that de-escalates or escalates the conflict (*Hypothesis 3*).

The above three hypotheses were put to the test by Onne Janssen, Martin Euwema and myself (1994; Janssen, 1994; Janssen & Van de Vliert, 1996; Janssen et al., 1996).

Method

Overview of the study.   The research enlisted students as subjects and consisted of four parts. First, we selected a realistic conflict issue to construct a scenario for conflict simulation. Second, after having instructed the subjects, we measured the independent variables of concern for one's own goal and concern for the opponent's goal. Third, we videotaped the subjects' conflict interactions. Finally, we had observers assess the dependent measures of each subject's conflict behaviour and contribution to escalation by scoring the tapes.

Subjects.   Videotaped data were obtained from 84 Dutch students in the behavioural sciences at the University of Utrecht. Random assignment to dyads resulted in 16 male/male dyads, 14 male/female dyads, and 12 female/female dyads. Subjects received 10 Dutch guilders (about $US6) for their participation.

Conflict simulation.   The two students in each dyad were asked to act out a role-play wherein they both wished to apply for a six-month trainee post as an organisational researcher in the personnel department of the University Hospital. In order to obtain this position they had to prepare a good and attractive research proposal. The experimenter told them that they had the choice of handing in a written proposal, or of giving an oral presentation before a committee. He further told one student to opt for the written proposal because of being a good writer, and the other to choose the oral presentation because of being good at oral presentations. This choice between written proposal and oral presentation produced the conflict issue that made salient each dyad member's goal to carry off the trainee post.

Positive versus negative goal interdependence was used to manipulate the subjects' dual goal concern. It should be kept in mind, however, that we were interested in conflict behaviour and conflict escalation as a function of dual goal concern and not of goal interdependence. In the condition of positive goal interdependence the dyads were told that the personnel department needed two trainees (two positions). The two members of the dyad had to prepare one joint written proposal or oral presentation to win or lose those two trainee posts together. This manipulation was reinforced by the prospect of future interaction for six months. In the condition of negative goal interdependence the dyads were told that only one researcher was needed. They were left with the choice of either both handing in their own written proposal or both giving their own oral presentation before a committee for that single trainee post. This manipulation was reinforced by the absence of expected future interaction.

After this general briefing the two subjects were separated. They got time to project themselves into the conflict scenario, and to complete a questionnaire that assessed the dual concern for one's own and for the other's goal. Finally, the dyad members interacted about their conflict for about ten minutes in front of a camera. Afterwards, subjects were debriefed and paid.

Independent measures: concerns.   In agreement with the suggestion put forward in this chapter, concern for one's own goal and concern for the other's goal were operationalised as a multiplicative function of outcome valence and outcome feasibility. As for outcome valence, the subject indicated on seven-point scales the attractiveness, desirability, importance, and allure of one's own goal to get the research post (Cronbach's $\alpha = .93$) and the other's goal to get the research post ($\alpha = .95$). As for outcome feasibility, the subject provided a percentage for the likelihood of obtaining the research post, and a percentage for the likelihood that the other student would obtain it.

Dependent measure: conflict behaviour.   Each video-recorded simulation was rated for the components of conflict behaviour by four neutral observers (three women and one man). After being trained for two days, each observer independently assessed the use of avoiding, accommodating, compromising, problem solving, and fighting by completing seven-point scales, anchored by *absolutely not used* (1) and *absolutely used* (7). They did so for each two-minute interval, for each dyad member separately, and for each of the five components of conflict behaviour. Two-minute time intervals were chosen because a dyad member's action followed by the other dyad member's reaction appeared usually to take about two minutes. The *intra*observer consistency across time intervals was acceptable: α ranged from .50 for fighting to .86 for problem solving (mean α = .78). Across time intervals, the *inter*observer reliability in terms of Kendall's *W* ranged from .57 for avoiding to .83 for problem solving (mean *W* = .74).

Dependent measure: (de-)escalation.   After the assessment of the conflict behaviour, the same observers independently gave each dyad overall scores for escalation in terms of substantive and relational outcomes (cf. Van de Vliert, Euwema, & Huismans, 1995). Each observer indicated on seven-point scales, anchored by *not at all* (1) and *very much* (7), the extent to which the seriousness of the conflict intensified, the issue was resolved, the mutual understanding worsened, the atmosphere became more antagonistic, and the mutual trust increased. The reliability coefficients were high for both the *intra*observer consistency (α ranged from .92 to .96) and the overall *inter*observer agreement (Kendall's *W* = .89). Each subject was assigned the overall escalation score of his or her dyad.

Results and Discussion

Examination of dual goal concern. As intended, the dyad members having to cooperatively prepare one joint proposal (positive goal interdependence) and those having to prepare their own competitive proposal (negative goal interdependence) experienced different levels of goal concern. The results were in line with the theoretical considerations and empirical evidence reviewed in this chapter. Positive goal interdependence, compared to negative goal interdependence, produced a considerably higher level of concern for the other's goal. Whereas positive goal interdependence tended to equalise the degrees of concern for one's own and for the other's goal (r = .67; $M_{\text{own goal}}$ = 4.56, SD = 1.24; $M_{\text{other's goal}}$ = 4.08, SD = 1.82), negative goal interdependence tended to produce opposite degrees of concern for one's own and the other's goal (r = –.65; $M_{\text{own goal}}$ = 3.68, SD = .80; $M_{\text{other's goal}}$ = .95, SD = .59).

Tests of hypotheses.   For the hypotheses to be confirmed, the conflict behaviours should intermediate the relation between the goal concerns and the de-escalation or escalation. As argued, first of all, a person's goal concerns should predict his or her conflict behaviours. Table 4.1 contains the results of regressing the conflict behaviours on the concern for one's own and the other's goals, and their interaction.

Higher concern for the other's goal, but no concomitant higher concern for one's own goal, appeared to be associated with relatively less avoiding, and much more compromising and problem solving. Thus, Hypothesis 1 was only partly supported because concern for one's own goal did not have any behavioural effect. In deviation from the conflict concerns theory, the interaction terms for avoiding and problem solving were not significant, while the significant interaction term for compromising indicates that higher concern for the other's goal and lower instead of higher concern for one's own goal elicit compromising.

The test of Hypothesis 2, stating that one-sided concern for one's own goals leads to less accommodating and more fighting, also provided mixed results. As the main effects in Table 4.1 indicate, more accommodating seems to be exclusively produced by higher concern for the other's goal and not by lower concern for one's own goal. However, as expected, the significant interaction term for accommodating ($\beta = -.40$) indicates that lower concern for one's own goal and higher concern for the other's goal did produce especially high levels of accommodating. As also predicted, higher concern for one's own goal and lower concern for the other's goal did result in more fighting, though the interaction term for fighting was not significant. Taking stock of these results, the evidence in favour of Hypothesis 2 outweighs the evidence against it.

Not shown in Table 4.1 are the regressions of (de-)escalation on the concern for one's own and the other's goals, and their interaction. As anticipated, concern for one's own goal appeared to escalate the conflict ($\beta = .25$, $\Delta R^2 = .04$, $p \leq .05$), whereas concern for the other's goal appeared to de-escalate it ($\beta = -.68$, $\Delta R^2 = .29$, $p \leq .001$; interactive effect: $\beta = .05$, $\Delta R^2 = .00$, n.s.). When the influence of the five components of conflict behaviour was controlled, the escalative effect of concern for one's own goal disappeared completely (from $\beta = .25$, $p \leq .05$, to $\beta = .12$, n.s.), and the de-escalative effect of concern for the other's goal reduced considerably (from $\beta = -.68$, $p \leq .001$, to $\beta = -.28$, $p \leq .05$). These reductions in predictive power were caused by the de-escalative intermediating influence of problem solving ($\beta = -.50$, $p \leq .001$) and the escalative intermediating influence of fighting ($\beta = .25$, $p \leq .05$).

The above results strongly suggest that, in agreement with Hypothesis 3, and due to the de-escalating influence of problem solving and the escalating influence of fighting, concern for the other's goal indeed accounted for much more of the variance in (de-)escalation than concern for one's own goal. As a noteworthy restriction, three out of the four neutral observers were female. This gender factor may be partly responsible for the finding that concern for the other's goal has a strong impact on the de-escalative or escalative course of the process. Men might judge the escalativeness of problem solving and fighting differently than women. Arguing against the seriousness of this limitation, however, is the correspondence between the above results and those from prior investigations

TABLE 4.1
Components of Conglomerated Conflict Behaviour as a Function of
Dual Goal Concern

	Integrative dimension					
	Avoiding		Compromising		Problem solving	
	β[a]	ΔR^2	β	ΔR^2	β	ΔR^2
A. Concern for one's own goal	−.16	.02	−.13	.01	−.08	.00
B. Concern for the other's goal	.34*	.03†	.64**	.15**	.68**	.26**
A × B	−.10	.01	−.27*	.06*	−.20	.03†

	Distributive dimension			
	Accommodating		Fighting	
	β	ΔR^2	β	ΔR^2
A. Concern for one's own goal	−.14	.01	.30*	.08**
B. Concern for the other's goal	.77**	.19**	−.68**	.15**
A × B	−.40**	.11**	.19	.02

Note: $N = 84$.
[a] Beta values from the regression equation including the two goal concerns and their interaction;   † $p \leq .10$, two-tailed;   * $p \leq .05$, two-tailed;   ** $p \leq .01$, two-tailed.

(e.g. Ben-Yoav & Pruitt, 1984a, 1984b; Burke, 1970; Butler, 1994; Pruitt et al., 1983; Renwick, 1977; Van de Vliert, Euwema, & Huismans, 1995).

Conclusion and discussion.   Systematic observations of videotaped conflict simulations by neutral observers both confirmed and disconfirmed parts of the conflict concerns theory. The predictions of specific components of conflict behaviour were only partly supported, notably with regard to strongly integrative and distributive behaviour; this deviates from earlier support for the behavioural predictions (Ben-Yoav & Pruitt, 1984a, 1984b; Butler, 1994; Pruitt et al., 1983). But the predictions of the behavioural consequences fared much better. Higher concern for the realisation of the other's ultimate goals appeared to de-escalate the conflict, both directly and through more problem solving and less fighting. Additionally, though much less markedly, higher concern for the realisation of one's own ultimate goals escalated the conflict through more fighting.

This study particularly demonstrates that both weak and strong concern for one's own goals may lead people to the de-escalative or to the escalative path. In contrast, weak concern for the other's goals tends to produce less de-escalative and more escalative behavioural components, whereas strong concern for the other's goals tends to produce more de-escalative and less escalative behavioural components. A principle of equifinality seems to operate in that concern for the other's goals can attain the same degree of (de-)escalation through different behavioural components. These findings break away from the paradigm that views escalative behaviour as the predominant result of too much concern for one's own goals (cf. Greenhalgh, 1987, 1995; Pruitt & Carnevale, 1993; Thompson, 1990). At the same time, they support the alternative paradigm of dual goal concern producing conglomerated conflict behaviour.

PROPOSITIONS

4a. A conflict issue gives rise to an assessment of one's own and the other's goals and subsequent concerns about attaining these goals (pp. 87–92).

4b. Concern for one's own goals and concern for the other's goals consist of goal valences and means–end feasibilities that motivate dominant conflict behaviour (pp. 85–87, 96).

4c. Positive goal interdependence between the parties tends to equalise the actor's degree of concern for one's own and the other's goals, whereas negative goal interdependence tends to produce opposite degrees of concern for one's own and the other's goals (pp. 90–91, 97).

4d. The dual goal concern intermediates the relation between the conflict issue and the dominant conflict behaviour (pp. 82–86).

4e. The concern dimensions co-determine the dominant conflict behaviour (pp. 76–79, 83, 94–95, 97–99; see Figure 4.1 for specific predictions of avoiding, accommodating, compromising, problem solving, and fighting).

4f. Concern for one's own goals determines *how* the conflict de-escalates or escalates, whereas concern for the other's goals determines whether and explains *why* the conflict de-escalates or escalates (pp. 92–95, 98–100).

CHAPTER FIVE

Fourth Step:
Complexity Explanations

Simple and stable conflict behaviour is a white crow. In Chapter 3 it was proposed that parties to a conflict handle a basic dilemma between either equal or differential treatment of oneself and the opponent by blending or alternating integrative and distributive moves. From Chapter 4 we have subsequently learned that their reactions are rooted in dual concern for one's own and for the other's goals. But, of course, the dilemma and concern viewpoints do not cover the whole story about behavioural complexity.

The present chapter seeks to describe and explain complex conflict behaviour in more detail. It departs from the viewpoint that a conglomeration of behavioural components cannot be described by a single combination of one degree of integration and one degree of distribution; neither can it be explained by a single level of concern for one's own goals combined with a single level of concern for the other's goals. As an introduction, behavioural complexity and some typical examples of behavioural conglomerations are examined. On the basis of this review, predictions of conglomerated behaviour and its consequences will then be worked out. Closing the chapter are two global reports of empirical demonstrations of the usefulness of the complexity perspective for an adequate understanding of behavioural effectiveness.

CONGLOMERATED CONFLICT BEHAVIOUR

No conflict behaviour is completely without complexity. Take a fight. Covert sabotage and hidden coalition formation make it an indirect fight. An underlying intention to reach agreement makes it a hard negotiation. An attempt at defeating the adversary while complying with agreed-upon rules makes it a fair fight. I have even observed the still more complex aggregation of an indirect fight to settle a disagreement in a fair way.

The following section pays closer attention to behavioural complexity, before—in the subsequent section—a conglomeration is defined as an aggregation of distinct components of conflict handling. We will see that each component can be described in terms of the degree to which it occurs, and its relationship with each of the other components. Some concrete examples of conglomerated conflict behaviour, including firm flexibility, are elaborated upon.

Complexity

Foreshadowings of complexity.   Ever since the publication of the conflict management grid, behavioural complexity has been around with no one there to stop and stare. Blake and Mouton (1964, 1970) discerned no less than 76 mixtures of their five pure types of conflict management appearing at the four corners and at the centre of the grid. They also devoted entire chapters to aggregated reactions, including paternalism and the two-hat approach (see Chapter 1). Indeed, on close inspection, even a seemingly exclusive reaction to a conflict is always a mix of conflict behaviours. As put nicely by Rubin, Pruitt, and Kim (1994, p. 4): "most conflict situations—be they armed exchanges, labor strikes, international negotiations, family squabbles, or the tacit exchanges that occur when two drivers vie for position at an unmarked intersection—call forth a *combination*, and often a *sequence* of the preceding strategies. Rarely is one strategy used to the exclusion of the others." The fact that, by definition, conflict behaviour contains both covert intentions and overt enactments further complicates the preceding considerations.

Simultaneous and sequential complexity.   A reaction can be simultaneously linked to another reaction, as in the case of a sarcastic compliment. In addition, a reaction can also be sequentially linked to another reaction, as in the case of fighting before compromising to reduce loss of face. Self-evidently, sequential complexity increases with larger time units of analysis, thus larger samples of behaviour. In a shout of anger the sequential complexity will be less than in an explanation of one's position, and much less than in an entire phase of a conflict. It is a good thing to keep this relationship with the unit of analysis at the back of one's mind when taking note of the definition of conglomerated conflict behaviour.

Definition

The term *conglomerated conflict behaviour* refers to a simultaneous or sequential aggregation of several behavioural components in varying degrees. A "component" is a holistic unit of action. Each component, in its turn, has an integrative and a distributive content. Whereas a conglomeration is heterogeneous and divisable into its components, a component is homogeneous and *un*splittable into its integrative and distributive content. Consider, for instance, indirect fighting and hard negotiating. Indirect fighting is a conglomeration of two solid bodies of reaction, to wit: avoiding open confrontation, and making one's way by attacks and defences in a roundabout way. Quite differently, hard negotiating constitutes a constellation of a displayed and an intended reaction, because overt contentious activity is embedded in a covert plan to settle the matter eventually.

Description

It is suggested here that an accurate picture of a conglomeration has to pay attention to the content, the occurrence, and the covariation of its components. The advantages of this approach are discussed after the details of the descriptive method have been presented.

Content of components. Conglomerated conflict behaviour does not have a fixed number of components. Which and how many components are most useful depends on the objectives of an investigation or intervention. Obviously, it is advisable to build the components out of the five-part typology of avoiding, accommodating, compromising, problem solving, and fighting, whenever appropriate. In any case, each component has a specific content that can be described in terms of both the intensity with which that component occurs, and its covariation with each of the other components. For all components together, two configurations result: a pattern of relative levels of occurrence and a pattern of relative levels of covariation.

Pattern of occurrence refers to the relative intensity with which each behavioural component occurs. N components produce a configuration of N degrees of occurrence for an individual or for a group. For instance,

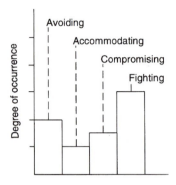

FIG. 5.1   A pattern of occurrence of components of indirect fighting.

indirect fighting to settle a disagreement in a fair way might be characterised by the following pattern of occurrence of four behavioural components: 20% avoiding, 10% accommodating, 15% compromising, 30%
fighting, and 25% unclassifiable reaction. Fighting, having the highest level
of occurrence, dominates this pattern (see also Fig. 5.1), thus designating
it as distributive rather than as integrative.

Pattern of covariation refers to the relative extent to which each behavioural component concurs with each of the other components in the
behavioural conglomeration. For multifaceted observations of conglomerated conflict behaviour, the pattern of covariation takes the form of a
degree of positive correlation between the two components in each pair of
behavioural components. N components produce a pattern of ½ N $(N-1)$
degrees of covariation. Thus, the above complex fight might consist of the
following six correlations: avoiding–accommodating –.10; avoiding–
compromising .05; avoiding–fighting .40; accommodating–compromising
–.20; accommodating–fighting –.30; compromising–fighting .25. In this
pattern, fighting, which occurs most, has a relatively high degree of positive
correlation with avoiding. Clearly, this behavioural conglomeration is characterised by a "dominant coalition" between fighting and avoiding.

The pattern of covariation may be visualised in the same way as the
interrelations between modes of conflict management were portrayed in
Figs 3.1 and 3.2. Multidimensional scaling techniques translate the pattern
of correlations into an elegant network of spatial distances. The resulting
picture is much easier to assimilate than the correlation matrix. It may
well also bring out features of a pattern that are obscured in the numerical
representation of the data. For the above example this pictorial approach

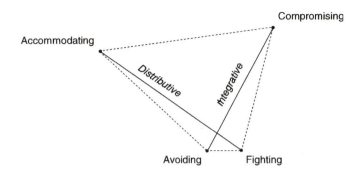

FIG. 5.2   A pattern of covariation of components of indirect fighting.

produces Fig. 5.2, wherein the dominant coalition between fighting and avoiding stands out. Note also that the distributive diagonal is somewhat longer than the integrative diagonal because it contributes more to an apt description of the pattern of interrelationships between the four cornerstone components of the conglomeration.

Combined pattern.   The combined sets of information on the occurrence and covariation of the behavioural components provide an even richer picture of a conglomeration than they do in separation. In particular, the pattern of covariation can be used to interpret the pattern of occurrence more adequately. It reveals what each particular component of behaviour means in terms of the other components. Figure 5.2 thus adds shades of meaning to Fig. 5.1. The fact that the dominant component of 30% fighting concurs most with avoiding ($r = .40$) characterises it as associated with fighting. Perhaps the fighter in this example scuffles in regard to some aspects of the issue, while escaping other topics. Or this fighter might stay away from direct clashes, adopting hidden moves that are guerrilla-like.

To facilitate the comparison of the patterns of occurrence and co-variation, they could be integrated into one picture. Figure 5.3 thus represents both the occurrence and the internal structure and meaning of all relevant parts of the conglomeration. Such an all-inclusive picture constitutes a very informative close-up snapshot of an incidence of conglomerated conflict behaviour.

A similar snapshot of the police sergeants' behaviour in Study 1, having a conflict with a constable or a warrant officer, is given in Fig. 5.4. As can be seen, indirect fighting, which occurs predominantly (thickest dot),

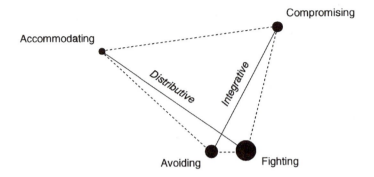

FIG. 5.3   A combined pattern of occurrence (thickness of dots) and covariation (closeness of dots) of components of indirect fighting.

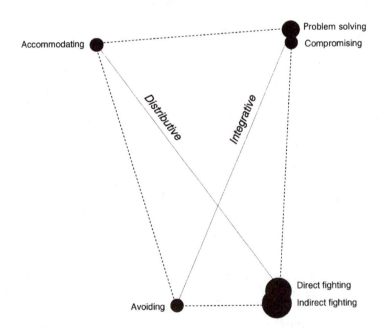

FIG. 5.4   Combined pattern of occurrence (thickness of dots) and covariation (closeness of dots) of police sergeants' components of fighting behaviour in Study 1.

concurs with direct fighting and avoiding (relatively small distances). This concurrence makes sense because indirect fighting is a blend or assemblage of attacking and defending, and avoiding of open confrontation. Direct fighting, the back-up component of behaviour (second thickest dot), also has ingredients of avoiding (relatively small distance). Taken together, the police sergeants manifest a "dominant coalition" of indirect fighting, direct fighting, and avoiding. Accommodating, compromising, and problem solving conglomerate into a "counter-coalition" that seems too weak to influence the course of the conflict.

Advantages of pattern approach.   Of course, the conceptualisation of conflict management in terms of conglomerated instead of single and pure conflict behaviour does not constitute a parsimonious paradigm. Relatedly, the required process of building complex theory will be difficult. I believe, however, that these disadvantages of using the concept of conglomerated conflict behaviour—lack of parsimony and laborious theory building—are counterbalanced by several advantages.

First of all, the patterns of occurrence and covariation mirror a person's behaviours much more adequately than the data on single types commonly reported. They do not ignore relevant forms of reaction that supplement and give meaning to the dominant response. Due to the many possible differences in a configuration of behavioural components, it is virtually unthinkable that conglomerations have identical patterns of occurrence and covariation. Put otherwise, each conglomerated conflict behaviour has its own patterns of occurrence and covariation, like each individual has his or her own D.N.A. pattern.

A second merit of the paradigm of conglomerated behaviour is that the patterns make a promising research device. The two patterns enable detailed comparisons of intended, reported, and actually manifested behaviours. They also constitute a relatively simple research device. The pattern of occurrence consists of a simple set of means, and the pattern of covariation consists of a simple set of correlations. As a third advantage, the pattern approach makes possible a pictorial method, which may facilitate the interpretation and dissemination of research results (cf. Figs 5.3 and 5.4).

Fourth, the pattern approach highlights effects of conflict issue, person, environment, and goal concerns on the relative rather than absolute occurrence and meaning of reactions. For instance, actors report a less competitive and more cooperative pattern of occurrence of their own behaviours than do their opponents (Thomas & Pondy, 1977). Also, actors report a pattern of greater similarity between their own competitive and cooperative behaviours than do observers (Van de Vliert & Prein, 1989).

Lastly, the de-escalative or escalative consequences of behaviours can be investigated and controlled more accurately by considering patterns of behavioural components as opposed to single behavioural types (see Studies 5 and 6 at the end of this chapter).

Retrospect and prospect. Unsplittable modes of conflict handling aggregate into a conglomeration of conflict behaviour with singular behavioural components having a degree of occurrence, as well as a degree of covariation, with each of the other components. The patterns of occurrence and covariation capture the uniqueness of the conglomeration; they carry the behaviour's identity card. Typical examples, to be discussed now, are walk-away negotiation, tacit coordination, firm flexibility, and using promises.

TYPICAL EXAMPLES

Walk-Away Negotiation

Buyers and sellers, recruiters and applicants, etc., often have alternative bargaining partners at their disposal. This availability of exit options makes goals and goal concerns salient. Giebels, De Dreu, and Van de Vliert (1995) showed that the mere availability of unilateral exit options, compared to bilateral exit options, led to lower joint outcomes, especially if the parties were having low concern for the other's outcomes. If the value of the exit option is also known, one usually develops a limit level or resistance point (e.g. Fisher & Ury, 1981; Neale & Bazerman, 1991; Pinkley, Neale, & Bennett, 1994). This resistance point is the minimum level of benefits, or the maximum level of costs, beyond which the bargainer will lose interest in the present partner and will break off the negotiation. Beyond that point no-agreement alternatives, if any, will become more attractive than the anticipated settlement (Lax & Sebenius, 1986; Lewicki & Litterer, 1985).

A related and popular negotiating tactic is to exaggerate how many no-agreement alternatives one has and how favourable they are. Many buyers, for instance, pretend that there are other attractive potential sellers, whereas many sellers pretend that there are other attractive potential buyers. This conjuring up of great alternatives comes with the threat that one will turn one's back on the present negotiation partner, whereas, in fact, one definitely wants a deal. Even if one goes so far as literally to walk away, that act may still represent a flowing move within a serious game of coming to terms. In such a conglomeration, avoiding seems to set the tone. However, avoiding is set alongside the really dominant intentions of furthering joint interests and fostering mutual satisfaction.

Basically, walk-away negotiation involves the manipulation of information, which seems more compatible with compromising than with problem solving. Indeed, compromising wears the mantle of walk-away negotiation relatively often, sometimes in combination with the stole and hat of give-and-take bargaining. Compromising has a chameleonic identity (see Chapter 3).

Tacit Coordination

Nonverbal communication through eye contact, facial expressions, and body language usually adds important components to conglomerated conflict behaviour (for details, see Borisoff & Victor, 1989; Pruitt, 1981). Time and again research shows that deeds speak louder than words. This deed–word asymmetry is especially interesting when a discrepancy exists between nonverbal and verbal communications. Nonverbal cues can leak information that a party attempts to conceal from the adversary. On the other hand, a party can use eyes, face, and body to pass on information that, in point of fact, should not or cannot be revealed.

Pruitt and Carnevale (1993) referred to nonverbal aspects of ending a controversy with a solution as "tacit coordination." Putnam (1990) described it as a merger of reactions in which one withholds information while revealing it through incremental disclosures and predictable patterns of behaviour. Although one refrains from verbal efforts to bring to the surface underlying interests and to develop solutions, one does drop pointed hints of a willingness to integrate somehow, sooner or later. What we have here is an intriguing conglomeration of simultaneously "moving away" from the issue and yet "moving toward" mutual understanding and agreement (Horney, 1945). Negotiating dominates the occurrence and internal structure of the conglomerated behavioural components because the deeds have more impact than the words.

Firm Flexibility

It is usually effective to show firmness with respect to one's own ultimate goals while being responsive and flexible regarding each party's immediate goals and the other's ultimate goals (Fisher & Ury, 1981; Leng, 1993; Pruitt, 1995; Rubin, Pruitt, & Kim, 1994; Tutzauer & Roloff, 1988). In fact, the advice reads: be hard on your own basic interests, whenever necessary, in conjunction with being soft on anything else, notably the opponent's positions and underlying desires. Thus, on closer consideration, the authors recommend a conglomeration in which fighting for the really important things, though dominant, is combined and contrasted with accommodative behaviour regarding all other things.

Conglomerations of firm flexibility pop up under different names. Blake and Mouton's (1964) "paternalism" couples 9,1 behaviour of dominance and tight control with 1,9 behaviour that fosters the well-being of people. Reacting benevolently yet autocratically, a paternalist demands compliance and offers security in return: fighting and accommodating operate in juxtaposition. "Instrumental interest/concern" (Lax & Sebenius, 1986; Rubin, Pruitt, & Kim, 1994), or setting a sprat to catch a mackerel, is yet another manifestation of fighting and accommodating operating in juxtaposition. Likewise, in "double-voice discourse" self-assertion and an orientation to one's own agenda is accomplished with linguistic mitigation and responsiveness to the addressee's point of view and to the mutual relationship (Sheldon & Johnson, 1994).

"Logrolling" may be considered a conglomeration of being *firm* about a benefit or cost that is important to oneself but unimportant to the opponent, while being *flexible* about a benefit or cost that is unimportant to oneself but important to the opponent. Negotiated package deals always have this structure of concurrently winning and losing on different issues or different aspects of the same issue. As for aspects of issues, recall that a trade-negotiation is a complex matter of three part-settlements dealing with the means of exchange, the rate of exchange, and the magnitude of exchange, not to mention the terms of delivery. So negotiators may also barter a gain on one part-settlement for a loss on another part-settlement, as is the case with a quantity rebate or a cash discount.

Pruitt (1995) summarises and discusses six common tactics in conflict episodes that are forms of firm flexibility: concede but only to a point, hold firm on one's position while seeking a way to compensate the other, hold firm on more important issues while conceding on less important issues, hold firm on one's interests while seeking novel ways to achieve these interests, hold firm on more important interests while abandoning less important interests, and hold firm if one's interests seem stronger than those of the other party and yield if the other's interests seem stronger. It is interesting to note that positive goal interdependence has high potential for such tactics of firm flexibility because the lower-order goals are incompatible whereas the higher-order goals are compatible. In contrast, negative goal interdependence has low potential for the implementation of firm flexibility because both the lower- and the higher-order goals are incompatible (see Chapter 4).

Using Promises

Fighters frequently use threats and promises as weapons. Like a threat, a promise is a declaration or assurance that one will act in a certain way if the opponent acts in a certain way (cf. Deutsch, 1973; Rubin, Pruitt, &

Kim, 1994). However, whereas a threat is a commitment to inflict punishment if the adversary disobeys, a promise is a commitment to supply a reward if the adversary obeys. Translated into grid concepts, a threat is a 9,1 fighting tactic that communicates a 9,1 intention of further fighting, while a promise is a 9,1 fighting tactic that communicates a 1,9 intention of shifting to accommodation (for a threat stated with an apology, see Shapiro & Bies, 1994).

The hypothesis that threats tend to consist of straightforward contentious components, whereas promises tend to be conglomerations of fighting and accommodating, has been put to an explorative test by Stanley Frankel and myself. We had 267 full-time employees enrolled in a part-time MBA programme at the Southern Illinois University describe a conflict in which they had been directly involved. They then completed a five-point rating-scale, anchored by *not at all likely* and *very likely*, on how likely they would be to use each of 23 tactics in that particular conflict, including the following two contentious tactics: "to somehow get some leverage over your opponent and *threaten* him or her with it"; and "to *promise* your opponent something he or she wants in return." This rating procedure was repeated for each of three conflicts, involving a superior, a co-worker, and a subordinate.

Applying the procedure from Studies 2 and 3 in Chapter 3, the correlations among the 23 tactics were visually reproduced in a two-dimensional space. This visualisation resulted in roughly the same pictures for superiors, co-workers, and subordinates. In all three conditions "threaten" and "promise" appeared to lie on the distributive dimension. "Threaten" determined the fighting pole, together with appealing to a higher authority. Voting by majority decision, voting by minority decision, and minimum winning size coalition took up less extreme contentious positions on that distributive dimension. The least contentious positions were taken up by "promise," logroll, handshake, and consensus decision. In accord with our theoretical point of departure, this position of "promise" was interpreted as an amalgamation of fighting and accommodating. Those results make it understandable that, in general, threats escalate the conflict more than do promises (Deutsch & Krauss, 1960; Rubin, Pruitt, & Kim, 1994).

In sum, a threat is a wolf while a promise is a wolf in sheep's clothing. A threat is a homogeneously contentious move, whereas a promise represents a heterogeneous conglomeration of fighting and accommodating. The findings also imply that the combined use of a threat and a promise represents an even more complex mode of conflict behaviour. Bowers (1974) coined the term "thromise" for the simultaneous application of future stick and future carrot as a compliance-gaining tactic. Though there is no research on hand yet about the impact of thromises, one may suspect that they are very effective, albeit in the direction of blind compliance rather than in the direction of attempts at mutual adjustment and innovation.

THEORY OF CONGLOMERATED CONFLICT BEHAVIOUR

The preceding chapter outlined that dual concern for one's own and the other's goals incites people to a dominant component of conflict behaviour. Here several combinations of dual goal concern together are thought of as determining several components of conglomerated conflict behaviour. The main point to be made is that instantaneous combinations of dual goal concern produce simultaneous conglomerations of conflict behaviour, and that changing combinations of dual goal concern produce sequential conglomerations of conflict behaviour (for concern-based behavioural change, see Gulliver, 1979; Keating et al., 1994; Nicotera, 1994; Putnam, 1990). To this end the sections that follow discuss the grate of concerns, introduced in Chapter 1, and predictions of conglomerated conflict behaviour based on it.

Grate of Concerns

Metatheory. The explanation of conglomerated behaviour is sought in the fourth face of the conflict management grid, the grate of concerns. The grate of concerns is a combination of domains of concern for one's own and the other's goals. All cells of dual goal concern are available to the actor, simultaneously as well as successively. This availability of multiple domains of dual goal concern allows the adoption of multiple components of conflict behaviour, which are mutually linked because they share integrative and distributive dimensions, and because they regard the same actor, the same conflict issue, and the same opponent.

The grate of concerns represents the metatheoretical perspective that the L-angle of concerns theory has to be applied repeatedly to predict a number of unique locations in the space of integrative and distributive reactions to conflict. Each dual concern cell in the conflict management grid may determine a component of conglomerated conflict behaviour. As a dominant reaction is determined by a combination of a single level of goal concern for oneself and a single level of goal concern for the other, conglomerated conflict behaviour is determined by a combination of multiple levels of goal concern for oneself and for the other. And just like the L-angle of concerns, the grate of concerns intermediates between the conflict issue and the more or less integrative and distributive reactions to it.

The following paragraphs will illustrate and acknowledge multiple goals as the birthplace of multiple goal concerns. Obviously, multiple goals may exist for oneself, for the opponent, or for both, the former two usually being less complex than the last one. The section concludes with the designing of prototypes of concerns complexity.

Birthplace of multiple goal concerns. In many conflicts, and in almost every negotiation, each side will have multiple interests, not just one (Fisher & Ury, 1981; Fukushima & Ohbuchi, 1996; Hocker & Wilmot, 1991; Roloff & Jordan, 1992). To cite Deutsch (1973, p. 21): "Most situations of everyday life involve a complex set of goals and subgoals." Those various goals are the cradle of multiple instantaneous or changing combinations of dual goal concern.

Consider the following example of concerns complexity. A conservative mayor falls out with members of a pressure group regarding a forbidden demonstration against a liberal policy toward drug abuse. Given his conservative attitude, he might be sympathetic to the ideal of a more preservationist policy that the demonstration hopes to bring nearer. He might even develop some supportive concern for the opponents' plan now to use the ban on the demonstration as a propaganda stunt. At the same time, the mayor may become highly concerned about loss of face when giving in by permitting the demonstration. Undoubtedly, this constellation of goal-based concerns will motivate the mayor to create conglomerated conflict behaviour. Through tacit coordination the opponents' propaganda stunt might be facilitated by both maintaining the ban and saving face, while valuable replacements for the demonstration might be negotiated.

The case is a reminder of the pity postulate "No goals, no goal concerns." Indeed, each level of goal concern can be traced back to a goal and goal circumstances that produce it (see Chapter 4). Different degrees of concern for one's own goals are caused by different goals set by oneself. Likewise, different degrees of concern for the other's goals are caused by different goals ascribed to the counterpart. The present chapter is focusing closely on the multiplexity of the goal concerns and their causal connections with instances of conglomerated conflict behaviour.

Deutsch's (1949, 1973, 1985) theory of goal interdependence, outlined in Chapter 4, touches upon concerns complexity without going into it. Deutsch assumed that individuals can be motivated (a) cooperatively, (b) competitively, (c) neither cooperatively nor competitively, and (d) both cooperatively and competitively (cf. McClintock, 1972, 1976; Kelley & Thibaut, 1978). In the case of (a) through (c), conflict behaviour can still be explained by a single level of concern for one's own goals combined with a single level of concern for the other's goals; that is, a behavioural explanation based on the L-angle of concerns is still possible. Only in the case of both a cooperative and a competitive motivation are two levels of concern for one's own goals combined with two levels of concern for the other's goals needed to explain the resulting behaviour. Unfortunately, neither Deutsch (1949, 1973, 1985) nor his followers (e.g. Johnson & Johnson, 1989; Tjosvold, 1989, 1990) have ever worked out this notion of motivational complexity.

Prototypes of concerns complexity. The grate of concerns has four corners, which can be connected through two horizontal lines, two vertical lines, and two diagonal lines. Six typical constrictions of dual concern combinations may be distinguished along the same lines.

The horizontal prototypes (see Fig. 5.5, above) refer to multiple concerns for one's own goals only, either in conjunction with low concern for the other's goals (1,1 to 9,1), or in conjunction with high concern for the other's goals (1,9 to 9,9). They may be labelled *own-sided concerns complexity.*

The vertical prototypes (see Fig. 5.5, middle) refer to multiple concerns for the other's goals only, either in conjunction with low concern for one's own goals (1,1 to 1,9), or in conjunction with high concern for one's own goals (9,1 to 9,9). They may be labelled *other-sided concerns complexity.*

The diagonal prototypes (see Fig. 5.5, below) refer to bilateral concerns complexity. Equal levels of dual goal concern, ranging from 1,1 to 9,9, may be labelled *symmetrical two-sided concerns complexity.* Opposite levels of dual goal concern, ranging from 1,9 to 9,1, may be labelled *complementary two-sided concerns complexity.*

Behavioural Predictions

As a complex predictor, the grate of concerns provides as many subpredictions as there are combinations of concern for one's own and the other's goals. Each pair of two concern combinations co-determines one component of the behavioural conglomeration. Relying on and extending the conflict concerns theory, this approach will now be applied to the prototypes of concerns complexity defined above.

Own-sided concerns complexity. Multiple levels of concern for one's own goals lead to *indirect fighting* in conjunction with low concern for the other's goals (1,1–9,1), but to *soft negotiating* in conjunction with high concern for the other's goals (1,9–9,9). Indirect fighting contains dominant components such as avoiding, separating, undermining esteem, coalescing, and forcing (cf. Fig. 3.2). In the case of soft negotiating, the fact that the disputant is very concerned about at least one objective of each side will evoke some integrative behaviour. At the same time, low concern for at least one other objective of self adds one or more components of conceding, stepping down, or reconciling oneself to the facts.

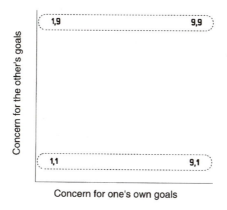

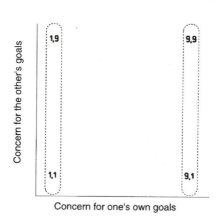

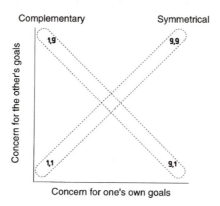

FIG. 5.5 Own-sided (above), other-sided (middle), and two-sided (below) concerns complexity.

Other-sided concerns complexity.   Multiple levels of concern for the other's goals lead to *indirect capitulating* in conjunction with low concern for one's own goals (1,1–1,9), but to *hard negotiating* in conjunction with high concern for one's own goals (9,1–9,9). Indirect capitulating is the avoidance of overt capitulation on an issue, often by the enlistment of a third party. Also, a constriction of low concern for the adversary's victory as such and high one-sided concern for the adversary realising his or her goals fosters covert accommodation. In contrast, the components of hard negotiating range from problem solving and confronting issues to position bargaining and fighting. The underlying intention to reach agreement makes this a predominantly integrative strategy.

Symmetrical two-sided complexity.   Equal levels of dual goal concern, ranging from 1,1 to 9,9, elicit *integrating conglomerated behaviour*. The strategies of walk-away negotiation and tacit coordination described earlier serve well as illustrations.

Walk-away negotiation results from the constriction of low dual concern for both parties' divergent standpoints, and high dual concern for both parties' underlying interests. Such a conglomeration prospers in situations where all lower-order goals are less important and feasible than all higher-order goals. Similarly, tacit coordination may be understood as caused by low dual concern about both parties' verbal statements, and high dual concern about both parties' nonverbal cues. Such a conglomeration prospers in situations where aims cloaked in deeds are more important and feasible than objectives wrapped in words.

Complementary two-sided complexity.   Opposite levels of dual goal concern, ranging from 1,9 to 9,1, evoke *distributing conglomerated behaviour*. The earlier examples of firm flexibility and using promises are cases in point.

Firm flexibility is rooted in high concern for one's own real interests but low concern for the other's evident standpoints, and moderate concern for the other's real interests but low concern for one's own evident standpoints. Such a conglomeration prospers in situations where one's own higher-order goals outweigh all other goals of both parties. Likewise, the use of a promise will be found with people motivated by high concern about one's present benefit from winning and low concern about the adversary's present cost of losing, together with low concern about the future cost of keeping one's promise and high concern about the adversary's future benefit from the remuneration. Such a conglomeration prospers in situations where some immediate influence on an opposing party is more attractive and realisable than a later debt towards this opponent is repulsive.

TABLE 5.1
Predictions of Conglomerated Conflict Behaviour for Six Prototypes of
Concerns Complexity

Prototype of complexity	Grate locations	Conglomerated behaviour
Own-sided concerns		
	1,1–9,1	Indirect fighting
	1,9–9,9	Soft negotiating
Other-sided concerns		
	1,1–1,9	Indirect capitulating
	9,1–9,9	Hard negotiating
Two-sided concerns		
Symmetrical	1,1–9,9	Integrating
Complementary	1,9–9,1	Distributing

Recapitulation.   A party to a conflict setting multiple goals for self and/ or ascribing multiple goals to the opponent has to come to terms with simultaneously active combinations of dual goal concern. The concerns complexity is handled by aggregating distinct reactions into simultaneously or sequentially conglomerated conflict behaviour. Six types of conglomerated conflict behaviour predicted by six prototypes of concerns complexity are summarised in Table 5.1. Not included in this table is the effectiveness of these behaviours, which is explained and discussed next.

EFFECTIVENESS OF CONGLOMERATED
CONFLICT BEHAVIOUR

Conflict behaviour is viewed as personally effective to the extent that an individual succeeds in realising the benefits or costs desired for oneself. Personal effectiveness may or may not be in accord with dyadic effectiveness: the extent to which conflict behaviour is producing better outcomes for the dyad by resolving the conflict issues, improving the relationship with the other party, or both (cf. Janssen & Van de Vliert, 1996; Thomas, 1992b; Tjosvold, 1991).

Up to 1994, two implicit assumptions guided our research and intervention projects directed at the effectiveness of conflict behaviour. The first one, that modes of conflict behaviour are pure and mutually independent variables, has been amply challenged above. The second implicit assumption holds that modes of conflict behaviour have pure and mutually independent relations with effectiveness. That is, different modes of behaviour do not intermediate or moderate each other's impact on the substantive and relational outcomes of the conflict. The one-best-way perspective, contingency perspective, and time perspective, to be discussed here, all share that assumption. Breaking with the prevailing approach, this section leads to a complexity perspective stating that components of conflict behaviour do have joint effects (cf. Van de Vliert, Euwema, & Huismans, 1995; Van de Vliert & Euwema, 1996).

One-Best-Way Perspective

Blake and Mouton (1970) stated that the high/high or 9,9 concurrence of the two concerns produces the most effective mode of conflict management for all parties involved. They also called the highly integrative 9,9 behaviour the "fifth achievement," and strongly recommended it because it was supposed to be the most constructive way of reacting to social discord. One decade later they even presented their grid theory as a "one-best-style approach" (Blake & Mouton, 1981, p. 441; for similar views, see Follett, 1940; Pneuman & Bruehl, 1982; Tjosvold, 1991).

There is much evidence in favour of this one-best-way perspective. Investigations of real-life superior–subordinate conflicts strongly suggest that, personally as well as dyadically, integrative methods are the most effective manner of conflict management (Barker, Tjosvold, & Andrews, 1988; Burke, 1970; Lawrence & Lorsch, 1967; Phillips & Cheston, 1979; Rahim, 1992; Renwick, 1977; Tjosvold, 1991; Volkema & Bergmann, 1989). More generally, it has also been documented that successful resolution leads to greater group productivity, more creative and constructive outcomes (Butler, 1994; Johnson, Johnson, & Smith, 1989; Likert & Likert, 1976; Rubin, Pruitt, & Kim, 1994; Tutzauer & Roloff, 1988), trust and openness (Deutsch, 1973, 1980; Zand, 1972), and de-personalisation of future conflicts (Filley, 1975).

The arguments against problem solving, however, are that often insufficient opportunities for integration exist, that it is too time and energy consuming, and that unilateral openness and drawing of attention to joint interests may escalate the conflict (Filley, 1975; Hocker & Wilmot, 1991; Walton, 1972, 1987). For example, Johnson and Lewicki (1969) showed that a superordinate goal initiated by a participant in the conflict became caught up in the competitiveness of the situation and escalated rather than de-escalated the conflict. Another boomerang effect has been suggested by Schweiger, Sandberg, and Ragan (1986): the price of better but laborious decisions may well be that the opponents fancy the idea of future co-operation less than before.

Contingency Perspective

A great number of authors have attacked the foregoing view, contending that no best mode of conflict management exists. Instead, the answer regarding what is personally or dyadically most successful can only be given in the light of situational realities (e.g. Axelrod, 1984; Gladwin & Walter, 1980; Hocker & Wilmot, 1991; Rahim, 1992; Robbins, 1974; Thomas, 1977, 1992b). For example, experienced managers reported that it would be appropriate to adopt each mode of conflict behaviour from the five-part typology in a number of specific situations including the following ones (Thomas, 1977): (a) avoiding when an issue is trivial, or more important issues are pressing; (b) accommodating to build social credits for later issues, especially when the present issue is more important to the opponent than to oneself; (c) compromising when goals are important but not worth the effort of more assertive modes, and under time pressure; (d) problem solving to gain commitment or to work through feelings that have interfered with a relationship; and (e) fighting when quick and decisive action is vital—i.e. emergencies—and when important but unpopular actions need implementing.

A well-known hypothesis states that the level of tension determines the occurrence as well as the individual and collective effectiveness of conflict behaviour (Brown, 1983; Levi, 1981; Poole, Shannon, & DeSanctis, 1992; Rahim, 1992; Robbins, 1974, 1991; Schroder, Driver, & Streufert, 1967; Walton, 1969). Walton (1969) discerned three levels of tension (low–medium–high) with differential effects on the utilisation of information and the outcomes of the conflict process. *Low tension level* conflicts lead to inactivity and avoidance, neglect of information, and low effectiveness as there is no sense of urgency and no necessity to act assertively (cf. Janis, 1982). In case of a *medium level of tension* the parties will seek and integrate more information, consider more alternatives, and experience a stronger impulse to improve the situation. The conflict increases their productivity. *High tension level* conflicts reduce the capacity to perceive, process, and evaluate information. This reduced capacity in turn produces aggressive and defensive interactions that result in less effective or downright destructive consequences, at least for the dyad.

In short, conflicts of either too low or too high intensity are liable to harm the parties rather than benefit them, while moderately escalated conflicts are likely to do the reverse. Consequently, too low a level of tension requires temporary escalation by fighting in order to promote dyadic effectiveness. In moderately escalated conflicts it is best to initiate negotiation or mediation if one wants to secure good joint outcomes. Finally, if the level of tension is too high, temporary inaction and accommodative moves to de-escalate the conflict are most appropriate for both the person and the dyad.

Time Perspective

Short-term wisdom may be long-term folly, and the other way around. This longitudinal perspective on desirable and undesirable behaviours has recently brought Thomas (1992a, 1992b) to the insight that the contingency viewpoint and the "problem solving ethic" are reconcilable by taking two time horizons into account.

The contingency perspective focuses on coping with the immediate conflict situation and provides answers to the short-term question of how best to cope with the here and now. It does not move beyond the limitations of the current conditions and is relatively pragmatic in flavour. In contrast, the one-best-way perspective of conflict resolution focuses on the longer-term task of creating desirable future circumstances. It emphasises that contextual variables are changeable rather than given, and that the ideal functioning of the social system should be brought nearer by all manner of means.

Complexity Perspective

In contrast to the one-best-way, contingency, and time perspectives, the complexity assumption in this book holds that mixed modes of conflict behaviour are very common, and that the behavioural components are meaningfully interrelated rather than discrete. Adopting the well-known part–whole principle of Gestalt psychology, the complexity perspective additionally holds that the perceived properties and effects of a behavioural component are largely determined by the whole pattern of behavioural components. Examples abound, including the following one building on Chapters 3 and 4. Compromising combined with problem solving, compared to compromising combined with direct fighting, has a less distributive meaning and a higher degree of dyadic effectiveness. In short, effectiveness is a function of various behavioural components that intermediate and moderate each other's impact. As a case in point, combinations of influence tactics are usually more personally effective than single tactics (Falbe & Yukl, 1992; Williams, 1983, 1993; Yukl, Falbe, & Young Youn, 1993).

Williams (1983, 1993) asked hundreds of experienced attorneys, for whom negotiating is a daily activity, to describe personally effective as well as personally ineffective peers. The single most important finding was that a cooperative approach was neither more nor less effective than an aggressive approach. Personal effectiveness as a negotiator appeared to be determined by a whole pattern of traits and behaviours, and not by a single component. More specifically, negotiators with a cooperative pattern appeared to be effective unless a number of overly cooperative components were added, including being trustful, gentle, obliging, patient, and forgiving. Ineffective cooperators were, in a manner of speaking, marshmallows. The aggressive pattern of win–lose negotiators, on the other hand, appeared to be rather effective if they were not arrogant, bluffing, quarrelsome, egoistic, and did not use take-it-or-leave-it offers. Though effective aggressors even used threats and were willing to stretch the facts, they never became insufferably obnoxious.

Unlike the time perspective, the paradigm of conglomerated conflict behaviour presumes that short-term and long-term goals and goal concerns operate simultaneously. Short-term and long-term goals together produce the six prototypes of concerns complexity from Fig. 5.5 and the subsequent conglomerated conflict behaviours from Table 5.1. An overall synthesis of one-best-way, contingency, and time perspectives into the complexity perspective thus comes within reach. The synthesis would be perfect if it could be shown that, in the long run, problem solving determines the personal and dyadic effectiveness more than other components, even when the latter components are more appropriate and occur more in particular situations. A novel research tack is necessary to tease out the relationships between the relative occurrence and covariation of conflict behavioural components, and the resulting effectiveness. The following studies commence this challenging line of research.

STUDY 5: EFFECTIVENESS AND BEHAVIOURAL COMPLEXITY

This investigation, which has been published in more detail elsewhere (Van de Vliert, Euwema, & Huismans, 1995), was an extension of Study 1 in Chapter 2 (see also Fig. 5.4). It used systematic observations of 116 videotaped conflict transactions involving police sergeants vis-à-vis a superior or subordinate. The ongoing effectiveness debate incited Martin Euwema and myself to examine whether the dyadic effectiveness of problem solving is intermediated or moderated by other components of the recorded behaviour. Specifically, we argued that the problem solving component controlled for the other behavioural components is positively related to the dyadic effectiveness of conglomerated conflict behaviour (*Hypothesis 1*). In addition, a qualification of this hypothesis was based on Walton's (1969) level of tension theory discussed above. We argued that the problem solving component controlled for the other behavioural components is more positively related to the dyadic effectiveness of conglomerated conflict behaviour at a medium level of the fighting component than at lower and higher levels of fighting (*Hypothesis 2*).

Method

Overview of the study.   First, we selected the incendiary conflict issue that the opponent took away and used a reserved car for more than an hour without reporting this to the station sergeant responsible for all cars. We defined three stages of escalating reactions to that conflict, and trained confederates to perform this sequence of behaviours. We then recruited police sergeants as subjects and videotaped their transaction with a subordinate or superior confederate. Finally, we had four observers assess the components of the conglomerated conflict behaviour by scoring the tapes for the occurrence of avoiding, accommodating, compromising, problem solving, indirect fighting, and direct fighting. No distinction between the simultaneous and sequential occurrence of these behavioural components was made. Descriptions of the subjects, the conflict issue, the confederates' behaviour, the assessment of the components of conflict behaviour, and the limitations of the study can be found in Chapter 2 (Study 1; for experimental procedures, reliability, and validity, see Van de Vliert, Euwema, & Huismans, 1995). The study was replicated with senior nurses handling a standardised conflict vis-à-vis a less powerful nurse or a more powerful physician (Van de Vliert & Euwema, 1996).

Effectiveness.   The four observers also rated the dyadic effectiveness of each videotaped conflict transaction on ten 5-point scales for substantive and relational outcomes. The *substantive outcomes* concerned the ultimate number of conflict issues, the severeness of those issues, proximity to a solution, the chances of recidivism, and the quality of concerted task performance. The *relational outcomes* concerned the attention given to communalities, the ultimate amount of mutual distrust and mutual understanding, as well as the ultimate atmosphere, and personal relationship. The ten scales could be combined into one measure of effectiveness (Kendall's W varied from .61 to .85; $M = .74$; overall Cronbach's $\alpha = .94$).

Results and Discussion

Table 5.2 gives the means indicating the pattern of occurrence of the six behavioural components, and the 15 correlations indicating the pattern of covariation of these components, broken down for superiors and subordinates.

Tests of hypotheses.   The first hypothesis was tested using multiple regression analysis, because this technique takes into account the fact that the components of conglomerated conflict behaviour may intermediate each other's impact. Regressions of the sergeants' dyadic effectiveness on the

TABLE 5.2

Means, Standard Deviations, and Intercorrelations of Six Components of Conglomerated Conflict Behaviour, and Dyadic Effectiveness, for Superiors (above the diagonal) and Subordinates (below the diagonal): Study 5

Behavioural components	Superiors M	SD	Subordinates M	SD	1	2	3	4	5	6	7
1. Avoiding	1.36[a]	.52	1.21	.33		-.16[b]	-.23	-.41	.29	.48	-.34
2. Accommodating	1.30	.40	1.36	.34	.16[b]		.14	.36	-.12	-.42	.49
3. Compromising	1.13	.23	1.19	.28	-.08	.33		.62	.05	.15	.14
4. Problem solving	1.92	.64	1.92	.57	-.15	.16	.47		.12	-.35	.58
5. Indirect fighting	3.36	.53	2.88	.46	.20	-.22	-.06	.16		.50	.15
6. Direct fighting	3.03	.82	2.48	.66	.15	-.27	.26	.00	.36		-.53
7. Effectiveness	3.01	.40	3.05	.41	-.31	.30	.15	.42	.03	-.50	

[a] 1 = not at all; 5 = to a great extent.

[b] Superiors: $N = 60$; $r \geq .25$, $p \leq .05$; $r \geq .33$, $p \leq .01$, two-tailed.
Subordinates: $N = 56$; $r \geq .26$, $p \leq .05$; $r \geq .34$, $p \leq .01$, two-tailed.

TABLE 5.3
Dyadic Effectiveness of Superiors and Subordinates as a Function of Six
Components of Conglomerated Conflict Behaviour: Study 5

Behavioural components	Superiors		Subordinates	
	β^a	R^2	β	R^2
Avoiding	−.07		−.27**	
Accommodating	.21*		.19	
Compromising	.05		.10	
Problem solving	.18		.25**	
Indirect fighting	.46**		.28**	
Direct fighting	−.58**		−.53**	
		.61**		.54**

Note: Superiors: $N = 60$. Subordinates: $N = 56$.
[a] Beta weights from the regression equation including all six behavioural components.
* $p \leq .05$, two–tailed; ** $p \leq .01$, two–tailed.

behavioural components produced Table 5.3. It shows that, as superiors, the sergeants treated their subordinate more effectively if they removed direct fighting ($\beta = -.58$, $p \leq .01$), or added indirect fighting ($\beta = .46$, $p \leq .01$) or accommodating ($\beta = .21$, $p \leq .05$). Together the behavioural components accounted for 61% of the variance in effectiveness. Table 5.3 also shows that, as subordinates, the sergeants responded to their superior more effectively if they removed direct fighting ($\beta = -.53$, $p \leq .01$) and avoiding ($\beta = -.27$, $p \leq .05$), or added indirect fighting ($\beta = .28$, $p \leq .05$) and problem solving ($\beta = .25$, $p \leq .05$). In this case the behavioural components accounted for 54% of the variance in effectiveness. The fact that a larger problem solving component increased the effectiveness of the conglomerated conflict behaviour supported Hypothesis 1, although this relationship was only significant for subordinate behaviour.

To investigate whether there exists a nonlinear interactive effect of the problem solving and fighting components on effectiveness, as predicted under Hypothesis 2, we inspected the regressions of effectiveness on problem solving at low, medium and high levels of direct and indirect fighting. Hypothesis 2 was not supported at all, either for superior or for subordinate behaviour. Instead, a marginally significant linear interactive effect emerged: increased problem solving by superiors vis-à-vis a subordinate was especially effective at high levels of direct fighting, $F (2,50) = 2.40$, $p \leq .10$. No other interactive effect was found.

Additional results. An exciting conclusion regarding the pattern of occurrence was that a small increase in relatively low levels of the problem solving component still enhanced effectiveness (for similar evidence, see Falbe & Yukl, 1992; Williams, 1983, 1993; Yukl, Falbe, & Young Youn, 1993). Also, small changes in negligible components of accommodating by superiors and avoiding by subordinates still changed joint outcomes and the relationship between the conflicting parties. All this contradicts the common view that the dominant type of conflict handling is also the dominant determinant of behavioural effectiveness. Instead, constructive conflict management is indeed determined by a whole composition of more and less salient reactions that intermediate each other's effectiveness.

As for the pattern of covariation, the zero-order correlations between the six behavioural components and effectiveness in Table 5.2 and the pattern of corresponding beta weights in Table 5.3 are far from identical. It means that the consequences of conflict behaviour can be investigated and controlled more accurately by considering patterns of behavioural components as opposed to isolated behavioural types; the "Gestalt" of components counts, not the sum of its parts. Notably, the assumption that each mode of behaviour has its own consequences would have led us to conclude that the component of indirect fighting is neither effective nor ineffective (see Table 5.2: for superiors $r = .15$, n.s.; for subordinates $r = .03$, n.s.). Our alternative assumption that components of conglomerated behaviour affect consequences jointly, however, uncovered the otherwise hidden fact that the component of indirect fighting is effective for both superiors (see Table 5.3: $ß = .46$, $p \le .01$) and subordinates ($ß = .28$, $p \le .05$). This finding contradicts the implicit common view that types of conflict handling are mutually independent determinants of behavioural effectiveness that do not intermediate each other's substantive and relational outcomes.

Unexpectedly, the problem solving component is less rather than more effective than the component of indirect fighting by controlling the process. This suboptimal position of problem solving cannot be explained by the fact that the conflict situation did not contain integrative potential, because some police sergeants did create solutions that provided high benefit to both parties (cf. Rubin, Pruitt, & Kim, 1994). Illustrations of such solutions included the future availability of another fall-back car and compensating the use of the sergeant's private car. Hence, the higher effectiveness of the component of indirect fighting also refutes Blake and Mouton's (1964, 1970, 1981) one-best-way postulate about problem solving.

More specifically, we detected that one may handle a conflict more constructively by climbing the following "ladder of effectiveness" of behavioural components: direct fighting, avoiding, compromising, accommodating, problem solving, and indirect fighting. The ladder is virtually identical for superior and subordinate police sergeants (see Table 5.3). It is worth noting that higher steps on this ladder are both more effective and less disagreeable (cf. Study 1 in Chapter 2). Perhaps the component of indirect fighting by controlling the process is so effective because it provides a way to prevail without creating a disagreeable impression in the eyes of the opponent. We also know that indirect fighting is neither an active component of making suggestions and showing solidarity ($r = .15$, n.s.) nor a passive component of asking for information and showing tension ($r = -.07$, n.s.; see Study 1 in Chapter 2, and Van de Vliert & Euwema, 1994). These results may well suggest that the component of indirect fighting by controlling the process is also effective because it provides a subtle, indirect route to holding sway over the opponent.

Replication. For reasons of generalisability, we demonstrated that the ladder of effectiveness of behavioural components found for male/male police dyads also holds for female/female, female/male, and male/male transactions in hospitals (Van de Vliert & Euwema, 1996).

This replication study also examined whether the problem solving and direct fighting components moderate each other's impact on the substantive and relational outcomes outlined above. As can be learned from Fig. 5.6, senior nurses were especially effective if they combined a great deal of problem solving with a great deal of direct fighting. This finding does not unconditionally support the one-best-way view that problem solving serves the organisation best. Nor does it support the contingency view that either problem solving or direct fighting will be most appropriate under certain circumstances. Instead, Fig. 5.6 clearly supports the paradigm of conglomerated conflict behaviour. The senior nurses operating most effectively peppered their problem solving moves with moves of direct fighting. They created a behavioural compound that might be seen as a form of constructive controversy (Cosier, 1978; Janis, 1982; Johnson, Johnson, & Smith, 1989; Schweiger, Sandberg, & Ragan, 1986; Schweiger, Sandberg & Rechner, 1989; Schwenk, 1990; Tjosvold, 1985; Van de Vliert, 1997; Walton, 1969).

Discussion of Figure 5.6. The apparent effectiveness of conglomerations of problem solving and direct fighting makes sense for at least two reasons. First of all, most conflict issues are so complex that problem solving might be more appropriate for some aspects of the discord, while direct fighting might be more appropriate for other aspects. For example, problem solving is especially appropriate for merging pieces of insight as well as working through a negative feeling, whereas direct fighting is especially appropriate for responding to an emergency element as well as implementing an important but unpopular decision (Rahim, 1992; Thomas, 1992b).

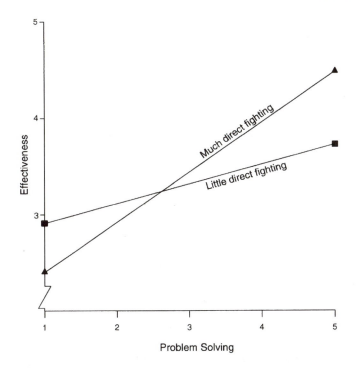

FIG. 5.6   Dyadic effectiveness of senior nurses' conglomerated conflict behaviour as a result of the components of problem solving and direct fighting.

As a consequence, the effectiveness might well increase if problem solving is competently interspersed with direct fighting, or vice versa.

Second, each component of conglomerated conflict behaviour comes with its own risks in terms of ineffectiveness. The risks of problem solving include the possibility that the parties' mutual relationship will block high joint outcomes, that the ultimate solution is not worth the necessary time and energy investment, or even that so-called win–win outcomes are out of the question (Hocker & Wilmot, 1991). The risks of direct fighting include escalation beyond acceptable cost limits, a deteriorating relationship, and stalemate following failure of contentious tactics (Rubin, Pruitt, & Kim, 1994). As a consequence, the juxtaposition or alternation of problem solving and direct fighting might reduce both types of risks. To paraphrase Walton, Cutcher-Gershenfeld, and McKersie (1994, p. 337), who developed a similar argument and reported some empirical support for it: the combination of the two strategies can enhance effectiveness by minimising the tendency of problem solving to produce stagnation and the tendency of forcing to produce escalation.

Conclusions. The assumption that conflict handling is a conglomeration of more and less effective behavioural components has been confirmed for severe conflict between superiors and subordinates in clear-cut hierarchical organisations. Four conclusions can be drawn. First, the dyadic effectiveness of conglomerated conflict behaviour is a function of the nature rather than the level of occurrence of its components. Second, the behavioural components intermediate and moderate each other's impact on dyadic effectiveness. Third, an increase in the component of problem solving tends to have a positive effect on the parties' joint outcomes and mutual relationship, especially if they combine it with an increase in the component of direct fighting. Finally, the components of indirect fighting and direct fighting by controlling the process have opposite positive versus negative effects on the parties' joint outcomes and mutual relationship.

STUDY 6: EFFECTIVENESS AND SEQUENTIAL COMPLEXITY

Study 5 supported our viewpoint that components of conglomerated conflict behaviour have joint effects. However, it did not distinguish between simultaneous and sequential conglomerations of behavioural components. Therefore the distinction between behavioural juxtaposition and behavioural alternation was made in a subsequent investigation, to be published in more detail elsewhere (Van de Vliert et al., in press). Specifically, based on the earlier findings, we expected the dyadic effectiveness of conglomerated conflict behaviour to be a positive function of problem solving (*Hypothesis 3*), a negative function of direct fighting (*Hypothesis 4*), and a positive function of problem solving in combination with direct fighting (*Hypothesis 5*). Additionally, we wondered whether the greater dyadic effectiveness of problem solving in combination with direct fighting is primarily caused by simultaneous or sequential complexity. And if alternation of problem and direct fighting is more effective, is this because problem solving precedes or follows direct fighting?

Method

Overview of the study. To begin with, we recruited work dyads from a wide variety of organisations to take part in a one-day workshop on conflict management that we organised for them. We designed a general and comprehensible conflict issue to be acted out by each dyad. The simulations were videotaped and later rated by two independent groups of observers. The first group assessed the occurrence of problem solving and direct fighting, while the second group assessed the effectiveness of the conglomerated conflict behaviour.

Subjects. Eleven male/male, 9 male/female, and 4 female/female dyads participated. The age of the subjects ranged from 25 to 52 years ($M = 39$ years), and 64% of them held a managerial position. All dyad members had either a superior–subordinate or a lateral co-working relationship in daily life.

Conflict simulation. Pilot studies (Nauta, 1996) resulted in the following role script:

> Two persons, A and B, form a selection committee whose task it is to hire a suitable candidate for a new job. Due to illness during a vacation in a foreign country, A has been absent for three weeks. When A returns, it emerges that B has continued screening candidates and there are only two left. A and B both feel frustrated because things have not proceeded satisfactorily. B believes that A let B do all the work alone. A feels let down by B because the two remaining candidates do not meet the requirements that A finds most important. They make an appointment to talk things over.

One dyad member prepared for role A while the other dyad member prepared for role B. Subjects had 12 minutes to handle the conflict.

Measurements. Each conflict interaction was videotaped and later transcribed. A transcript contained 55 speaking turns on average, where a speaking turn is defined as everything a person says between the other's last utterance and the other's next utterance. Four observers were trained to assess the occurrence of the behavioural components of problem solving and direct fighting for each of A's and B's speaking turns separately. The interobserver reliability coefficients were good for A's and B's problem solving ($\alpha = .78$) as well as direct fighting ($\alpha = .90$). The correspondence between A's and B's average scores across observers and speaking turns (problem solving $r = .35$, $p < .05$; direct fighting $r = .71$, $p < .001$) allowed us to treat the dyad as a whole, instead of differentiating between A and B.

A completely independent group of four observers watched the videotapes once again to assess the substantive and relational outcomes with the help of seven items from Study 5. The inter-rater agreement was satisfactory (α ranged from .76 to .87). Averaged across coders, the seven-item scale provided a reliable overall criterion of dyadic effectiveness ($\alpha = .96$).

Predictors.   Each speaking turn was categorised as reflecting no prob-lem solving versus problem solving, as well as no direct fighting versus direct fighting. Next, we created three types of categorised speaking turns. First, *problem solving* (P): problem solving with no direct fighting. Second, *direct fighting* (F): direct fighting with no problem solving. Third, *concur-rence* (C): problem solving combined with direct fighting. For each dyad, we then computed the percentage of speaking turns coded as P, F, and C, respectively. These three predictors dealt with the absence or presence of *simultaneous conglomeration* of problem solving and direct fighting within speaking turns.

A number of additional predictors dealt with the *sequential conglomera-tion* of problem solving and direct fighting in one dyad member's speaking turn at time t and problem solving and direct fighting in the same dyad member's next speaking turn at time t+2 (after the other dyad member's speaking turn at t+1). The fourth predictor was each dyad's percentage of two subsequent own speaking turns coded as P at time t and F at time t+2 (PF). Conversely, the fifth predictor was each dyad's percentage of two subsequent own speaking turns coded as F at time t and P at time t+2 (FP). Four similar predictors indicated P at time 1 and C at time 2 (PC), F at time 1 and C at time 2 (FC), C at time 1 and P at time 2 (CP), and C at time 1 and F at time 2 (CF).

Results and Discussion

Table 5.4 contains the descriptive statistics. Note that direct fighting is used much more than problem solving, concurrence, and sequences of problem solving and direct fighting. Similarly to Study 5, problem solving and direct fighting have opposite positive and negative relations with effectiveness, respectively. In addition, concurrence of problem solving and direct fighting, problem solving followed by direct fighting, direct fighting fol-lowed by problem solving, and concurrence followed by problem solving, all have significant positive relations with effectiveness.

Regression analysis based on the z-scores of all the variables showed that direct fighting ($\Delta R^2 = 56\%$, B = $-.75$, $F = 28.14$, $p < .001$) and direct fighting followed by problem solving ($\Delta R^2 = 10\%$, B = $.31$, $F = 5.99$, $p < .05$) account for 66% of the variance in effectiveness. These results imply a disconfirmation of Hypothesis 3 because, in and of itself, problem solving does not predict effectiveness over and above the successful predictors. The two effects support Hypotheses 4 and 5, respectively. The less dyad mem-bers used direct fighting, and the more they used direct fighting followed by problem solving, the more effectively they handled their conflict. Thus dyads avoided the detriment of direct fighting when they combined their direct fighting moves with problem solving moves. No unique contribution

TABLE 5.4
Means, Standard Deviations, and Intercorrelations of Problem Solving, Direct Fighting, and Dyadic Effectiveness: Study 6

	M	SD	F	C	PF	FP	PC	FC	CP	CF	E
Simultaneous											
Problem solving (P)	2.56	3.11	−.71**	.41*	.89**	.41*	.39*	.14	.78**	.04	.64**
Direct fighting (F)	66.01	15.97		−.78**	−.64**	−.05	−.32	−.51**	−.79**	−.35*	−.75**
Concurrence (C)	20.70	8.42			.33	.04	.31	.71**	.46*	.59**	.51**
Sequential											
P first, F next (PF)	1.63	2.44				.19	.08	.26	.68**	.05	.55**
F first, P next (FP)	1.01	1.32					.53**	−.24	.00	−.00	.35*
P first, C next (PC)	.37	.93						−.14	.34	−.01	.33
F first, C next (FC)	13.95	4.74							.20	.69**	.23
C first, P next (CP)	.64	1.35								.03	.56**
C first, F next (CF)	11.56	3.71									.04
Effectiveness (E)	4.81	1.30									

Note: $N = 24$ dyads; scales indicate percentages of speaking turns (P, F, C) or transitions of preceding speaking turns to following speaking turns (PF, FP, PC, FC, CP, CF).
 * $p < .05$; ** $p < .01$.

to effectiveness could be established for concurrence of problem solving and direct fighting, problem solving followed by direct fighting, and concurrence followed by problem solving. Additional analyses with A's or B's individual use of problem solving and direct fighting as predictors of dyadic effectiveness yielded the same pattern of results.

As in Study 5, the results support the conclusion that the behavioural components of problem solving and direct fighting have interdependent effects on conflict outcomes. More importantly, however, Study 6 shows that dyadic effectiveness depends not only on what combination of tactics is used but also on how the tactics are sequenced throughout the conflict interaction. It is important to note that our successful predictor of direct fighting followed by problem solving rests on the observation of repeated behavioural patterns rather than once-only behavioural shifts. The corresponding recommendation states that the sequence of "first direct fighting then problem solving" may have to be repeated to enhance effectiveness. Supplementary analyses of the total "wave" of direct fighting–problem solving–direct fighting–problem solving indicate that effectiveness is especially sensitive to ending with problem solving.

The findings provide additional and more specific scientific underpinning for the crude behavioural recommendation that social conflict pays (Johnson, Johnson, & Smith, 1989; Tjosvold, 1985, 1991; Van de Vliert, 1985, 1997). As outlined in our discussion of Fig. 5.6, problem solving and direct fighting supplement each other with respect to appropriateness for specific aspects of conflict as well as reduction of risks in terms of ineffectiveness. For those reasons, the mixture of constructive problem solving and controversy in the form of direct fighting might be best.

The findings provide a more refined operationalisation of the rule of thumb that integrative and distributive moves should be mixed (cf. Putnam, 1990; Lax & Sebenius, 1986). In order to be effective, controversy in the form of direct fighting should precede constructive exploration in the form of problem solving. This behavioural sequence resembles the well-documented effectiveness of the "reformed sinner strategy" (Deutsch, 1973; Harford & Solomon, 1967), and the within-person "black-hat/white-hat routine" (Hilty & Carnevale, 1993; Rafaeli & Sutton, 1991). In all such cases, a phase of differentiation precedes a phase of integration (Walton, 1987). On closer consideration, however, the reformed sinner strategy and the strategy of taking off one's black hat and putting on one's white hat address once-only behavioural shifts. In contrast, our findings are based on the continuous alternation of direct fighting and problem solving. Apparently, the move from direct fighting to problem solving has a more de-escalatory and effective nature than the reverse move from problem solving to direct fighting has an escalatory and ineffective nature.

Conclusions.   Study 6 contributes to the conflict management field in several regards. First of all, at dyadic level, the occurrence of problem solving and the occurrence of direct fighting have been studied together—as twins—rather than as separate entities. Breaking away from the prevailing assumption of conflict behaviours as mutually isolated modes of reaction, problem solving and direct fighting were successfully conceptualised as components of complex conflict behaviour (cf. Falbe & Yukl, 1992; Knapp, Putnam, & Davis, 1988; Rubin, Pruitt, & Kim, 1994; Yukl, Falbe, & Young Youn, 1993; Van de Vliert, Euwema, & Huismans, 1995; Van de Vliert et al., in press). Second, the effectiveness of problem solving and the *in*effectiveness of direct fighting have been studied as twins rather than loners. Challenging the prevailing assumption of conflict behaviours as mutually isolated determinants of substantive and relational outcomes, it was demonstrated that problem solving and direct fighting are more effective, or less ineffective, in combination than they are in isolation (cf. Falbe & Yukl, 1992; Putnam, 1990; Van de Vliert, Euwema, & Huismans, 1995; Van de Vliert et al., in press). Finally, for the first time, the simultaneous and the sequential occurrence of problem solving and direct fighting have been studied in tandem. The continuous repetition of direct fighting, followed by simultaneous problem solving and direct fighting, is an especially effective conglomeration of conflict behaviour.

PROPOSITIONS

5a. In the same way that a single goal for oneself and a single goal for the other party elicit a single combination of dual goal concern, multiple short- and long-term goals for oneself and for the other party elicit multiple combinations of dual goal concern (pp. 112–117).

5b. Multiple combinations of dual goal concern determine the aggregation of various degrees of several reactions into conglomerated conflict behaviour (pp. 114–117; see Table 5.1 for specific predictions of indirect fighting, soft negotiating, indirect capitulating, hard negotiating, integrating, and distributing).

5c. Conglomerated conflict behaviour can be represented by a pattern of occurrence of its components, and a pattern of covariation of these components (pp. 103–108).

5d. The pattern of covariation reveals what each component of conglomerated conflict behaviour means in terms of the other components (pp. 105–107).

5e. Personal and dyadic effectiveness are a function of conglomerated conflict behaviour in that the behavioural components intermediate or moderate each other's impact (pp. 117–121).

5f. The behavioural component of problem solving is more effective if simultaneously combined with or sequentially preceded by direct fighting (pp. 121–133).

PART FOUR

Conclusion

CHAPTER SIX

Renewed View

Working and writing on theoretical frontiers involve taking chances, as one exchanges familiar ground for alien territory. The main aim of this monograph is the introduction of a new paradigm to guide research and intervention in the domain of interpersonal conflict behaviour. I left behind the common assumption that a conflicting individual uses only one single and pure mode of behaviour, replacing it with the assumption that any reaction consists of multiple components of behaviour manifested simultaneously or sequentially. In addition, I also left behind the common assumption that modes of conflict behaviour have mutually independent effects, replacing it with the assumption that components of behaviour intermediate or moderate each other's impact on the substantive and relational outcomes of the conflict (for an illustration of both behavioural complexity and complexity of behavioural effects, see the Box "Constructive Controversy by a Senior Nurse").

The book has not been devised as a collage of loosely coupled chapters and sections with regard to this paradigm shift. Rather than being organised at a nominal level of structure, the topics display a theoretically meaningful sequence of themes. Each chapter has been designed so as to build on the preceding chapter, comprising a step forward in the direction of fathoming the phenomenon of conglomerated conflict behaviour, as well as a step upward in the direction of higher theoretical value.

In this last chapter the steps forward and upward are explored further. Attention is paid to several leading ideas about complex conflict behaviour. Next, the four-step theoretical ladder from Chapter 1 is critically reviewed.

Constructive Controversy by a Senior Nurse

As part of one of our experimental studies (Van de Vliert & Euwema, 1996), briefly mentioned in Chapter 5, a female senior nurse found an elderly female patient very upset, complaining about a male physician who had treated the patient in a rude manner. The patient asked for more medicine, but did not get it, and was told to accept the pain and stop nagging. Though the patient started to cry, the physician just left the room. When the nurse tackled the physician about his conduct, he began by trivialising the incident, continued by indicating his disagreement with the underlying organisational policy, and ended with a personal attack on the behaviour of the nurse. The following complex and effective conflict transaction unfolded during the third stage of escalation:

> The nurse is persistent: "But what can we do for the patient?" The physician becomes personal: "Listen, you haven't even been there! You don't know what happened, and now you are telling me what to do?" Nurse: "I want to hear both stories and I want to let you know what the effects of your behaviour are on the patient. I want to stand up for the patient. I think we should do something for her." The physician suggests the staff should discuss this. The nurse then amiably explores this issue. Next, the physician looks at his watch. The nurse responds: "I understand you're in a hurry. At this moment I would like to stress two issues. First, I would appreciate it very much, both for the patient and for the nursing staff, that you meet with the patient again today. Second, I am willing to explore this issue with you more broadly and bring it into the staff meeting. Can I trust you to see the patient today?" Physician: "O.K., I will see what I can do."

In this dialogue the nurse blends and assembles the component of *problem solving* (But what can we do for the patient? I am willing to explore this issue with you more broadly) and the component of *direct fighting* (I want to stand up for the patient. Can I trust you to see the patient today?) without blaming the physician. The nurse remains descriptive, explorative, and content-oriented, even after the person-oriented remarks of her opponent and his signs of leaving. At the same time she pressurises the physician to call on the patient that very day. She clearly acts on behalf of the patient and the staff, which makes her both dyadically and organisationally effective. The juxtaposition of problem solving and direct fighting yields effectiveness by maximising both the tendency of problem solving to produce issue-focused togetherness, and the tendency of direct fighting to produce other-focused agitation.

LEADING IDEAS ABOUT COMPLEX
CONFLICT BEHAVIOUR

The steps made in outlining the paradigm of conglomerated conflict behaviour reflect both commonality and diversity. In Chapter 1, the commonality has been highlighted by stressing that objectively the same conflict management grid has four manifestations or faces. In the subsequent chapters the diversity and separateness of the four faces have been highlighted. The first part of this last chapter deals with some aspects of the unity and connectedness of the four steps that have received, at most, implicit attention. Specifically, handling conflict will be characterised as processing issues, developing goal concerns, overcoming choices, and producing (de-)escalation.

Handling Conflict is Processing Issues

Both a strong and a weak side of the conflict management grid in Fig. 1.1 is the absence, or more precisely the implicit presence, of the conflict issue. On the one hand, the "issuelessness" is a merit because the grid, quite correctly, does not assume that a certain issue produces a particular reaction to the conflict. On the other hand, the invisibility of the issue is a shortcoming of the grid paradigm, because the cognitive/affective nature of the discord is a necessary but incomplete antecedent of any component of conflict behaviour. Managing conflict is handling perceptions, conceptions, and emotions embedded in the subject matter of social obstruction or irritation.

Several components of conflict management in Chapter 2 reflect cognitive—but not affective—aspects of the conflict issue, which seem to be lacking completely at first sight. Accommodating is defined as giving in to the other's *point of view or demand*. Problem solving refers to the reconciliation of the counterparts' *basic interests*. And direct fighting includes demanding the opponent's attention to the *topic of the discord*, also termed issue fighting (Van de Vliert & Euwema, 1994). Such descriptions clearly show how difficult it is to pass over the substance and seriousness of the conflict without comment, when delineating what the disputants do. For that reason Nicotera (1993) suggested the use of two issue dimensions— attention to one's own and attention to the other's view—as main descriptors of conflict behaviour.

The integrative and distributive dimensions in Chapter 3, though less easily recognisable, transmit the same message of the omnipresence of the conflict issue. Recall that integration is dealing with the variable size of a joint pie, whereas distribution is dealing with the division of a fixed pie. Obviously a pie is just a metaphor for a cognitive side of a conflict issue.

Hence, the joint and fixed pie nature of a component of conflict behaviour reflects the perceived variable-sum and constant-sum nature of the issue that is managed. And, by implication, proposition 3e may be formulated slightly differently. It reads: distinct components of conflict handling are interrelated in terms of the magnitude of their integrative and distributive behavioural content. Because integration refers to the perceived size of joint pie while distribution refers to the perceived distribution of fixed pie, it may also be read as: distinct components of conflict handling are inter-related in terms of the magnitude of the perceived variable-sum and constant-sum characteristics of the conflict issue.

After gleaming in Part Two, the sun of the psychic content of the conflict begins to rise in Part Three of the book. Without assuming that a certain issue produces a particular reaction, Chapters 4 and 5 recognise and dignify cognitions and emotions as the ultimate origins of conflict management. The cognitive and emotional aspects of the conflict issue make goals and goal concerns salient. Consequently neither person nor environment, without regard to the subject and the intensity of the problem, can be construed as the sole source from which conglomerated conflict behaviour arises.

Given that the subject matter characterises and partly causes the way a conflict is handled, it is remarkable that a cogent grounding of conflict behaviour in issue-based theory and research is missing, including in this book. In particular, the impact of affective discord on behaviour and outcomes remains one of the least studied areas of conflict management, including negotiation and third-party intervention (see, however, Baron et al., 1990; Carnevale & Isen, 1986; Carnevale et al., 1989; Jehn, 1997).

What we do know is that disagreements about scarce resources are distributive-prone, thus predestinated to cause accommodating, compromising, or direct fighting about the outcomes. Also, recently, much progress has been made on determinants of responses to feelings of injustice (e.g. Felstiner, Abel, & Sarat, 1980; Lind & Tyler, 1988; Sheppard, Lewicki, & Minton, 1992). Apart from that, still surprisingly little is known about how, for instance, incompatible personalities, displaced frustrations, and mis-understandings influence interactions differently (for types of issues, see Chapter 1; Coombs, 1987; Deutsch, 1973; Glasl, 1980).

Handling Conflict is Developing Goal Concerns

This section first summarises what we have learned about developing and taking account of concerns for one's own and the other's goals. As is discussed next, a party who is unaware of the aims behind the other party's action may misread the other's goals and may therefore develop concern for the other's goals in a mismatched way. Looking for a new impetus for further research, critical comments about the loss-versus-gain content and the complexity of the goal concerns will complete this section.

Processing goal concerns. Chapter 4 stated that the cognitive or affective discord making up the conflict issue alerts a conflict party to endangered goals of self and other. Deliberately or inadvertently a party to a conflict sets goals for itself in addition to perceiving or assuming goals for the other party. By making the parties' goals salient, the conflict issue itself, rather than the person or the environment, is the birthplace of goals and subsequent goal concerns.

Chapters 4 and 5 further dealt with the important part that goal concerns play in at least three respects. First, concern for one's own goals has an impact on behaviour in conjunction with concern for the other's goals. The concern-based reaction benefits or harms oneself as well as the other party. Second, one typically develops multiple goals and goal concerns for both oneself and the other party. This complexity of goal concerns causes conglomerated conflict behaviour. Finally, positively interdependent goals promote much goal concern for the other party and predominantly cooperative behaviour, whereas negatively interdependent goals promote little goal concern for the other party and predominantly competitive behaviour.

Misreading the other's goals. As stated in Chapter 2, observed components of conflict handling can be categorised more easily as avoiding, accommodating, compromising, problem solving, indirect fighting, or direct fighting to the extent that an actor's behavioural intention is known better or attributed with more certainty. By implication, a principal party can read the other party's degrees of integrative and distributive transaction better if that party's goals of nonconfrontation, agreement or prevalence are more overt, distinct, and stable. Due to ambiguity of the opponent's goals, however, a party may sometimes interpret predominantly integrative behaviour as mainly distributive, or the other way around, to the effect that concern for the wrong goals is developed.

Recall that effectuation of integrative goals requires the parties to behave symmetrically with both parties avoiding or negotiating, whereas effectuation of distributive goals requires them to behave complementarily with one party accommodating and the other party fighting (proposition 3c). Consequently, when the opponent's predominant integration is mistaken for distribution, one might well become predisposed to react complementarily on the distributive dimension although symmetry on the integrative dimension would produce mutual adjustment. Conversely, when the other party's predominant distribution is mistaken for integration, one might well become predisposed to react symmetrically on the integrative dimension although complementarity on the distributive dimension would produce mutual adjustment. This line of reasoning refines Thomas and Pondy's (1977) point of view that each party's attribution of the other's intent feeds the inter-action process between the disputants (see also De Dreu et al., 1995).

Losses versus gains.   Goals are desired outcomes for oneself and for one's opponent to be concerned about. A relevant factor, as yet not ad-dressed, is whether the goals are conceptualised as costs or as benefits. By now it is common knowledge that, depending on the reference point used, objectively the same potential outcomes may be framed as losses or as gains. For example, if one gets $1000 for something, one "loses" $700 if one expected to receive $1700, but one "gains" $700 if one expected to receive $300. A most important but somewhat different manifestation of this loss-versus-gain frame is a conflict party's prospect of losing face versus gaining face if the issue is settled in a certain way (cf. Brown, 1977; Folger & Poole, 1984; Pruitt, 1981; Tjosvold & Huston, 1978).

Because one's losses are more aversive than one's gains are attractive (Kahneman & Tversky, 1979; Tversky & Kahneman, 1981), people become more concerned about their own goals when they anticipate losses than when they anticipate gains (e.g. De Dreu, 1993; Kahneman, 1992; Taylor, 1991). As a consequence of the higher concern for their own interests, they react more assertively. In agreement with this, researchers repeatedly found that a prospect of losses led negotiators to less concessionary behaviour and a lower settlement rate than did a prospect of gains (Bazerman et al., 1985; Carnevale & Pruitt, 1992; De Dreu et al., 1994, 1995; De Dreu, Emans, & Van de Vliert, 1992b; Neale & Bazerman, 1985, 1991; Neale, Huber, & Northcraft, 1987).

Other empirical evidence likewise suggests that participants in a conflict, especially when they have a rather cooperative orientation, become more concerned about the other party's goals when they foresee that the oppo-nent will have to swallow a loss than when they foresee that the opponent will enjoy a profit (De Dreu, Emans, & Van de Vliert, 1992a; De Dreu, Lualhati, & McCusker, 1994). As a consequence of this higher concern for the other's interests, they appear to react more cooperatively. So, one's own goals, and in certain circumstances the other's goals as well, elicit higher concern when they are framed as losses than when they are framed as gains. Those findings argue for enriching the conflict concerns theory by includ-ing the differential impact of goals that are seen as losses versus goals that are seen as gains.

Complexity of goal concerns.   A serious shortcoming of all present theo-ries on conflict handling is that they pass over the complexity of the parties' goal concerns. To be sure, Thomas (1992b) recently addressed the effective-ness of modes of conflict behaviour in relation to concerns for short- and long-term goals. Also, the theory of conglomerated conflict behaviour in Chapter 5 moves somewhat towards a better understanding of how people handle the multiplexity of their goals and goal concerns during conflict. However, to date, nobody has investigated to what extent and to what effect multiple goals of conflicting parties are processed, let alone understood when and why sequential rather than simultaneous conglomerations of conflict behaviour are selected (for types of goals, see Chapter 4; Lax & Sebenius, 1986; Roloff & Jordan, 1992; Thomas, 1982, 1992b).

A leap forward might be made if more thorough attention was paid to the conflict issue as the origin of multiple goal concerns. Often the conflict issue is complex, and different aspects might give rise to different goal concerns regarding oneself as well as different concerns about goals associated with the other party. However, even a single issue might trigger multiple goal concerns dealing with, for instance, saving face, the clearance of earlier or parallel feelings of discord, and setting a sprat to catch a mackerel. Relying on Thomas (1982, 1992b), the most basic choice to be made is whether to regard some conflicting action as directed at intrinsic or instrumental goals. Another useful point of departure is that characteristics of the acting person and characteristics of the perceived environment alter the relationship between the conflict issue and concerns about conflict management goals (cf. Fig. 4.3). For example, when facing public opposition, a junta leader will develop different goal concerns than an elected president, and in times of peace both will develop different goal concerns than in times of war.

Recapitulation. In sum, handling conflict is developing concern for one's own and the other's goals. One judges and cares about one's own potential losses or gains, and one also assesses and cares about the opponent's potential losses or gains. In general, one's own goals as well as the other's goals elicit higher concern when they are framed as losses than when they are framed as gains. As a consequence, goals framed as losses stand a better chance of being realised than equally high goals framed as gains. Conglomerated behaviour results as a party pursues a number of goals rather than a single goal, either simultaneously or sequentially.

Handling Conflict is Overcoming Choices

Consider another example. A chairman might avoid an explosive issue in the main because it would take too much time to explore and reconcile everybody's goals and concerns. In that case, he makes the choice to adopt a large component of avoidance and to reject a large component of conflict resolution. The chairman might also bypass the choice between avoiding and problem solving by imposing a voting procedure or by setting up an advisory committee. In that case, he is adopting and rejecting none of the initial behavioural alternatives. At the same time, he is facing a selection without actually executing that selection. Instead, a decision is made that overcomes the choice. The decision honours the intellectual capability of human beings to break out of a seemingly fixed definition of opposite courses of action, without incorporating the opposing standpoints and interests into a compromise or a resolution. The next paragraphs further explain why the process of overcoming choices is the beating heart of complex human conflict behaviour, notably including negotiating.

Overcoming choice in conflict behaviour.   The family of conflict frameworks presented in the preceding chapters is characterised by making decisions that overcome choices. The X-cross model in Chapter 3 highlights that the behavioural dilemma between integration and distribution is transformed into singular conflict behaviour having an integrative and distributive content. To be sure, one of those types of content might be insignificant, but the X-cross model maintains that minimum amounts of both are always present. Put conversely and more specifically, 100% non-integration through avoiding, 100% defeat through accommodating, and 100% victory through direct fighting never occur. This nonexistence of pure behaviours is the essence of conglomerated conflict behaviour.

Similarly, the conflict concerns theory in Chapter 4 emphasises that a conflict is characterised by an inescapable tension between concern for one party's goals and concern for the other party's goals. This choice between the two motives cannot really be made, which gives the conflict its complex motivational nature. The choice is overcome by transforming the two concerns into an unsplittable dual goal concern and unsplittable conflict behaviour (for a related research recommendation, see the Box "Theoretical Flaws of Cooperative and Competitive Orientations"). More specifically, the choice is overcome by transforming a combination of dual goal concern into a component of conglomerated conflict behaviour.

Finally, in Chapter 5, the extension of the concerns theory focuses on the choice between multiple concerns for one's own goals (own-sided concerns complexity), for the other's goals (other-sided concerns complexity), or both (two-sided concerns complexity). None of the levels of goal concern, either within or between the two classes of concern, is however selected over any other. Instead, the choice is once more overcome. The initially loose concerns are restricted to create a conglomeration of conflict behaviour. Behavioural components are woven together into a complex tapestry characterised by a pattern of occurrence and a pattern of co-variation of its components.

Interestingly, for the purpose of improving the effectiveness of task groups, techniques have been developed to implement processes of over-

Theoretical Flaws of Cooperative and Competitive Orientations

The conflict concerns theory identifies two basic social motives: concern for one's own goals, and concern for the other's goals. The theory further states that a 100% choice in favour of one of these concerns is impossible. Conflicting parties simply cannot escape from mixing the two elemental concerns into a complex motive composed of an element dealing with the self and a similar element dealing with the opponent. Especially noteworthy cases of such complex motives are the so-called cooperative orientation to maximise both one's own and the other's outcomes, and the so-called competitive orientation to maximise the relative advantage of one's own over the other's outcomes (e.g. Deutsch, 1949, 1973, 1985; Griesinger & Livingston, 1973; Johnson & Johnson, 1989; Kuhlman, Brown, & Teta, 1992; Liebrand, 1982; Liebrand & Van Run, 1985; MacCrimmon & Messick, 1976; McClintock, 1972, 1976; Tjosvold, 1989, 1990; Van der Togt & Van de Vliert, 1996; Van Lange, 1991, 1992).

It is important to note explicitly that the two elemental concerns have a very different relationship with these two complex orientations. In the cooperative orientation, concern for one's own goals and concern for the other's goals are both high. In contrast, in the competitive orientation, concern for one's own goals is much higher than concern for the other's goals. Consequently, concern for the other's goals rather than concern for one's own goals discriminates between a cooperative and a competitive orientation. This reveals two serious shortcomings of research designs that manipulate cooperative versus competitive orientation. First, low concern for one's own goals is left out of consideration. Though one often adds a condition of individualistic orientation, this condition is then characterised by high concern for one's own goals. Second, the manipulation is unnecessarily complex as high versus low altruistic orientation could replace cooperative versus competitive orientation.

The cooperative, competitive, and individualistic orientations are frequently used as behavioural determinants in research designs that do not also include an altruistic orientation. Viewed from the perspective of the conflict concerns theory, the absence of predominant concern for the other's goals raises questions about the interpretation of the research findings. Does an effect of a cooperative motive result mainly from fairly high valence and feasibility of one's own goals, of the other's goals, or both? Similarly, does an effect of a competitive motive result mainly from higher valence and feasibility of one's own goals, from lower valence or feasibility of the other's goals, or both? If the two orientations are contrasted, the questions become even more complicated. Does a difference between the cooperative and the competitive motive result mainly from higher or lower valence and/or feasibility of one's own goals in the cooperative compared

> to the competitive condition, of the other's goals in the cooperative compared to the competitive condition, or both?
>
> To prevent such ambiguity of findings, researchers are advised to use the elemental concerns for one's own and for the other's goals rather than the complex cooperative and competitive orientations. Predominant concern for the other's goals or altruistic orientation is the most promising factor, also given the fact that it determines the de-escalation or escalation of the conflict (see proposition 4f).

coming choices. Those interventions include the involvement of opposing outsiders, the formulation of competing proposals, and the application of devil's advocacy (e.g. 't Hart, 1990; Janis, 1982; Johnson & Tjosvold, 1989; Katzenstein, 1996; Schweiger, Sandberg, & Rechner, 1989; Schwenk, 1990; Schwenk & Cosier, 1993; Tjosvold, 1991). Compared to consensus-seeking groups, groups using such techniques made significantly higher-quality decisions. The results suggested that debate itself, through its presence rather than through its format, improves group performance by formalising and legitimising escalative behaviours that create solutions that overcome choices.

Overcoming choice in negotiation.   Negotiating, without or with the help of a third party, is a clear example of facing behavioural choices but making a decision that goes beyond the initial options. To paraphrase Follett (1940, p. 33): the trick with compromising and problem solving is not to let one's thinking stay within the boundaries of two alternatives that are mutually exclusive. It helps when, from the outset, the opposite interactions are firmly embedded in the intention to reach an agreement. According to Mastenbroek (1989), to be successful, negotiators have to face and should overcome four dilemmas between opposite activities.

The first choice, between conceding and stubborn reactions, must be passed by in favour of a firm presentation of facts and arguments. The second choice, between bending and domineering, must be passed by to bring about a balance of power. The third choice, between jovial and hostile ways of acting, must be passed by to promote a constructive climate. The last choice, between exploring and avoiding, must be passed by to obtain procedural flexibility.

In Chapter 3 all such dilemmas were substantiated in the statement that compromising represents both a mixture of avoiding and problem solving and a point of balance between accommodating and fighting. Mixture and balance reflect the overarching decision to settle, which exceeds the behavioural options on which the settlement rests.

Recapitulation. The management of conflict comes with inescapable, but essentially impossible, choices between integration and distribution, and between goal concerns for one party and goal concerns for the other party. Negotiating is probably the most salient illustration of this process of facing a choice without making that choice.

Handling Conflict is Producing (De-)Escalation

Inevitably, conflict management has (de-)escalative consequences (e.g. De Dreu, Nauta, & Van de Vliert, 1995; Glasl, 1980; Rubin, Pruitt, & Kim, 1994). The seriousness of the issue increases or decreases, the levels of concern for one's own and the other's goals go up or down, the subsequent behaviour is more or less integrative and distributive, and the ultimate outcomes are more advantageous or disadvantageous. Key to those conflict dynamics are concerns for the other's goals (Butler, 1995; Janssen & Van de Vliert, 1996). After having reasoned why this is supposed to be so, some attention is paid to turning points from de-escalation to escalation or vice versa.

Key to (de-)escalation. Study 5 in Chapter 5 revealed that direct fighting and avoiding are the most ineffective and escalative components of conglomerated conflict behaviour. Consequently, as indicated in Chapter 3, a marked process of de-escalation typically proceeds up the integrative dimension, from 1,1 avoiding towards 9,9 problem solving, and/or across the distributive dimension, from 9,1 direct fighting towards 5,5 compromising and 1,9 accommodating. Conversely, a clear-cut escalating process proceeds down the integrative dimension, and/or across the distributive dimension towards direct fighting.

De-escalative movement up the integrative dimension is caused by an increasing concern for both one's own and the other's goals (see arrow 1 in Fig. 6.1). De-escalative movement across the distributive dimension, on the other hand, is caused by decreasing concern for one's own goals in conjunction with increasing concern for the other's goals (arrow 2). For escalative movements reverse formulations apply, as indicated by arrows 3 and 4 in Fig. 6.1. Following on logically from these basics of (de-)escalation, more concern for one's own goals may or may not intensify the conflict, whereas more concern for the other's goals will generally mitigate the conflict. Conversely, less concern for one's own goals may or may not mitigate the conflict, whereas less concern for the other's goals will generally intensify the conflict.

This line of deductive reasoning underpins proposition 4f once more: concern for one's own goals determines *how* the conflict de-escalates or escalates, whereas concern for the other's goals determines whether and explains *why* the conflict de-escalates or escalates. It boils down to the fact

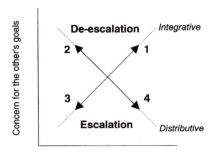

FIG. 6.1 Escalation as a direct function of integrative and distributive components of conglomerated conflict behaviour, and as an indirect function of concern for one's own and the other's goals.

that concerns for the other's goals are crucial to steering conflict behaviour having (de-)escalative effects.

Turning points.   A (de-)escalative effect can be immediate, as is sometimes the case with conflict resolution or vengeful behaviour. However, consequences are often indirect: conflict management first influences a (de-)escalative state, such as weaker or stronger discord, which in its turn influences subsequent (de-)escalative behaviour (Nauta, 1996). Interestingly, as will be elaborated below, some components of conflict management tend to produce short-term de-escalation but long-term escalation. Conversely, some other components of conflict management tend to produce short-term escalation but long-term de-escalation. All such behaviours arguably have a built-in turning point, so to speak.

Unilateral openness intended as a de-escalative tactic, drawing attention to overall interests during a fight, and tough negotiating all tend to have a boomerang effect (Filley, 1975; Johnson & Lewicki, 1969; Walton, 1987). Likewise, it often turns out after a while that powerful people who want to prevent further conflict by suppressing the current disagreement in fact obtain the opposite result (Deutsch, 1973). And avoidance of any confrontation may well have the consequence that, in the end, a more destructive unspoken or underground conflict arises (Glasl, 1980; Hocker & Wilmot, 1985). Thus, like the hierarchical suppression of conflict, avoidance may have a direct, barely escalative effect for some time, but in the longer run will have an indirect, escalating effect.

The reverse process, that escalative behaviour leads indirectly to less rather than to more conflict, also occurs. From the discussion of the level of tension theory in Chapter 5, as well as from the aforementioned techniques to implement processes of overcoming choices, it is apparent that, in the end, moderate escalation can be conducive to integrative behaviour (cf. Fisher, 1997; Van de Vliert, 1997). Also, there is Coser's (1956) proposition that contentious behaviour brings the parties closer together, and that it restores the unity and stability among them unless the relationship is affected in a seriously negative manner. This proposition received support in Bach and Wyden's (1969) practical experiences while teaching couples how to fight fairly.

In future research it is essential to map the many uncharted areas around turning points from direct de-escalative consequences to indirect escalative consequences, and vice versa. Here are some intriguing questions with which to begin. All other things being equal, do de-escalative cycles turn into escalative cycles more or less easily than escalative cycles turn into de-escalative cycles? Or, put in terms of the above key to (de-)escalation, is it harder to change from low to high concern for the other's goals than it is to change from high to low concern for the other's goals? And do the findings equally apply to conflicts about anticipated losses and conflicts about anticipated gains (De Dreu et al., 1994, 1995), and to conflicting parties in the roles of plaintiff and defendant (Nauta, 1996; Peirce, Pruitt, & Czaja, 1993)? If we are serious about answering such questions, longitudinal studies of conflict processes are urgently needed. Longitudinal studies may, moreover, improve our insight into the behavioural sequences and phases of (de-)escalating conflicts, provided that we overcome some major problems of measuring change (cf. Van de Vliert, Huismans, & Stok, 1985).

Recapitulation. High concern for the other's goals produces de-escalative behavioural components, whereas low concern for the other's goals produces escalative behavioural components. Those components of conglomerated conflict behaviour include reactions associated with short-term de-escalation but long-term escalation, or short-term escalation but long-term de-escalation. Against this background the question arises as to whether it is harder to continue a de-escalating high concern for the other's goals than it is to continue an escalating low concern for the other's goals.

THEORETICAL LADDER

In this book I have not only attempted to introduce, describe and explain complex conflict behaviour. An overarching purpose was to promote the quality of research and intervention regarding conflict management by presenting steps or levels of conceptualisation. At the lower theoretical levels, behavioural components are not or are only superficially related to their causes or effects, including the topic of the dissent. Frameworks that do interrelate the behavioural components and their determinants or consequences are considered higher-level theories.

Underlying the main purpose of improving quality in theory development and application is the basic argument that too few scholars of conflict are able to recognise adequately the degrees of scientific contribution. They are too readily satisfied with low levels of theory construction and utilisation. They get stuck, so to speak, on the bottom rungs of the theoretical ladder.

A more detailed description of the four upward steps in Fig. 6.2, put together in the preceding chapters in passing, will further clarify what I mean. Next, a glance at the main historical stages of the development of the conflict management grid will illustrate the view that, with ups and downs, we are collectively climbing this four-step ladder for building and rebuilding theory. In the end, an attempt is made to answer two remaining questions. Is higher up the ladder always better? How solid is this ladder anyway?

Four Upward Steps

At the thin end of the wedge in Chapter 1 the bottom definition of conflict behaviour as a goal-directed reaction to a conflict issue experienced is introduced. The first step from that definition to typological descriptions of behavioural components adds three things: it identifies the characteristics and particulars of components of conflict behaviour; it arranges those behavioural components into a system of categories; and it provides a corresponding nomenclature. Classifications such as the five-part and six-part taxonomies in Chapter 2 enable us to analyse and typify complex conflict behaviours and to communicate about them. Such typologies lift us up to a nominal level of descriptive knowledge.

The progression from the typologies to the dimensional model in Chapter 3 refines the description of how people handle conflict by going from the particular types of behavioural components to the general dimensions without losing the particular in the general. This step also adds three things: it identifies whether components of conglomerated conflict behaviour are integrative and/or distributive; it does so on continuous rather than on discrete scales; and it combines the two descriptors to represent the uniqueness of the behavioural components in a precise and comprehensible way. The X-cross model enables us to investigate consciously and interrelate components of conglomerated conflict behaviour in terms of their main similarities and differences. Such a model lifts us up to an ordinal, or possibly an interval, level of descriptive knowledge.

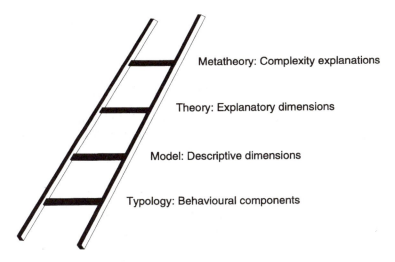

FIG. 6.2   The four-step theoretical ladder of conglomerated conflict behaviour.

The following ascent, leading into and onto the explanatory theory of dual goal concern in Chapter 4, exceeds the pure description of conflict handling. It adds the proposition that the concerns for one's own and the other's goals are continuous rather than discrete factors that co-determine a single and dominant component of de-escalative or escalative behaviour. Those additions enable us to investigate the concerns as the ultimate dual determinant of predominant conflict behaviour and conflict (de-)escalation. The concerns theory lifts us up to a level of knowledge that specifies multiple causes of *single effects* on (de-)escalative conflict management.

The fourth advancement, from theory to metatheory, from the explanation of a single component to the explanation of multiple components, is in a way the reverse of the advancement from typological to dimensional descriptions. Whereas that second step goes from the particular to the general without losing the particular in the general, the complexity explanations go from the general concerns to the particular componential concerns without losing the general in the particular. It adds that multiple combinations of dual goal concern operate simultaneously, that they produce the aggregation of reactions, and that problem solving is a relatively effective component of the resulting conglomerated conflict behaviour. Those additions enable us to predict and portray with even greater accuracy what conflicting parties do, and to understand the course and the outcomes of the process more thoroughly. The metatheory of effective conglomerations lifts us up to a level of knowledge that specifies multiple causes of *multiple effects* on (de-)escalative conflict management.

In sum, then, the theoretical ladder has four steps, leading from bare and simple circumscriptions of components of conflict behaviour to advanced explanations of complex conflict behaviour. As scientists, we are climbing this ladder together. With the best of intentions yet lacking in caution, we sometimes take steps backward and downward. Throughout this book past work on the conflict management grid has gradually revealed itself as a sad case in point.

History at a Glance

Decades ago, Blake and Mouton (1964, 1970) climbed the theoretical ladder to a point where nobody could or would follow them at that time. It is likely that even Blake and Mouton may not have seen through the important implications and the full theoretical significance of their grid paradigm. Granted, as exemplified in Chapter 1, their grid complex constitutes an ambiguous stimulus configuration that lends itself to several figure–ground perceptions. However that, in and of itself, does not justify or even clarify the fact that back in the 1960s people were only able or ready to see and act upon the lowest rung of the ladder. Blake and Mouton's contemporaries picked up the grid exclusively as a five-part typology of components of (conflict) management.

As the Box "Historical Milestones of the Conflict Management Grid" illustrates, the subsequent steps up the theoretical ladder match nicely the historical stages of advancement of the conflict management grid. During the early years Blake and Mouton (1964, 1970) and Hall (1969), in particular, developed the five-part typology. From 1964 onwards it took Thomas (1976) and Prein (1976) more than a decade to reach the next rung on the ladder. Recall that at that level, the level of the X-cross model, all descriptions of behavioural components can be interrelated in terms of the common factors of integration and distribution. After almost another decade Ben-Yoav and Pruitt (1984a, 1984b), followed shortly after by Carnevale (1986), were the first to set foot on the level where the L-angle of concerns makes it possible to explain components of managing conflict and their (de-)escalative consequences. A third decade has passed and we are now beginning to see signs that a fourth step might be made. In fact, some tottering first moves may have been made in this book when I tried to predict conglomerated conflict behaviour using Blake and Mouton's seminal ideas about mixed grid theories as a point of departure.

In conclusion, for thirty years the conflict management grid has been theoretically underdeveloped and undervalued. The five-part typology and the X-cross model represent very restricted interpretations of Blake and

---

Historical Milestones of the Conflict Management Grid

First Step

1964   Blake and Mouton published "The managerial grid."
1969   Hall introduced the first full-fledged self-assessment instrument on the basis of the five-part typology of conflict management.
1970   Blake and Mouton claimed that the grid theory applies to all social conflicts.

Second Step

1976   Thomas gave the grid a central position in his handbook chapter on conflict management and discovered that the diagonals constitute an integrative and a distributive dimension.
1976   Prein demonstrated that the integrative and distributive dimensions describe conflict behaviour best.

Third Step

1984   Ben-Yoav and Pruitt showed that concerns for one's own and the other's goals predict conflict strategies and outcomes.
1986   Carnevale used the goal concerns from the grid framework to predict mediator intervention.

Fourth Step

1994   It is about time that conflict handling is conceptualised as a complex pattern of behavioural components rather than as pure and single behaviour (cf. Chapter 5).

Mouton's (1964, 1970) original ideas. It makes more sense to locate the founders of the grid paradigm on the explanatory third and fourth rungs of the theoretical ladder that we are climbing together.

Is Higher Always Better?

In this text a conceptual framework—that is, a typology, a model, a theory, or a metatheory—has theoretical value in so far as it represents fruitful rules of correspondence between conflict behaviours and their antecedents or consequences. From the outset, in the introductory chapter, the position has been taken that the theoretical value increases with each step from behavioural definition to typology, from typology to model, from model to theory, and from theory to metatheory (cf. Fig. 6.2). Thus, by implication, higher up the theoretical ladder is always considered scientifically better. On closer consideration, this seems an exaggeration, because there is theoretical virtue in such divergent qualities as simplicity, widespread applicability or generality, and exactness or accuracy of rules of correspondence. And, as Thorngate (1976; see also Van de Vliert, 1977; Weick, 1979) convincingly argued, it is impossible for a theory of social behaviour to be simultaneously simple, general, and accurate. The more accurate a general theory is, for example, the less simple it will be in describing and explaining behaviours.

This interesting thought might well imply that each of the conceptual frameworks in this book has theoretical worth in some respects but not in others. Indeed, the main value of the five-part typology in Chapter 2 lies in its description of simple and pure behavioural components, notably at the expense of its accuracy. Conversely, the main value of the theory of conglomerated conflict behaviour in Chapter 5 lies in its accuracy of predictions of complex behaviour, notably at the expense of its simplicity. In between, Chapters 3 and 4 present the X-cross model of integration and distribution, and the dual concern theory. By emphasising the two-dimensional nature of the complex conflict management grid at the expense of specific behavioural components and goal concerns, these frameworks give priority to general and still rather simple features while sacrificing some accuracy. In short, climbing the theoretical ladder is moving from simplicity through generality to accuracy. That is to say, each rung of the ladder inevitably has its scientific strengths and weaknesses.

All this does not deny that descriptions have less theoretical quality than explanations, in that descriptive adequacies are prerequisites for viable explanatory efforts (Chomsky, 1965). It only tries to make the additional point that accuracy, often realised by means of experimental studies and advanced statistics, should not be treated as the sacred cow of the social sciences. Sometimes, for example during a conflict intervention, simple typological descriptions are to be preferred to complex behavioural pictures. And sometimes, for example when studying countless conflict incidents rather than a particular case, general approaches in terms of dimensions are to be preferred to specific descriptions and explanations of behavioural components.

A Solid Ladder?

This last section addresses a final question: to what extent does the theoretical ladder itself meet Thorngate's (1976; Weick, 1979) criteria of simplicity, generality, and accuracy?

A first, elegant, feature holds that each step of the ladder has been constructed from basically the same material, namely through a subjective transformation of objectively the same conflict management grid (see Chapter 1). This characteristic emphasises the commonality of descriptions of behavioural components, descriptive dimensions, explanatory dimensions, and complexity explanations. In other words, each step of the ladder views exactly the same complex conflict behaviour from a different viewpoint. This is a very distinctive and simple mark of the ladder. However, the conflict management grid as the common root of the ladder's steps is not a generally applicable principle. Moreover, the process of the objective-to-subjective transformation is described with insufficient accuracy and does not specify the circumstances under which each type of transformation takes place.

A second feature, involving the sequential order among the four steps of the ladder, flows from the section "History at a Glance." The proposed sequence of these steps correlates perfectly with the historical stages of theoretical advancement of the conflict management grid. Hence, the following corollary: each step of the ladder represents a necessary but insufficient condition for the next step of the ladder. This simple rather than accurate observation might well reflect a general principle of stepwise theory building.

A third feature lies in the fact that the steps of the ladder represent a hierarchical order in terms of description versus explanation, and components of behaviour versus dimensions (see Chapter 1). This is not a simple principle, as the description of a single behavioural component is located at the lowest rung of the ladder, while the full-fledged explanation of conglomerated behaviours is located at the highest rung. In contrast, the rather accurate ranking order of descriptions of behavioural components, descriptive dimensions, explanatory dimensions, and complexity explanations seems generalisable to theory building in behavioural domains other than conflict handling.

Finally, the theoretical quality of each rung of the ladder, as specified in the section "Is Higher Always Better?", implies a fourth feature of some importance. In general, higher rungs of the theoretical ladder initially have higher degrees of generality and accuracy, followed by lower degrees of simplicity and generality later on. This somewhat curvilinear relationship is far from simple, but it has an air of general applicability and accuracy. Recall that the theoretical virtues of simplicity, generality, and accuracy tend to drive each other out. No step of the ladder can cover them all. For that reason, the optimum might well be reached when all steps together cover simplicity, generality, and accuracy. And exactly that seems to be the case.

In a similar vein, none of the aforementioned features of the ladder in and of itself can cover simplicity, generality, and accuracy. The observation that each step views the same conflict behaviour from a different viewpoint derives its theoretical value primarily from simplicity. The observation that each step represents a necessary but insufficient condition for the next higher step derives its theoretical value primarily from both simplicity and generality. The observations that the lowest step is simple but not accurate, that the middle steps have the highest degree of generality, and that the highest step is accurate but not simple, derive their theoretical value primarily from accuracy. As a result, all features of the theoretical ladder together seem to cover an optimal array of simplicity, generality, and accuracy. From this diversity of scientific virtues I hope to have proposed a ladder that is useful for building modern theory on conflict behaviour.

PROPOSITIONS

6a.   Handling conflict is processing issues, developing concerns, overcoming choices, and producing (de-)escalation (pp. 139–149).

6b.   One's own goals as well as the other's goals elicit higher concern when they are framed as losses than when they are framed as gains (pp. 142–143).

6c.   Whereas some components of conflict behaviour tend to produce short-term de-escalation but long-term escalation, others tend to produce short-term escalation but long-term de-escalation (pp. 148–149).

6d.   The theoretical value of descriptions of behavioural components lies in simplicity rather than in generality and accuracy (pp. 153–154).

6e.   The theoretical value of descriptive and explanatory dimensions lies in simplicity and generality rather than accuracy (pp. 153–154).

6f.   The theoretical value of complexity explanations lies in accuracy rather than in simplicity and generality (pp. 153–154).

Thirty-Four Propositions

Each chapter in this essay has been summarised into a number of inter-related propositions. Among them are *axioms* taken as being true (e.g. propositions 1a through 1c), *core suppositions* which represent testable, central ideas (e.g. propositions 3e, 4e, 5b, and 6c), and *corollaries* which stem from or extend the axioms or core suppositions (e.g. propositions 2d, 4f, 5e, and 6f). There are 34 propositions in total, brought together here to sketch a bird's-eye view of the book.

PREVIEW

1a. Conflict refers to an individual's cognitive and/or affective discord due to a socially induced issue, which elicits goal-directed reactions and subsequent outcomes for all parties involved (pp. 4–7).

1b. As a rule, a conflict issue elicits a complex aggregation of intended or displayed behavioural components, referred to as conglomerated conflict behaviour (pp. 3, 6).

1c. Blake and Mouton's (1964, 1970) conflict management grid has four distinct manifestations or faces, which can be used to describe and explain conglomerated conflict behaviour (pp. 14–19).

1d. The theoretical value of the four grid manifestations increases in the following order: descriptions of behavioural components, descriptive dimensions, explanatory dimensions, complexity explanations (pp. 19–22).

1e.   The dimensions of the grid's diagonals *describe* conglomerated conflict behaviour, whereas the goal concern dimensions of the grid's sides also *explain* it (pp. 20–22).

FIRST STEP: DESCRIPTION OF BEHAVIOURAL COMPONENTS

2a.   Components of conglomerated conflict behaviour can be categorised more easily as avoiding, accommodating, compromising, problem solving, and indirect or direct fighting if the actor's behavioural intention is known better (p. 30).

2b.   Two kinds of compromising components exist: claim-negotiating resulting in an allocation of something nobody owns, and trade-negotiating resulting in an exchange of belongings (pp. 35–36).

2c.   A component of fighting is direct to the extent that it is overt and straightforward, and fair to the extent that it follows mutually agreed upon behavioural rules to defeat the other party (pp. 30, 32, 39–40).

2d.   A fair fighting component is different from a negotiating component in that it is based on an agreement about right and wrong behaviour, but is not directed at a further agreement in the form of a compromise or a resolution (pp. 34–35, 40).

2e.   The dichotomy of cooperative and competitive components, the trichotomy of moving away–toward–against, and the typology of avoiding, accommodating, compromising, problem solving, and indirect or direct fighting are interrelated in terms of the agreeableness and activeness of the postulated components (pp. 41–48).

SECOND STEP: DESCRIPTIVE DIMENSIONS

3a.   The integrative dimension ranging from the component of avoiding to the component of problem solving, and the distributive dimension ranging from the component of accommodating to the component of fighting, have a positive or neutral rather than a negative relationship of co-occurrence (pp. 54–56, 66–67, 70).

3b. The integrative dimension represents variations in anticipated variable-sum outcomes, whereas the distributive dimension represents variations in anticipated constant-sum outcomes for the conflicting parties (pp. 51–53).

3c. Effectuation of variable-sum outcomes on the integrative dimension requires behavioural symmetry on the part of the opponent with both parties avoiding or negotiating, whereas effectuation of constant-sum outcomes on the distributive dimension requires behavioural complementarity on the part of the opponent with one party accommodating and the other party fighting (pp. 58–59, 61).

3d. Conflicting parties handle behavioural dilemmas between equal and differential treatment of oneself and the opponent by conglomerating more and less integrative and distributive components of conflict behaviour (pp. 56–61).

3e. Distinct components of conflict handling are interrelated in terms of the magnitude of their integrative and distributive behavioural content (pp. 56, 61, 69–70).

3f. For the conflicting parties together, on the integrative dimension compromising is suboptimal in relation to conflict resolution, but on the distributive dimension compromising is optimal in relation to victory and defeat (pp. 52–54, 63, 71).

THIRD STEP: EXPLANATORY DIMENSIONS

4a. A conflict issue gives rise to an assessment of one's own and the other's goals and subsequent concerns about attaining these goals (pp. 87–92).

4b. Concern for one's own goals and concern for the other's goals consist of goal valences and means–ends feasibilities that motivate dominant conflict behaviour (pp. 85–87, 96).

4c. Positive goal interdependence between the parties tends to equalise the actor's degree of concern for one's own and the other's goals, whereas negative goal interdependence tends to produce opposite degrees of concern for one's own and the other's goals (pp. 90–91, 97).

4d.   The dual goal concern intermediates the relation between the conflict issue and the dominant conflict behaviour (pp. 82–86).

4e.   The concern dimensions co-determine the dominant conflict behaviour (pp. 76–79, 83, 94–95, 97–99; see Fig. 4.1 for specific predictions of avoiding, accommodating, compromising, problem solving, and fighting).

4f.   Concern for one's own goals determines *how* the conflict de-escalates or escalates, whereas concern for the other's goals determines whether and explains *why* the conflict de-escalates or escalates (pp. 92–95, 98–100).

FOURTH STEP: COMPLEXITY EXPLANATIONS

5a.   In the same way that a single goal for oneself and a single goal for the other party elicit a single combination of dual goal concern, multiple short- and long-term goals for oneself and for the other party elicit multiple combinations of dual goal concern (pp. 112–117).

5b.   Multiple combinations of dual goal concern determine the aggregation of various degrees of several reactions into conglomerated conflict behaviour (pp. 114–117; see Table 5.1 for specific predictions of indirect fighting, soft negotiating, indirect capitulating, hard negotiating, integrating, and distributing).

5c.   Conglomerated conflict behaviour can be represented by a pattern of occurrence of its components, and a pattern of covariation of these components (pp. 103–108).

5d.   The pattern of covariation reveals what each component of conglomerated conflict behaviour means in terms of the other components (pp. 105–107).

5e.   Personal and dyadic effectiveness are a function of conglomerated conflict behaviour in that the behavioural components intermediate or moderate each other's impact (pp. 117–121).

5f.   The behavioural component of problem solving is more effective if simultaneously combined with or sequentially preceded by direct fighting (pp. 121–133).

RENEWED VIEW

6a. Handling conflict is processing issues, developing concerns, overcoming choices, and producing (de-)escalation (pp. 139–149).

6b. One's own goals as well as the other's goals elicit higher concern when they are framed as losses than when they are framed as gains (pp. 142–143).

6c. Whereas some components of conflict behaviour tend to produce short-term de-escalation but long-term escalation, others tend to produce short-term escalation but long-term de-escalation (pp. 148–149).

6d. The theoretical value of descriptions of behavioural components lies in simplicity rather than in generality and accuracy (pp. 153–154).

6e. The theoretical value of descriptive and explanatory dimensions lies in simplicity and generality rather than in accuracy (pp. 153–154).

6f. The theoretical value of complexity explanations lies in accuracy rather than in simplicity and generality (pp. 153–154).

References

Amason, A.C., & Schweiger, D.M. (1997). The effects of conflict in strategic decision making effectiveness and organizational performance. In C.K.W. De Dreu & E. Van de Vliert (Eds.), *Using conflict in organizations*, 101–115. Newbury Park, Calif.: Sage.

Axelrod, R. (1984). *The evolution of cooperation*. New York: Basic Books.

Bach, G.R., & Wyden, P. (1969). *The intimate enemy*. New York: Morrow.

Bacharach, S.B., & Lawler, E.J. (1981). *Bargaining: Power, tactics, and outcomes*. San Francisco: Jossey-Bass.

Bales, R.F. (1950). *Interaction process analysis: A method for the study of small groups*. Reading, Mass.: Addison-Wesley.

Barker, J., Tjosvold, D., & Andrews, I.R. (1988). Conflict approaches of effective and ineffective project managers: A field study in a matrix organization. *Journal of Management Studies, 25*, 167–178.

Baron, R.A. (1984). Reducing organizational conflict: An incompatible response approach. *Journal of Applied Psychology, 69*, 272–279.

Baron, R.A. (1989). Negative effects of destructive criticism: Impact on conflict, self-efficacy, and task performance. In M.A. Rahim (Ed.), *Managing conflict: An interdisciplinary approach*, 21–31. New York: Praeger.

Baron, R.A., Fortin, S.P., Frei, R.L., Hauver, L.A., & Shack, M.L. (1990). Reducing organizational conflict: The role of socially-induced positive affect. *International Journal of Conflict Management, 1*, 133–152.

Bartos, O.J. (1995). Modeling distributive and integrative negotiations. *Annals of the American Academy of Political and Social Science, 542*, 48–60.

Bartunek, J.M., Kolb, D.M., & Lewicki, R.J. (1992). Bringing conflict out from behind the scenes. In D.M. Kolb & J.M. Bartunek (Eds.), *Hidden conflict in organizations: Uncovering behind-the-scenes disputes*, 209–228. Newbury Park, Calif.: Sage.

Baxter, L.A. (1982). Conflict management: An episodic approach. *Small Group Behavior, 13*, 23–42.

Bazerman, M.H. (1983). Negotiator judgment: A critical look at the rationality assumption. *American Behavioral Scientist, 27*, 211–228.

Bazerman, M.H., Magliozzi, T., & Neale, M.A. (1985). The acquisition of an integrative response in a competitive market. *Organizational Behavior and Human Performance, 34*, 294–313.

Bazerman, M.H., & Neale, M.A. (1983). Heuristics in negotiation: Limitations to dispute resolution effectiveness. In M.H. Bazerman & R.J. Lewicki (Eds.), *Negotiating in organizations*, 51–67. Beverly Hills, Calif.: Sage.

Bell, E.C., & Blakeney, R.N. (1977). Personality correlates of conflict resolution modes. *Human Relations, 30*, 849–857.

Ben-Yoav, O., & Pruitt, D.G. (1984a). Resistance to yielding and the expectation of cooperative future interaction in negotiation. *Journal of Experimental Social Psychology, 20*, 323–335.

Ben-Yoav, O., & Pruitt, D.G. (1984b). Accountability to constituents: A two-edged sword. *Organizational Behavior and Human Performance, 34*, 283–295.

Bies, R.J. (1989). Managing conflict before it happens: The role of accounts. In M.A. Rahim (Ed.), *Managing conflict: An interdisciplinary approach*, 83–91. New York: Praeger.

Bies, R.J., & Moag, J.S. (1986). Interactional justice: Communication criteria of fairness. In R.J. Lewicki, B.H. Sheppard & M.H. Bazerman (Eds.), *Research on negotiation in organizations, Vol. 1*, 43–55. Greenwich, Conn.: JAI Press.

Bisno, H. (1988). *Managing conflict*. Newbury Park, Calif.: Sage.

Blake, R.R., & Mouton, J.S. (1964). *The managerial grid*. Houston, Tex.: Gulf.

Blake, R.R., & Mouton, J.S. (1970). The fifth achievement. *Journal of Applied Behavioral Science, 6*, 413–426.

Blake, R.R., & Mouton, J.S. (1981). Management by grid principles or situationalism: Which? *Group and Organization Studies, 6*, 439–455.

Blalock, H.M., Jr. (1989). *Power and conflict: Toward a general theory*. Newbury Park, Calif.: Sage.

Bobko, P. (1985). Removing assumptions of bipolarity: Towards variation and circularity. *Academy of Management Review, 10*, 99–108.

Borisoff, D., & Victor, D.A. (1989). *Conflict management: A communication skills approach*. Englewood Cliffs, N.J.: Prentice Hall.

Bowers, J.W. (1974). Guest editor's introductions: Beyond threats and promises. *Speech Monographs, 41*, ix–xi.

Brockner, J., & Rubin, J.Z. (1985). *Entrapment in escalating conflicts: A social psychological analysis*. New York: Springer Verlag.

Brown, B.R. (1977). Face-saving and face-restoration in negotiation. In D. Druckman (Ed.), *Negotiations: Social-psychological perspectives*, 275–299. Beverly Hills, Calif.: Sage.

Brown, C.T., Yelsma, P., & Keller, P.W. (1981). Communication-conflict predisposition: Development of a theory and an instrument. *Human Relations, 34*, 1103–1117.

Brown, L.D. (1983). *Managing conflict at organizational interfaces*. Reading, Mass.: Addison-Wesley.

Burke, R.J. (1970). Methods of resolving superior–subordinate conflict: The constructive use of subordinate differences and disagreements. *Organizational Behavior and Human Performance, 5*, 393–411.

Burton, J.W. (1990). *Conflict: Resolution and prevention*. New York: St. Martin's Press.

Butler, J.K., Jr. (1994). Conflict styles and outcomes in a negotiation with fully-integrative potential. *International Journal of Conflict Management, 5*, 309–325.

Butler, J.K., Jr. (1995). Behaviors, trust, and goal achievement in a win–win negotiating role play. *Group & Organization Management, 20*, 486–501.

Cahn, D.D. (1994). *Conflict in personal relationships*. Hillsdale, N.J.: Lawrence Erlbaum Associates Inc.

Cannon, W.B. (1929). *Bodily changes in pain, hunger, fear, and rage*. New York: Appleton.

Carnevale, P.J. (1986). Strategic choice in mediation. *Negotiation Journal, 2*, 41–56.

Carnevale, P.J. (1992). The usefulness of mediation theory. *Negotiation Journal, 8*, 387–390.

Carnevale, P.J., Conlon, D.E., Hanisch, K.A., & Harris, K.L. (1989). Experimental research on the strategic-choice model. In K. Kressel & D.G. Pruitt (Eds.), *Mediation research: The process and effectiveness of third-party intervention*, 344–367. San Francisco: Jossey-Bass.

Carnevale, P.J., & Isen, A.M. (1986). The influence of positive affect and visual access on the discovery of integrative solutions in bilateral negotiation. *Organizational Behavior and Human Decision Processes, 37*, 1–13.

Carnevale, P.J., & Probst, T.M. (1997). Good news about competitive people. In C.K.W. De Dreu & E. Van de Vliert (Eds.), *Using conflict in organizations*, 129–146. Newbury Park, Calif.: Sage.

Carnevale, P.J., & Pruitt, D.G. (1992). Negotiation and mediation. *Annual Review of Psychology, 43*, 531–582.

Chomsky, N. (1965). *Aspects of the theory of syntax*. Cambridge, Mass.: MIT Press.

Cialdini, R.B., Schaller, M., Houlihan, D., Arps, K., Fultz, J., & Beaman, A.L. (1987). Empathy-based helping: Is it selflessly or selfishly motivated? *Journal of Personality and Social Psychology, 52*, 749–758.

Coombs, C.H. (1987). The structure of conflict. *American Psychologist, 42*, 355–363.

Coombs, C.H., & Avrunin, G.S. (1988). *The structure of conflict*. Hillsdale, N.J.: Lawrence Erlbaum Associates Inc.

Coser, L. (1956). *The functions of social conflict*. Glencoe, Ill.: Free Press.

Cosier, R.A. (1978). The effects of three potential aids for making strategic decisions on prediction accuracy. *Organizational Behavior and Human Performance, 22*, 295–306.

Cosier, R.A., & Ruble, T.L. (1981). Research on conflict-handling behaviour: An experimental approach. *Academy of Management Journal, 24*, 816–831.

Craig, J.H., & Craig, M. (1974). *Synergic power: Beyond domination and permissiveness*. Berkeley, Calif.: Proactive Press.

Dallinger, J.M., & Hample, D. (1995). Personalizing and managing conflict. *International Journal of Conflict Management, 6*, 273–289.

Daves, W.F., & Holland, C.L. (1989). The structure of conflict behaviour of managers assessed with self- and subordinate ratings. *Human Relations, 42*, 741–756.

De Dreu, C.K.W. (1993). *Gain and loss frames in bilateral negotiation: Concession aversion following the adoption of other's communicated frame*. Unpublished dissertation, University of Groningen, The Netherlands.

De Dreu, C.K.W., Carnevale, P.J., Emans, B.J.M., & Van de Vliert, E. (1994). Gain–loss frames in negotiation: Loss aversion, mismatching, and frame adoption. *Organizational Behavior and Human Decision Processes, 60*, 90–107.

De Dreu, C.K.W., Carnevale, P.J., Emans, B.J.M., & Van de Vliert, E. (1995). Outcome frames in bilateral negotiation: Resistance to concession making and frame adoption. In W. Stroebe & M. Hewstone (Eds.), *European Review of Social Psychology, Vol. 6*, 97–125. Chichester: Wiley.

De Dreu, C.K.W., Emans, B.J.M., & Van de Vliert, E. (1991). De invloed van referentiekaders op de utiliteit van verdeling van geld [The influence of frames of reference on the utility of own–other outcome-distributions]. *Gedrag en Organisatie, 6*, 429–443.

De Dreu, C.K.W., Emans, B.J.M., & Van de Vliert, E. (1992a). Frames of reference and co-operative social decision-making. *European Journal of Social Psychology, 22*, 297–302.

De Dreu, C.K.W., Emans, B.J.M., & Van de Vliert, E. (1992b). The influence of own cognitive and other's communicated gain or loss frame on negotiation behavior. *International Journal of Conflict Management, 3*, 115–132.

De Dreu, C.K.W., Lualhati, J., & McCusker, C. (1994). Effects of gain–loss frames on satisfaction with self–other outcome differences. *European Journal of Social Psychology*, *24*, 497–510.

De Dreu, C.K.W., Nauta, A., & Van de Vliert, E. (1995). Self-serving evaluations of conflict behavior and escalation of the dispute. *Journal of Applied Social Psychology*, *25*, 2049–2066.

De Dreu, C.K.W., & Van Lange, P.A.M. (1995). The impact of social value orientations on negotiator cognition and behavior. *Personality and Social Psychology Bulletin*, *21*, 1178–1188.

De Ridder, R., & Tripathi, R.C. (Eds.) (1992). *Norm violation and intergroup relations*. Oxford: Oxford University Press.

Deutsch, M. (1949). A theory of cooperation and competition. *Human Relations*, *2*, 129–151.

Deutsch, M. (1973). *The resolution of conflict: Constructive and destructive processes*. New Haven, Conn.: Yale University Press.

Deutsch, M. (1980). Fifty years of conflict. In L. Festinger (Ed.), *Retrospections on social psychology*, 46–77. New York: Oxford University Press.

Deutsch, M. (1985). *Distributive justice: A social-psychological perspective*. New Haven, Conn.: Yale University Press.

Deutsch, M., & Krauss, R.M. (1960). The effect of threat on interpersonal bargaining. *Journal of Abnormal and Social Psychology*, *61*, 181–189.

Donohue, W.A. (1991). *Communication, marital dispute, and divorce mediation*. Hillsdale, N.J.: Lawrence Erlbaum Associates Inc.

Donohue, W.A., & Roberto, A.J. (1996). An empirical examination of three models of integrative and distributive bargaining. *International Journal of Conflict Management*, *7*, 209–229.

Douglas, A. (1962). *Industrial peacemaking*. New York: Columbia University Press.

Euwema, M.C. (1992). *Conflicthantering in organisaties* [Conflict handling in organizations]. Amsterdam: VU Press.

Euwema, M.C., & Van de Vliert, E. (1990). Gedrag en escalatie bij hiërarchische conflicten [Behavior and escalation in the case of hierarchical conflicts]. In A.P. Buunk, D. van Kreveld, & R. van der Vlist (Eds.), *Sociale psychologie en stereotypen, organisaties, gezondheid*, 28–42. 's-Gravenhage: Vuga.

Euwema, M.C., & Van de Vliert, E. (1994a). The influence of sex on managers' reactions in conflict with their subordinates. In A. Taylor & J. Beinstein Miller (Eds.), *Gender and conflict*, 119–140. Cresskill, N.J.: Hampton Press.

Euwema, M.C., & Van de Vliert, E. (1994b). *The influence of sex on subordinates' reactions in conflict with their superiors*. Unpublished manuscript, University of Groningen, The Netherlands.

Falbe, C.M., & Yukl, G. (1992). Consequences for managers of using single influence tactics and combinations of tactics. *Academy of Management Journal*, *35*, 638–652.

Felstiner, W.L.F., Abel, R.L., & Sarat, A. (1980). The emergence and transformation of disputes: Naming, blaming, claiming... *Law and Society Review*, *15*, 631–654.

Filley, A.C. (1975). *Interpersonal conflict resolution*. Glenview, Ill.: Scott, Foresman.

Fink, C.F. (1968). Some conceptual difficulties in the theory of social conflict. *Journal of Conflict Resolution*, *12*, 412–460.

Fisher, R. (1964). Fractionating conflict. In R. Fisher (Ed.), *International conflict and behavioral science: The Craigville papers*, 91–110. New York: Basic Books.

Fisher, R., & Ury, W. (1981). *Getting to yes: Negotiating agreement without giving in*. London: Hutchinson.

Fisher, R.J. (1990). *The social psychology of intergroup and international conflict resolution*. New York: Springer Verlag.

Fisher, R.J. (1994). Generic principles for resolving intergroup conflict, *Journal of Social Issues*, *50*, 47–66.

Fisher, R.J. (1997). Third party consultation as the controlled stimulation of conflict. In C.K.W. De Dreu & E. Van de Vliert (Eds.), *Using conflict in organizations*, 192–207. Newbury Park, Calif.: Sage.

Fiske, S.T. (1980). Attention and weight in person perception: The impact of negative and extreme behavior. *Journal of Personality and Social Psychology*, 38, 889–906.

Fiske, S.T., & Taylor, S.E. (1984). *Social cognition*. New York: Random House.

Fitzpatrick, M.A. (1988). Negotiation, problem solving and conflict in various types of marriages. In P. Noller & M.A. Fitzpatrick (Eds.), *Perspectives on marital interaction*, 245–270. Clevedon: Multilingual Matters.

Folger, J.P., & Poole, M.S. (1984). *Working through conflict: A communication perspective*. Glenview, Ill.: Scott, Foresman.

Folger, R., Sheppard, B.H., & Buttram, R.T. (1995). Equity, equality, and need. In B.B. Bunker, J.Z. Rubin, & Associates (Eds.), *Conflict, cooperation, and justice: Essays inspired by the work of Morton Deutsch*. San Francisco: Jossey-Bass.

Follett, M.P. (1940). Constructive conflict. In H.C. Metcalf & L. Urwick (Eds.), *Dynamic administration: The collected papers of Mary Parker Follett*, 30–49. New York: Harper.

Freud, S. (1933). Why war? In A. Einstein & S. Freud (Eds.), *Why war?*, 23–57. Paris: International Institute of Intellectual Cooperation, League of Nations.

Fukushima, O., & Ohbuchi, K. (1996). Antecedents and effects of multiple goals in conflict resolution. *International Journal of Conflict Management*, 7, 199–208.

Giebels, E., De Dreu, C.K.W., & Van de Vliert, E. (1995). *Exit options in integrative negotiation: Mediating role of social motivation*. Paper presented at the eighth conference of the International Association for Conflict Management, Helsingor, Denmark, June 11–14.

Gladwin, T.N., & Walter, I. (1980). *Multinationals under fire: Lessons in the management of conflict*. New York: Wiley.

Glasl, F. (1980). *Konfliktmanagement: Diagnose und Behandlung von Konflikten in Organisationen* [Conflict management: Diagnosis and treatment of conflicts in organizations]. Bern: Haupt.

Greenhalgh, L. (1987). Interpersonal conflicts in organizations. In C. L. Cooper & I.T. Robertson (Eds.), *International review of industrial and organizational psychology*, 229–271. Chichester: Wiley.

Greenhalgh, L. (1995). Competition in a collaborative context: Toward a new paradigm. In R.J. Bies, R.J. Lewicki, & B.H. Sheppard (Eds.), *Research on negotiation in organizations, Vol. 5*, 251–270. Greenwich, Conn.: JAI Press.

Greenhalgh, L., Neslin, S.A., & Gilkey, R.W. (1985). The effects of negotiator preferences, situational power, and negotiator personality on outcomes of business negotiations. *Academy of Management Journal*, 28, 9–33.

Griesinger, D.W., & Livingston, J.W., Jr. (1973). Toward a model of interpersonal motivation in experimental games. *Behavioral Science*, 18, 173–188.

Gulliver, P.H. (1979). *Disputes and negotiations: A cross-cultural perspective*. San Diego, Calif.: Academic Press.

Hall, J. (1969). *Conflict management survey*. Conroe, Tex.: Teleometrics International.

Harford, T., & Solomon, L. (1967). "Reformed sinner" and "lapsed saint" strategies in the prisoner's dilemma game. *Journal of Conflict Resolution*, 11, 104–109.

't Hart, P. (1990). *Groupthink in government: A study of small groups and policy failure*. Unpublished dissertation, University of Leiden, The Netherlands.

Hilty, J.A., & Carnevale, P.J. (1993). Black-hat/white-hat strategy in bilateral negotiation. *Organizational Behavior and Human Decision Processes*, 55, 444–469.

Hocker, J.L., & Wilmot, W.W. (1985). *Interpersonal conflict*, 2nd ed. Dubuque, Iowa: William C. Brown.

Hocker, J.L., & Wilmot, W.W. (1991). *Interpersonal conflict*, 3rd ed. Dubuque, Iowa: William C. Brown.

Hofstede, G.H. (1980). *Culture's consequences: International differences in work-related values.* Beverly Hills, Calif.: Sage.

Horney, K. (1945). *Our inner conflicts: A constructive theory of neurosis.* New York: W.W. Norton.

Janis, I.L. (1982) *Groupthink*, 2nd ed. Boston, Mass.: Houghton Mifflin.

Janssen, O. (1994). *Hoe interdependentie motiveert tot conflictgedrag* [How interdependence motivates conflict behavior]. Unpublished dissertation, University of Groningen, The Netherlands.

Janssen, O., Euwema, M.C., & Van de Vliert, E. (1994). Interdependentie, zelf–ander motivatie en conflictgedrag [Interdependence, self-other motivation and conflict behaviour]. *Nederlands Tijdschrift voor de Psychologie, 49*, 15–26.

Janssen, O., & Van de Vliert, E. (1996). Concern for the other's goals: Key to (de-)escalation of conflict. *International Journal of Conflict Management, 7*, 99–120.

Janssen, O., Van de Vliert, E., Euwema, M.C., & Stroebe, W. (1996). *How interdependence motivates conflict behavior.* Unpublished manuscript, University of Groningen, The Netherlands.

Jehn, K.A. (1997). Affective and cognitive conflict in work groups: Increasing performance through value-based intragroup conflict. In C.K.W. De Dreu & E. Van de Vliert (Eds.), *Using conflict in organizations*, 87–100. Newbury Park, Calif.: Sage.

Johnson, D.W., & Johnson, R.T. (1987). *Joining together: Group theory and group skills*, 3rd ed. Englewood Cliffs, N.J.: Prentice-Hall.

Johnson, D.W., & Johnson, R.T. (1989). *Cooperation and competition: Theory and research.* Edina, Minn.: Interaction Book Company.

Johnson, D.W., Johnson, R.T., & Smith, K. (1989). Controversy within decision making situations. In M.A. Rahim (Ed.), *Managing conflict: An interdisciplinary approach*, 251–264. New York: Praeger.

Johnson, D.W., & Lewicki, R.J. (1969). The initiation of superordinate goals. *Journal of Applied Behavioral Science, 5*, 9–24.

Johnson, D.W., Maruyama, G., Johnson, R.T., Nelson, D., & Skon, S. (1981). Effects of cooperative, competitive, and individualistic goal structures on achievement: A meta-analysis. *Psychological Bulletin, 89*, 47–62.

Johnson, D.W., & Tjosvold, D. (1989). Constructive controversy: The key to effective decision-making. In D. Tjosvold & D.W. Johnson (Eds.), *Productive conflict management: Perspectives for organizations*, 46–68. Minneapolis, Minn.: Team Media.

Kabanoff, B. (1987). Predictive validity of the MODE conflict instrument. *Journal of Applied Psychology, 72*, 160–163.

Kabanoff, B., & Van de Vliert, E. (1993). *Behaviour symmetry in conflicting dyads and its relation to interpersonal power and conflict outcomes.* Unpublished manuscript, University of New South Wales, Australia, and University of Groningen, The Netherlands.

Kagan, S., & Knight, G.P. (1981). Social motives among Anglo American and Mexican American children: Experimental and projective measures. *Journal of Research in Personality, 15*, 93–106.

Kahn, R.L., Wolfe, D.M., Quinn, R.P.., Snoek, J.D., & Rosenthal, R.A. (1964). *Organizational stress: Studies in role conflict and ambiguity.* New York: Wiley.

Kahneman, D. (1992). Reference points, anchors, norms, and mixed feelings. *Organizational Behavior and Human Decision Processes, 51*, 96–312.

Kahneman, D., & Tversky, A. (1979). Prospect theory: An analysis of decisions under risk. *Econometrica, 47*, 263–291.

Katzenstein, G. (1996). The debate on structured debate: Toward a unified theory. *Organizational Behavior and Human Decision Processes, 66*, 316–332.

Keating, M.E., Pruitt, D.G., Eberle, R.A., & Mikolic, J.M. (1994). Strategic choice in everyday disputes. *International Journal of Conflict Management, 5,* 143–157.

Kelley, H.H., & Stahelski, A.J. (1970). Social interaction basis of cooperators' and competitors' beliefs about others. *Journal of Personality and Social Psychology, 16,* 66–91.

Kelley, H.H., & Thibaut, J.W. (1978). *Interpersonal relations.* New York: Wiley.

Kilmann, R.H., & Thomas, K.W. (1977). Developing a forced-choice measure of conflict-handling behavior: The "MODE" instrument. *Educational and Psychological Measurement, 37,* 309–325.

Kluwer, E.S., Heesink, J.A.M., & Van de Vliert, E. (1996). Marital conflict about the division of household labor and paid work. *Journal of Marriage and the Family, 58,* 958–969.

Knapp, M.L., Putnam, L.L., & Davis, L.J. (1988). Measuring interpersonal conflict in organizations: Where do we go from here? *Management Communication Quarterly, 1,* 414–429.

Kramer, R.M., McClintock, C.G., & Messick, D.M. (1986). Social values and cooperative response to a simulated resource conservation crisis. *Journal of Personality, 54,* 576–592.

Kramer, R.M., Pommerenke, P., & Newton, E. (1993). The social context of negotiation: Effects of social identity and interpersonal accountability on negotiatior decision making. *Journal of Conflict Resolution, 37,* 633–654.

Kravitz, J.H. (1987). *Conflict management during crisis and non-crisis situations: An examination of managerial preferences.* Paper presented at the first conference of the International Association for Conflict Management, Fairfax, Virginia, June 22–25.

Kuhlman, D.M., Brown, C, & Teta, P. (1992). Judgments of cooperation and defection in social dilemmas: The moderating role of judge's social orientation. In W.B.G. Liebrand, D.M. Messick, & H.A.M. Wilke (Eds.), *Social dilemmas: Theoretical issues and research findings,* 111–132. Oxford: Pergamon Press.

Kuhlman, D.M., Camac, C.R., & Cunha, D.A. (1986). Individual differences in social orientation. In H.A.M. Wilke, D.M. Messick, & C.G. Rutte (Eds.), *Experimental social dilemmas,* 151–174. Frankfurt: Verlag Peter Lang.

Kuhlman, D.M., & Marshello, A. (1975). Individual differences in game motivation as moderators of preprogrammed strategic effects in prisoner's dilemma. *Journal of Personality and Social Psychology, 32,* 922–931.

Kuhn, T.S. (1970). *The structure of scientific revolutions,* 2nd ed. Chicago: University of Chicago Press.

Landy, F. (1978). Conflict management survey. In O.K. Buros (Ed.), *Eighth Mental Measurements Yearbook, Vol. 2,* 1173–1174. Highland Park, N.J.: Gryphon.

Laskewitz, P., Van de Vliert, E., & De Dreu, C.K.W. (1994). Organizational mediators siding with or against the powerful party? *Journal of Applied Social Psychology, 24,* 176–188.

Lawrence, P.R., & Lorsch, J.W. (1967). *Organization and environment: Managing differentiation and integration.* Boston, Mass.: Harvard University Press.

Lax, D.A., & Sebenius, J.K. (1986). *The manager as negotiator: Bargaining for cooperation and competitive gain.* New York: Free Press.

Lazarus, R.S., & Launier, R. (1978). Stress-related transactions between person and environment. In L.A. Pervin & M. Lewis (Eds.), *Perspectives in interactional psychology,* 287–327. New York: Plenum.

Leary, T. (1957). *Interpersonal diagnosis of personality.* New York: Ronald Press.

Leng, R.J. (1993). *Interstate crisis behavior, 1816–1980: Realism versus reciprocity.* Cambridge: Cambridge University Press.

Levi, L. (1981). *Preventing work stress.* Reading, Mass.: Addison-Wesley.

Lewicki, R.J., & Litterer, J.A. (1985). *Negotiation.* Homewood, Ill.: Irwin.

Lewicki, R.J., Weiss, S.E., & Lewin, D. (1992). Models of conflict, negotiation and third party intervention: A review and synthesis. *Journal of Organizational Behavior, 13,* 209–252.

Liebrand, W.B.G. (1982). *Interpersonal differences in social dilemmas: A game theoretical approach*. Unpublished dissertation, University of Groningen, The Netherlands.

Liebrand, W.B.G., & Van Run, G.J. (1985). The effect of social motives across two cultures on behavior in social dilemmas. *Journal of Experimental Social Psychology, 21*, 86–102.

Liebrand, W.B.G., Wilke, H.A.M., Vogel, R., & Wolters, F.J.M. (1986). Value orientation and conformity in three types of social dilemma games. *Journal of Conflict Resolution, 30*, 77–97.

Likert, R., & Likert J.G. (1976). *New ways of managing conflict*. New York: McGraw-Hill.

Lind, E.A., & Tyler, T.R. (1988). *The social psychology of procedural justice*. New York: Plenum Press.

Lingoes, J.C., & Roskam, E.E. (1973). A mathematical and empirical analysis of two multidimensional scaling algorithms. *Psychometrika, 38* (4, pt. 2): Monograph supplement.

Loewenstein, G.F., Thompson, L.L., & Bazerman, M.H. (1989). Social utility and decision making in interpersonal contexts. *Journal of Personality and Social Psychology, 57*, 426–441.

Luce, R.D., & Raiffa, H. (1957). *Games and decisions: Introduction and critical survey*. New York: Wiley.

MacCrimmon, K.R., & Messick, D.M. (1976). A framework for social motives. *Behavioral Science, 21*, 86–100.

March, J.G., & Simon, H.A. (1958). *Organizations*. New York: Wiley.

Martijn, C., Spears, R., Van der Pligt, J., & Jakobs, E. (1992). Negativity and positivity effects in person perception and inference: Ability versus morality. *European Journal of Social Psychology, 22*, 453–463.

Mastenbroek, W.F.G. (1989). *Negotiate*. Oxford: Basil Blackwell.

McClintock, C.G. (1972). Social motives: A set of propositions. *Behavioral Science, 17*, 438–454.

McClintock, C.G. (1976). Social motivations in settings of outcome interdependence. In D. Druckman (Ed.), *Negotiations: Social-psychological perspectives*, 49–77. Beverly Hills, Calif.: Sage.

McClintock, C.G., & Allison, S. (1989). Social value orientation and helping behavior. *Journal of Applied Social Psychology, 19*, 353–362.

McClintock, C.G., & Liebrand, W.B.G. (1988). The role of interdependence structure, individual value orientation, and other's strategy in social decision making: A transformational analysis. *Journal of Personality and Social Psychology, 55*, 396–409.

Messick, D.M., & Sentis, K.P. (1985). Estimating social and non-social utility functions from ordinal data. *European Journal of Social Psychology, 15*, 389–399.

Mills, J., Robey, D., & Smith, L. (1985). Conflict-handling and personality dimensions of project-management personnel. *Psychological Reports, 57*, 1135–1143.

Mintzberg, H. (1979). *The structuring of organizations*. Englewood Cliffs, N.J.: Prentice-Hall.

Morley, I., & Stephenson, G. (1977). *The social psychology of bargaining*. London: Allen & Unwin.

Nauta, A. (1996). *Oog om oog en baas boven baas: Interactiepatronen bij interpersoonlijk conflict op bureaucratische en organische organisatie-afdelingen* [Battle and bossiness in business: Interaction patterns in interpersonal conflict within bureaucratic and organic organisation departments]. Unpublished dissertation, University of Groningen, The Netherlands.

Neale, M.A., & Bazerman, M.H. (1985). The effects of framing and negotiation overconfidence on bargaining behaviors and outcomes. *Academy of Management Journal, 28*, 34–49.

Neale, M.A., & Bazerman, M.H. (1991). *Cognition and rationality in negotiation*. New York: Free Press.

Neale, M.A., Huber, V.L., & Northcraft, G.B. (1987). The framing of negotiations: Contextual versus task frames. *Organizational Behavior and Human Decision Processes, 39*, 228–241.

Nichols, L.C. (1984). Identification of conflict management styles of board of education member negotiators. Doctoral dissertation, Kansas State University. *Dissertation Abstracts International, 45* (04), 1004.

Nicotera, A.M. (1993). Beyond two dimensions: A grounded theory model of conflict-handling behavior. *Management Communication Quarterly, 6*, 282–306.

Nicotera, A.M. (1994). The use of multiple approaches to conflict: A study of sequences. *Human Communications Research, 20*, 592–621.

O'Reilly, C.A., & Weitz, B.A. (1980). *Conflict styles and sanction use.* Unpublished manuscript, Los Angeles: University of California.

Peirce, R.S., Pruitt, D.G., & Czaja, S.J. (1993). Complainant–respondent differences in procedural justice. *International Journal of Conflict Management, 4*, 199–222.

Phillips, E., & Cheston, R. (1979). Conflict resolution: What works ? *California Management Review, 21*, 76–83.

Pinkley, R.L., Neale, M.A., & Bennett, R.J. (1994). The impact of alternatives to settlement in dyadic negotiation. *Organizational Behavior and Human Decision Processes, 57*, 97–116.

Pneuman, R.W., & Bruehl, M.E. (1982). *Managing conflict.* Englewood Cliffs, N.J.: Prentice-Hall.

Poole, M.S., Shannon, D.L., & DeSanctis, G. (1992). Communication media and negotiation processes. In L.L. Putnam & M.E. Roloff (Eds.), *Communication and negotiation*, 46–66. Newbury Park, Calif.: Sage.

Prein, H.C.M. (1976). Stijlen van conflicthantering [Styles of conflict management]. *Nederlands Tijdschrift voor de Psychologie, 31*, 321–346.

Pruitt, D.G. (1981). *Negotiation behavior.* New York: Academic Press.

Pruitt, D.G. (1983). Strategic choice in negotiation. *American Behavioral Scientist, 27*, 167–194.

Pruitt, D.G. (1995). Flexibility in conflict episodes. *Annals of the American Academy of Political and Social Science, 542*, 100–115.

Pruitt, D.G., & Carnevale, P.J. (1993). *Negotiation in social conflict.* Milton Keynes: Open University Press.

Pruitt, D.G., Carnevale, P.J., Ben-Yoav, O., Nochajski, T.H., & Van Slyck, M. (1983). Incentives for cooperation in integrative bargaining. In R. Tietz (Ed.), *Aspiration levels in bargaining and economic decision making*, 22–34. Berlin: Springer.

Pruitt, D.G., & Kimmel, M.J. (1977). Twenty years of experimental gaming: Critique, synthesis, and suggestions for the future. *Annual Review of Psychology, 28*, 363–392.

Pruitt, D.G., & Rubin, J.Z. (1986). *Social conflict: Escalation, stalemate, settlement.* New York: Random House.

Putnam, L.L. (1990). Reframing integrative and distributive bargaining: A process perspective. In B.H. Sheppard, M.H. Bazerman, & R.J. Lewicki (Eds.), *Research on negotiation in organizations, Vol. 2*, 3–30. Greenwich, Conn.: JAI Press.

Putnam, L.L. (1997). Productive conflict: Negotiation as implicit coordination. In C.K.W. De Dreu & E. Van de Vliert (Eds.), *Using conflict in organizations*, 147–160. Newbury Park, Calif.: Sage.

Putnam, L.L., & Jones, T.S. (1982). Reciprocity in negotiations: An analysis of bargaining interaction. *Communication Monographs, 49*, 171–191.

Putnam, L.L., & Wilson, C.E. (1982). Communicative strategies in organizational conflicts: Reliability and validity of a measurement scale. In M. Burgoon (Ed.), *Communication Yearbook, Vol. 6*, 629–652. Beverly Hills, Calif.: Sage.

Putnam, L.L., & Wilson, S.R. (1989). Argumentation and bargaining strategies as discriminators of integrative outcomes. In M.A. Rahim (Ed.), *Managing conflict: An interdisciplinary approach*, 121–141. New York: Praeger.

Rafaeli, A., & Sutton, R.I. (1991). Emotional contrast strategies as means of social influence: Lessons from criminal interrogators and bill collectors. *Academy of Management Journal*, *34*, 749–775.

Rahim, M.A. (1983a). *Rahim organizational conflict inventories*. Palo Alto, Calif.: Consulting Psychologists Press.

Rahim, M.A. (1983b). A measure of styles of handling interpersonal conflict. *Academy of Management Journal*, *26*, 368–376.

Rahim, M.A. (1992). *Managing conflict in organizations*, 2nd ed. Westport, Conn.: Praeger.

Rahim, M.A., & Magner, R.A. (1995). Confirmatory factor analysis of the styles of handling interpersonal conflict: First-order factor model and its invariance across groups. *Journal of Applied Psychology*, *80*, 122–132.

Raiffa, H. (1982). *The art and science of negotiation*. Cambridge, Mass.: Harvard University Press.

Renwick, P.A. (1975a). Impact of topic and source of disagreement on conflict management. *Organizational Behavior and Human Performance*, *14*, 416–425.

Renwick, P.A. (1975b). Perception and management of superior–subordinate conflict. *Organizational Behavior and Human Performance*, *13*, 444–456.

Renwick, P.A. (1977). The effects of sex differences on the perception and management of superior–subordinate conflict: An exploratory study. *Organizational Behavior and Human Performance*, *19*, 403–415.

Ritzer, G. (1972). *Man and his work: Conflict and change*. Englewood Cliffs, N.J.: Prentice-Hall.

Robbins, S.P. (1974). *Managing organizational conflict: A nontraditional approach*. Englewood Cliffs, N.J.: Prentice-Hall.

Robbins, S.P. (1991). *Organizational behavior: Concepts, controversies, and applications*, 5th ed. Englewood Cliffs, N.J.: Prentice-Hall.

Roloff, M.E., & Jordan, J.M. (1992). Achieving negotiation goals: The "fruits and foibles" of planning ahead. In L.L. Putnam & M.E. Roloff (Eds.), *Communication and negotiation*, 1–45. Newbury Park, Calif.: Sage.

Ross, R.G., & DeWine, S. (1988). Assessing the Ross–DeWine conflict management message style (CMMS). *Management Communication Quarterly*, *1*, 389–413.

Rubin, J.Z., & Brown, B.R. (1975). *The social psychology of bargaining and negotiation*. New York: Academic Press.

Rubin, J.Z., Pruitt, D.G., & Kim, S.H. (1994). *Social conflict: Escalation, stalemate, and settlement*. New York: McGraw-Hill.

Ruble, T.L., & Cosier, R.A. (1982). A laboratory study of five conflict-handling modes. In G.B.J. Bomers & R.B. Peterson (Eds.), *Conflict management and industrial relations*, 158–171. Boston, Mass.: Kluwer & Nijhoff.

Ruble, T.L., & Thomas, K.W. (1976). Support for a two-dimensional model of conflict behavior. *Organizational Behavior and Human Performance*, *16*, 143–155.

Satir, V. (1972). *Peoplemaking*. Palo Alto, Calif.: Science and Behavior Books.

Schaap, C., Buunk, B.P., & Kerkstra, A. (1988). Marital conflict resolution. In P. Noller & M.A. Fitzpatrick (Eds.), *Perspectives on marital interaction*, 203–244. Clevedon: Multilingual Matters.

Schelling, T.C. (1960). *The strategy of conflict*. Cambridge, Mass.: Harvard University Press.

Schroder, H.M., Driver, M.J., & Streufert, S. (1967). *Information processing systems in individuals and groups*. New York: Holt, Rinehart & Winston.

Schweiger, D.M., Sandberg, W.R., & Ragan, J.W. (1986). Group approaches for improving strategic decision making: A comparative analysis of dialectical inquiry, devil's advocacy, and consensus. *Academy of Management Journal*, *29*, 51–71.

Schweiger, D.M., Sandberg, W.R., & Rechner, P.L. (1989). Experiential effects of dialectical inquiry, devil's advocacy, and consensus approaches to strategic decision making. *Academy of Management Journal, 32,* 745–772.

Schwenk, C.R. (1990). Effects of dialectical inquiry and devil's advocacy on decision-making. *Organizational Behavior and Human Decision Processes, 47,* 161–176.

Schwenk, C.R., & Cosier, R.A. (1993). Effects of consensus and devil's advocacy on strategic decision-making. *Journal of Applied Social Psychology, 23,* 126–139.

Shapiro, D.L., & Bies, R.J. (1994). Threats, bluffs, and disclaimers in negotiations. *Organizational Behavior and Human Decision Processes, 60,* 14–35.

Sheldon, A., & Johnson, D.W. (1994). Preschool negotiators: Linguistic differences in how girls and boys regulate the expression of dissent in same-sex groups. In R.J. Lewicki, B.H. Sheppard, & R.J. Bies (Eds.), *Research on negotiation in organizations, Vol. 4,* 37–67. Greenwich, Conn.: JAI Press.

Sheppard, B.H. (1984). Third party conflict intervention: A procedural framework. In B.M. Staw & L.L. Cummings (Eds.), *Research in organizational behavior, Vol. 6,* 141–190. Greenwich, Conn.: JAI Press.

Sheppard, B.H., Lewicki, R.J., & Minton, J.W. (1992). *Organizational justice: The search for fairness in the workplace.* New York: Lexington Books.

Sherif, M. (1966). *In common predicament.* Boston, Mass.: Houghton Mifflin.

Shockley-Zalabak, P. (1988). Assessing the Hall Conflict Management Survey. *Management Communication Quarterly, 1,* 302–320.

Simon, H.A. (1967). Motivational and emotional controls of cognition. *Psychological Review, 74,* 29–39.

Sitkin, S.B., & Bies, R.J. (1993). Social accounts in conflict situations: Using explanations to manage conflict. *Human Relations, 46,* 349–370.

Skowronski, J.J., & Carlston, D.E. (1987). Social judgment and social memory: The role of cue diagnosticity in negativity, positivity, and extremity biases. *Journal of Personality and Social Psychology, 52,* 689–699.

Sternberg, R.J., & Dobson, D.M. (1987). Resolving interpersonal conflicts: An analysis of stylistic consistency. *Journal of Personality and Social Psychology, 52,* 794–812.

Sternberg, R.J., & Soriano, L.J. (1984). Styles of conflict resolution. *Journal of Personality and Social Psychology, 47,* 115–126.

Straus, M.A. (1979). Measuring intrafamily conflict and violence: The conflict tactics (CT) scales. *Journal of Marriage and the Family, 41,* 75–88.

Tajfel, H., & Turner, J.C. (1979). An integrative theory of intergroup conflict. In W.G. Austin & S. Worchel (Eds.), *The social psychology of intergroup relations.* Monterey, Calif.: Brooks/Cole.

Taylor, S. (1991). Asymmetrical effects of positive and negative events: The mobilization-minimization hypothesis. *Psychological Bulletin, 10,* 67–85.

Teger, A.I. (1980). *Too much invested to quit.* New York: Pergamon Press.

Terhune, K.W. (1970). The effects of personality in cooperation and conflict. In P.G. Swingle (Ed.), *The structure of conflict.* New York: Academic Press.

Thomas, K.W. (1976). Conflict and conflict management. In M.D. Dunnette (Ed.), *Handbook of industrial and organizational psychology,* 889–935. Chicago: Rand McNally.

Thomas, K.W. (1977). Toward multidimensional values in teaching: The example of conflict behaviors. *Academy of Management Review, 2,* 484–490.

Thomas, K.W. (1979). Organizational conflict. In S. Kerr (Ed.), *Organizational Behavior,* 151–181. Columbus, Ohio: Grid Publications.

Thomas, K.W. (1982). Manager and mediator: A comparison of third-party roles based upon conflict-management goals. In G.B.J. Bomers & R.B. Peterson (Eds.), *Conflict management and industrial relations,* 141–157. Boston, Mass.: Kluwer & Nijhoff.

Thomas, K.W. (1988). The conflict-handling modes: Toward more precise theory. *Management Communication Quarterly, 1,* 430–436.

Thomas, K.W. (1992a). Conflict and conflict management: Reflections and update. *Journal of Organizational Behavior*, *13*, 265–274.

Thomas, K.W. (1992b). Conflict and negotiation processes in organizations. In M.D. Dunnette & L.M. Hough (Eds.), *Handbook of industrial and organizational psychology*, 2nd ed., 651–717. Palo Alto, Calif.: Consulting Psychologists Press.

Thomas, K.W., & Kilmann, R.H. (1974). *The Thomas–Kilmann conflict mode instrument*. Tuxedo, N.Y.: Xicom.

Thomas, K.W., & Kilmann, R.H. (1978). Comparison of four instruments measuring conflict behavior. *Psychological Reports*, *42*, 1139–1145.

Thomas, K.W., & Pondy, L.R. (1977). Toward an "intent" model of conflict management among principal parties. *Human Relations*, *30*, 1089–1102.

Thompson, L.L. (1990). Negotiation behavior and outcomes: Empirical evidence and theoretical issues. *Psychological Bulletin*, *108*, 515–532.

Thompson, L.L., & Hastie, R. (1990). Social perception in negotiation. *Organizational Behavior and Human Decision Processes*, *47*, 98–123.

Thorngate, W. (1976). "In general" vs. "it depends": Some comments on the Gergen–Schlenker debate. *Personality and Social Psychology Bulletin*, *2*, 404–410.

Ting-Toomey, S. (1988). Intercultural conflict styles: A face-negotiation theory. In Y. Kim & W. Gudykunst (Eds.), *Theories in intercultural communication*, 213–235. Newbury Park, Calif.: Sage.

Ting-Toomey, S., Gao, G., Trubisky, P., Yang, Z., Kim, H.S., Lin, S.L., & Nishida, T. (1991). Culture, face maintenance, and styles of handling interpersonal conflict: A study in five cultures. *International Journal of Conflict Management*, *2*, 275–296.

Tjosvold, D. (1985). Implications of controversy research for management. *Journal of Management*, *11*, 221–238.

Tjosvold, D. (1988). Cooperative and competitive dynamics within and between organizational units. *Human Relations*, *41*, 425–436.

Tjosvold, D. (1989). Interdependence approach to conflict management in organizations. In M.A. Rahim (Ed.), *Managing conflict: An interdisciplinary approach*, 41–50. New York: Praeger.

Tjosvold, D. (1990). The goal interdependence approach to communication in conflict: An organizational study. In M.A. Rahim (Ed.), *Theory and research in conflict management*, 15–27. New York: Praeger.

Tjosvold, D. (1991). *The conflict-positive organization: Stimulate diversity and create unity*. Reading, Mass.: Addison-Wesley.

Tjosvold, D., & Deemer, D.K. (1980). Effects of controversy within a cooperative or competitive context on organizational decision making. *Journal of Applied Psychology*, *65*, 590–595.

Tjosvold, D., & Huston, T. (1978). Social face and resistance to compromise in bargaining. *Journal of Social Psychology*, *104*, 57–68.

Tracy, L., & Peterson, R.B. (1986). A behavioral theory of labor negotiations: How well has it aged? *Negotiation Journal*, *2*, 93–108.

Triandis, H.C., Bontempo, R., Villareal, M.J., Asai, M., & Lucca, N. (1988). Individualism and collectivism: Cross-cultural perspectives on self–ingroup relationships. *Journal of Personality and Social Psychology*, *54*, 323–338.

Turner, M.E., & Pratkanis, A.R. (1997). Mitigating groupthink by stimulating constructive conflict. In C.K.W. De Dreu & E. Van de Vliert (Eds.), *Using conflict in organizations*, 53–71. Newbury Park, Calif.: Sage.

Tutzauer, F., & Roloff, M.E. (1988). Communication processes leading to integrative agreements: Three paths to joint benefits. *Communication Research*, *15*, 360–380.

Tversky, A., & Kahneman, D. (1981). The framing of decisions and the rationality of choice. *Science*, *211*, 453–458.

Van Lange, P.A.M. (1991). *The rationality and morality of cooperation.* Unpublished dissertation, University of Groningen, The Netherlands.

Van Lange, P.A.M. (1992). Rationality and morality in social dilemmas: The influence of social value orientations. In W.B.G. Liebrand, D.M. Messick & H.A.M. Wilke (Eds.), *Social dilemmas: Theoretical issues and research findings*, 133–146. Oxford: Pergamon Press.

Van de Vliert, E. (1977). Inconsistencies in the Argyris intervention theory. *Journal of Applied Behavioral Science, 13*, 557–564.

Van de Vliert, E. (1981). Siding and other reactions to a conflict: A theory of escalation toward outsiders. *Journal of Conflict Resolution, 25*, 495–520.

Van de Vliert, E. (1985). Escalative intervention in small-group conflicts. *Journal of Applied Behavioral Science, 21*, 19–36.

Van de Vliert, E. (1990a). Sternberg's styles of handling interpersonal conflict: A theory-based reanalysis. *International Journal of Conflict Management, 1*, 69–80.

Van de Vliert, E. (1990b). Small group conflicts. In J.B. Gittler (Ed.), *The annual review of conflict knowledge and conflict resolution, Vol. 2*, 83–118. New York: Garland.

Van de Vliert, E. (1992). Questions about the strategic choice model of mediation. *Negotiation Journal, 8*, 379–386.

Van de Vliert, E. (1996). Interventions in conflicts. In M.J. Schabracq, J.A.M. Winnubst & C.L. Cooper (Eds.), *Handbook of work and health psychology*, 405–425. Chichester: Wiley.

Van de Vliert, E. (1997). Enhancing performance by conflict-stimulating intervention. In C.K.W. De Dreu & E. Van de Vliert (Eds.), *Using conflict in organizations*, 209–222. Newbury Park, Calif.: Sage.

Van de Vliert, E. (in press). Conflict and conflict management. In H. Thierry, P.J.D. Drenth, & C.J. de Wolff (Eds.), *A new handbook of work and organisational psychology*. Hove: Psychology Press.

Van de Vliert, E., & Euwema, M.C. (1994). Agreeableness and activeness as components of conflict behavior. *Journal of Personality and Social Psychology, 66*, 674–687.

Van de Vliert, E., & Euwema, M.C. (1996). *Sex composition and effectiveness of conglomerated conflict behavior in Dutch hospitals.* Unpublished manuscript, University of Groningen, The Netherlands.

Van de Vliert, E., Euwema, M.C., & Huismans, S.E. (1995). Managing conflict with a subordinate or a superior: Effectiveness of conglomerated behavior. *Journal of Applied Psychology, 80*, 271–281.

Van de Vliert, E., & Hordijk, J.W. (1989). A theoretical position of compromising among other styles of conflict management. *Journal of Social Psychology, 129*, 681–690.

Van de Vliert, E., Huismans, S.E., & Stok. J.J.L. (1985). The criterion approach to unraveling beta and alpha change. *Academy of Management Review, 10*, 269–275.

Van de Vliert, E., & Kabanoff, B. (1990). Toward theory-based measures of conflict management. *Academy of Management Journal, 33*, 199–209.

Van de Vliert, E., Nauta, A., Giebels, E., & Janssen, O. (in press). Constructive conflict at work. *Journal of Organizational Behavior.*

Van de Vliert, E., & Prein, H.C.M. (1989). The difference in the meaning of forcing in the conflict management of actors and observers. In M.A. Rahim (Ed.), *Managing conflict: An interdisciplinary approach*, 51–63. New York: Praeger.

Van de Vliert, E., Schwartz, S.H., Huismans, S.E., Hofstede, G., & Daan, S. (1996). *Temperature, cultural masculinity, and domestic political violence: A cross-national study.* Unpublished manuscript, University of Groningen, The Netherlands.

Van der Togt, J.J.W., & Van de Vliert, E. (1996). *A self–other concerns model for group effectiveness: Separating the effects of concerns orientation and concerns strength.* Unpublished manuscript, University of Groningen, The Netherlands.

Väyrynen, R. (1991). To settle or to transform? Perspectives on the resolution of national and international conflicts. In R. Väyrynen (Ed.), *New directions in conflict theory: Conflict resolution and conflict transformation*. Newbury Park, Calif.: Sage.

Volkema, R.J., & Bergmann, T.J. (1989). Interpersonal conflict at work: An analysis of behavioral responses. *Human Relations, 42*, 757–770.

Vroom, V.H. (1964). *Work and motivation*. New York: Wiley.

Wagenaar, W.A., & Padmos, P. (1971). Quantitative interpretation of stress in Kruskal's multi-dimensional scaling technique. *British Journal of Mathematical and Statistical Psychology, 24*, 101–110.

Wall, J.A., Jr. (1985). *Negotiation: Theory and practice*. Glenview, Ill.: Scott, Foresman.

Walton, R.E. (1969). *Interpersonal peacemaking: Confrontations and third party consultation*. Reading, Mass.: Addison-Wesley.

Walton, R.E. (1972). Interorganizational decision making and identity conflict. In M. Tuite, R. Chisholm, & M. Radnor (Eds.). *Interorganizational decision making*, 94–111. Chicago: Aldine.

Walton, R.E. (1987). *Managing conflict: Interpersonal dialogue and third-party roles*, 2nd ed. Reading, Mass.: Addison-Wesley.

Walton, R.E., Cutcher-Gershenfeld, J.E., & McKersie, R.B. (1994). *Strategic negotiations: A theory of change in labor–management relations*. Boston, Mass.: Harvard Business School Press.

Walton, R.E., & McKersie, R.B. (1965). *A behavioral theory of labor negotiations: An analysis of a social interaction system*. New York: McGraw Hill.

Weick, K.E. (1979). *The social psychology of organizing*, 2nd ed. Reading, Mass.: Addison-Wesley.

Weider-Hatfield, D. (1988). Assessing the Rahim Organizational Conflict Inventory-II (ROCI-II). *Management Communication Quarterly, 1*, 350–366.

Weingart, L.R., Thompson, L.L., Bazerman, M.H., & Carroll, J.S. (1990). Tactical behavior and negotiation outcomes. *International Journal of Conflict Management, 1*, 7–31.

Williams, G.R. (1983). *Legal negotiation and settlement*. St. Paul, Minn.: West.

Williams, G.R. (1993). Style and effectiveness in negotiation. In L. Hall (Ed.), *Negotiation: Strategies for mutual gain*, 151–174. Newbury Park, Calif.: Sage.

Wilson, S.R. (1992). Face and facework in negotiation. In L.L. Putnam & M.E. Roloff (Eds.), *Communication and negotiation*. Newbury Park, Calif.: Sage.

Wilson, S.R., & Waltman, M.S. (1988). Assessing the Putnam–Wilson Organizational Communication Instrument (OCCI). *Management Communication Quarterly, 1*, 367–388.

Womack, D.F. (1988). Assessing the Thomas–Kilmann conflict MODE survey. *Management Communication Quarterly, 1*, 321–349.

Woodtli, M.A. (1982). The perceptions of deans of nursing of selected sources of conflict and conflict-handling modes. Doctoral dissertation, Illinois State University. *Dissertation Abstracts International, 44* (01), 87.

Yukl, G., Falbe, C.M., & Young Youn, J. (1993). Patterns of influence behavior for managers. *Group & Organization Management, 18*, 5–28.

Zand, D.E. (1972). Trust and managerial problem solving. *Administrative Science Quarterly, 17*, 229–239.

Zartman, I.W. (Ed.) (1976). *The 50% solution*. New Haven, Conn.: Yale University Press.

Zartman, I.W., & Berman, M.R. (1982). *The practical negotiator*. New Haven, Conn.: Yale University Press.

Glossary

ACCOMMODATING Nonconfrontation by giving in to the other party's point of view or demand.

ALTRUISTIC ORIENTATION Low concern for one's own goals and high concern for the other's goals.

AVOIDING Nonconfrontation by preventing or terminating efforts to yield, to negotiate, or to win.

BEHAVIOURAL COMPLEMENTARITY Dissimilarity of a party's reaction to the other party's preceding reaction to the conflict issue experienced.

BEHAVIOURAL SYMMETRY Similarity of a party's reaction to the other party's preceding reaction to the conflict issue experienced.

CLAIM-NEGOTIATION Pursuing a mutually agreed allocation of benefits or costs that nobody "owns."

COMPETITION Aspiring to defeat the other party in a covert and devious, or in an overt and straightforward, way.

COMPROMISING Negotiation by pursuing a mutually acceptable settlement in which each party makes some concession.

CONCERN FOR ONE'S OWN GOALS Valence and feasibility of attaining one's own objectives.

CONCERN FOR THE OTHER'S GOALS Valence and feasibility of attaining the other's objectives.

CONFLICT An individual's experience of obstruction or irritation by one or more other people reacted to in a beneficial or costly way.

CONFLICT BEHAVIOUR   An individual's intended or displayed outward re-action to a conflict issue.

CONFLICT HANDLING   Conflict behaviour.

CONFLICT ISSUE   An individual's experience of a subject matter of discord due to obstruction or irritation by one or more other people.

CONFLICT MANAGEMENT   Conflict behaviour.

CONFLICT MANAGEMENT GRID   A theory describing complex interpersonal conflict behaviours as more or less integrative and distributive, and as a function of concerns for one's own and the other party's goals.

CONFLICT OUTCOME   An end state of benefits or costs for both oneself and the other party.

CONGLOMERATED CONFLICT BEHAVIOUR   An individual's aggregation of several intended or displayed outward reactions in various degrees to a conflict issue.

CONSOLIDATION   Aspiring to defend oneself against the other party.

COOPERATION Nonconfronting through avoidance or accommodation, or negotiating a compromise or a resolution.

DE-ESCALATION Conflict-mitigating consequences of increasing concern for the other's goals.

DIRECT FIGHTING   Competition by aspiring to defeat the other party in an overt and straightforward way.

DISTRIBUTION   Minimising or maximising one's relative benefits or costs vis-à-vis the other party.

EFFECTIVENESS   Having produced outcomes desired for oneself and for the other party (personal effectiveness). Having reduced the conflict is-sues or having improved one's relationship with the other party (dyadic effectiveness).

ESCALATION   Conflict-intensifying consequences of decreasing concern for the other's goals.

FAIR FIGHTING   Competition by aspiring to defeat the other party on the basis of mutually agreed rules about right and wrong behaviour.

FIGHTING   Competition by aspiring to defeat the other party.

FIRM FLEXIBILITY   Standing resolute on one's own ultimate goals while trying to be responsive to the other party's immediate and ultimate goals.

FIVE-PART TYPOLOGY   The conflict management grid's description of con-glomerated conflict behaviour in terms of avoiding, accommodating, compromising, problem solving, and fighting.

GOAL FEASIBILITY   Likelihood of obtaining objectives.

GOAL INTERDEPENDENCE   Attaining one's own objectives facilitates or hampers the attainment of the other party's objectives, and vice versa.

GOAL VALENCE   Degree of reward for obtaining objectives.

GRATE OF CONCERNS   The conflict management grid's multiple motives to attain one's own and the other party's objectives, which determine and thus explain multiple components of conglomerated conflict behaviour.

INDIRECT FIGHTING   Competition by aspiring to defeat the other party in a covert and devious way.

INDIVIDUALISTIC ORIENTATION   High concern for one's own goals and low concern for the other's goals.

INTEGRATION   Minimising or maximising the benefits or costs for both parties.

L-ANGLE OF CONCERNS   The motivational sides of the conflict management grid to attain one's own and the other party's objectives, which determine and thus explain a single component of conglomerated conflict behaviour.

METATHEORY   One or more overarching rules of correspondence regarding one or more distinct theories.

MODEL   A set of leading ideas about the nature of conflict handling and the similarities and differences among distinct components of conglomerated conflict behaviour.

NEGATIVE GOAL INTERDEPENDENCE   Attaining one's own objectives hampers the attainment of the other party's objectives, and vice versa.

NEGOTIATION   Pursuing a mutually acceptable or completely satisfactory agreement.

NONCONFRONTATION   Withdrawing, doing nothing, or yielding.

PATTERN OF COVARIATION   The relative extent to which each behavioural component concurs with each of the other components in conglomerated conflict behaviour.

PATTERN OF OCCURRENCE   The relative intensity of each behavioural component in conglomerated conflict behaviour.

POSITIVE GOAL INTERDEPENDENCE   Attaining one's own objectives facilitates the attainment of the other party's objectives, and vice versa.

PROBLEM SOLVING   Negotiation by seeking a complete reconciliation of both parties' basic interests.

PROMISE   The declaration of a commitment to supply a reward if the other party obeys.

SPONTANEOUS CONFLICT BEHAVIOUR   An individual's outward reaction to a conflict issue that is not deliberately directed towards the acquisition of benefits or the prevention of costs.

STRATEGIC CONFLICT BEHAVIOUR   An individual's outward reaction to a conflict issue that is deliberately directed towards the acquisition of benefits or the prevention of costs.

TACIT COORDINATION   Realising a satisfactory agreement through nonverbal communication.

THEORETICAL VALUE   Usefulness of rules of correspondence between variables, notably in terms of simplicity, generality, and accuracy.

THEORY   A set of rules of correspondence between components of con-glomerated conflict behaviour and their determinants or consequences.

THIRD PARTY   Anyone who tries to get one or more principal parties to avoid, to accommodate, to negotiate, or to fight.

THREAT   The declaration of a commitment to inflict a punishment if the other party disobeys.

THROMISE   The declaration of a commitment to supply a reward if the other party obeys, and to inflict a punishment if the other party disobeys.

TRADE-NEGOTIATION   Pursuing a mutually agreed exchange of benefits or costs that one party "owns" for benefits or costs that the other party "owns."

TYPOLOGY   A classification based on characteristics and particulars of distinct components of conglomerated conflict behaviour.

WALK-AWAY NEGOTIATION   Pursuing a mutually acceptable agreement through avoiding.

X-CROSS MODEL   The variable-sum and constant-sum diagonals of the conflict management grid, which describe conglomerated conflict behaviour.

Author Index

Subject Index